Every Woman's Guide to
Romance in Paris

Caroline O'Connell

SQUAREONE
PUBLISHERS

In-House Editor: Joanne Abrams
Cover Designer: Jeannie Tudor
Typesetter: Gary A. Rosenberg

Square One Publishers
115 Herricks Road
Garden City Park, NY 11040
(516) 535–2010 • (877) 900–BOOK
www.squareonepublishers.com

Library of Congress Cataloging-in-Publication Data

O'Connell, Caroline.
  Every woman's guide to romance in Paris / Caroline O'Connell.—3rd ed.
     p. cm.
  Includes index.
  ISBN 978-0-7570-0234-2 (pbk.)
  1. Paris (France)—Guidebooks. 2. Women—Travel—France—Paris—Guidebooks.
I. Title.
  DC708.O25 2012
  914.4'36048412—dc23
                          2011037535

Printed in the United States of America

10   9   8   7   6   5   4   3   2   1

Contents

Acknowledgments

All books are collaborative efforts, and I am very lucky to have such a "hands on" team at Square One Publishers. They really are among the best in the business.

My editor, Joanne Abrams, stands out for her huge contribution in time and expertise, offering great ideas for listings to include and working painstakingly on the complicated layout. It has been wonderful having a partner like Joanne in this process.

Publisher Rudy Shur has also been intimately involved in brainstorming and key decisionmaking and came up with excellent ideas for two important new sections—the Save Some Money boxes and the graphics of central métro lines.

In Paris, four friends were instrumental in unlocking the secrets of their city.

Frédéric Reglain has contributed professional photos and been an ongoing source of advice on the ever-changing cultural scene—from jazz clubs to sporting events to trendy nightspots.

Yves Bénard graciously shared his considerable knowledge of the world of champagne and Parisian insider dining spots.

Jean Berchon, at Moët & Chandon, knows every top chef and was kind enough to introduce to me to Joël Robuchon, Alain Ducasse, Guy Savoy, Michel Rostang, and many others.

Carole Bricout, a good friend for more than twenty years, provided invaluable insight on *La Vie Parisienne* while I lived and visited there.

Milles merci, mes amis.

I've had the good fortune to take numerous trips to Paris with four close girlfriends—Liza Garfield, Sue Cameron Cosser, Elke Owens, and Christine McClure—who shared their sense of French style and *joie de vivre,* while living up to the phrase "shop 'til you drop."

Two other dear friends, Andrea Levine and Ginny Davis, share my interest in art history and contributed valuable advice on Paris' museums and travel deals.

And finally, my mother, Claire O'Connell, is the most supportive, encouraging parent any writer could want. Thank you, Mom.

CREDITS

Excerpts

The excerpt on page 66 is from "Hammams, North African Spas in Paris" by Angela Doland, Associated Press writer.

The excerpts on pages 70, 73, and 126 are from *French Chic* by Susan Sommers. Reprinted by permission of the author (www.dresszing.com).

The excerpt on page 117 is from an article in *European Travel & Life* by Marian McEvoy.

The excerpt on page 133 is from *Pierre Deux's French Country* by Pierre Moulin, Pierre Le Vec, and Linda Dannenberg.

The excerpt on page 174 is from the *National Geographic Traveler* article "Normandy Invasion" by Alan Richman.

The excerpt on page 181 is from the *National Geographic Traveler* article "On the Souvenir Trail" by Daisann McLane.

Maps

The maps on pages 10 to 11, 46 to 47, 167, and 196 to 202 are reprinted with permission from Michelin, copyright No. AGFA-NUBRUL.

Photos

Caroline O'Connell: pages 36, 40, 54, 69, 71, 76, 90, 120, 125, 130, 133, 135, 141, 176, 182.

Alexandre de Paris: page 62.

Hammam Pacha Paris: page 67.

Galeries Lafayette: page 116.

Fat Tire Bike Tours: page 146.

Duc des Lombards: page 156.

Moët & Chandon: pages 163 and 165.

About This Book

My love affair with Paris began a number of years ago on a five-week trip with a girl-friend, and that attraction to the City of Light has grown and endured ever since. Like most first-time visitors, I was enthralled by the beauty and excitement of the city. There were lively cafés and mouthwatering *pâtisseries* (bakeries) on every block. The shopping and dining were *très elegant*. The nightlife was glamorous. The sights and first-class museums traced the fascinating history of a civilization that has been influencing the rest of the world for centuries. I was hooked.

On subsequent trips, some lasting months, I immersed myself in the French culture, studied the language, and made lifelong friends with Parisians who were gracious enough to open their homes to me and share their day-to-day life in this breathtaking city. Along the way, I was able to increase my knowledge of fashion, cuisine, art, language, and history. The tastes and customs I adopted added a new dimension to my life, and I vowed to capture the essence of that unique world and "bottle it" for my friends. This guide is the culmination of those efforts. My goal is to maximize the limited time you'll have to enjoy this fabulous city and what it has to offer. So these pages will steer you to the heart of Paris, where the major sights and shops are within a short walk, and point out hidden gems you won't want to miss.

There are many reasons for my decision to focus on romance in Paris. First, if you are traveling with an *amour*, I don't know of a more romantic city for you to enjoy *ensemble* (together). Candlelit dinners in gourmet restaurants, beautiful gardens to stroll through arm-in-arm, fashionable boutiques to indulge your every whim, and fascinating monuments at every turn make this one of the most charming and captivating places in the world. Second, from luxurious beauty salons to specialty stores devoted to custom-made lingerie and signature perfumes, Paris presents a wealth of opportunities for women to be pampered, so it's an exciting, fun place whether you're with a loved one or traveling with friends. And finally, the vibrant nightlife of Paris offers dinner and dancing, boat tours of illuminated riverbank monuments, risqué cabaret shows, jet-set nightclubs, and intimate jazz in underground cellars. This city doesn't sleep, and you won't either.

The order of this guide follows the logical progression of your trip, starting with preparation and travel arrangements. Every important category is included—hotels, restaurants, museums and historic sights, shopping, parks and sports, nightlife, and day trips near Paris. Each listing includes the name, address, phone number, website, *arrondissement* (district), métro (subway) stop, and credit card information. But this guide, unlike most, recommends only those places that will provide you with a once-in-a-lifetime trip. Instead of encyclopedic listings of hotels, museums, restaurants, and other attractions, *Romance in Paris* offers my A lists—the very best of what the City of Light has to offer. In addition, there are features not found in other Paris guidebooks, including special mentions of romantic hideaways; advice from Parisians on favorite pastimes, such as spending a few hours in a hammam (Arabic-style steam bath) or having lunch at the renowned wine store Lavinia; tips on French fashion; and explanations of French customs. A special inset titled "Making Your Trip Memorable" clues you into ten great activities that are bound to be "peak moments" of your trip. There is even a mini-guide to beautiful destinations right outside the city, such as France's Champagne country. French terms are included in each chapter and, for easy reference, they are repeated in a glossary at the end of the book.

Several criteria were used to select the listings included in this book, starting with location. I chose to focus most of my attention on the five *arrondissements* (districts) that border one another in the center of the city and straddle the Seine River. This strategy places you near the main attractions and ensures that you will have the full Parisian experience the moment you step foot outside your hotel. I included places that are popular with the French, so that you'll be able to get a deeper sense of *la vie Parisienne,* as well as places that have charm and are rewarding experiences. Many of the restaurants in this guide are less well known and "off the beaten track."

As often as possible, each category, from hotels to restaurants and stores, offers moderately priced and budget listings to help offset the costly exchange rate of US dollar to euro. In the section on hotels (see Chapter 1), I have categorized each option as Deluxe, Expensive, Moderate, or Bargain so that you can narrow the field and home in on the best choices. In many other cases, such as the section on restaurants (Chapter 5), I have listed the price (in euros) of some popular options, such as a *prix fixe* (fixed price) dinner or a glass of wine. So whether you're interested in a grand splurge or a moderately priced meal, you'll be able to find an excellent choice that fills the bill. Of course, prices are always changing, so all cost-related information should be used as a guide only.

Throughout *Romance in Paris,* you'll find unique "Save Some Money" boxes that provide euro-saving tips. There are many ways in which you can spend less even while staying in a top-flight hotel, visiting a world-famous museum, indulging in French fashion accessories, enjoying evening entertainment, or taking part in a range of other activities. The "Save Some Money" features will help you experience Paris to the max without maxing out your credit cards.

Because taking transportation to points of interest is often a challenge to travelers, I have created a special section called "Sightseeing Via the Métro" (see page 48). This offers easy-to-understand charts of three métro (subway) lines that run through the heart of the city, and guides you to the most noteworthy cultural sights, shopping, and restaurants found at various stops. It is designed not only to help you reach my top picks, but also to make sure that you fully enjoy the many exceptional neighborhoods that Paris has to offer.

Whenever they are available, each listing within this book includes a website that can provide you with further information. Because of the language difference, you may be a little reluctant to make use of these sites, but in most cases, it will be much easier than you think. Many websites enable you to choose the language in which the information is provided. Just look for the United Kingdom flag or the word "English," click on it, and the translation will appear. If the website doesn't offer this choice, use the Google search engine to find a hotel, restaurant, or other place of interest, and Google will provide a "translate this page" option. Click on the offered link, and the website information will be provided in English. To further help you find the information you need to plan your dream vacation, I have created the website www.romanceinparis.net. Visit it to find updated information as well as links to the home pages of many of the places and activities suggested in this guide.

Because you'll have to use a credit card to make hotel reservations, each hotel listing in Chapter 1 tells you which cards are accepted. When planning your trip, be sure to read the section in Chapter 1 that discusses the use of cards (see page 28), as certain steps are needed to make sure that they will work in Paris. To avoid problems, I carry both American Express and Visa, and I have found that most Paris businesses accept one or the other. In a few instances, you'll need euros to make a purchase. For clarity, the listings in Chapters 2 through 11 state either "Cards: Accepted" or "Cards: Not Accepted" so that you will know when to have extra cash on hand.

Throughout *Every Woman's Guide to Romance in Paris,* the heart ♥ rating highlights my favorites in each category. In the case of hotels and restaurants, the heart indicates those places with an especially romantic ambience, and in some cases, it highlights especially good values. You'll find that every listing opens another door to your personal dream trip come true.

From the moment you arrive, Paris will embrace you.

Bon voyage!

Caroline O' Connell

1. Les Preparatifs

Maximize Your Trip by Planning Ahead

Paris is beautiful year-round, but spring and fall are the best times to go. The weather is mild and delightful for strolling hand in hand and exploring the city. Sidewalk cafés are bustling with customers soaking up the sun while enjoying a *café au lait* and watching the passing street scene—a great show that goes on for hours.

In summertime, temperatures soar and not all places have air conditioning. Since August is the month of vacation in France, tourists almost outnumber the Parisians. Summer is also the high season for airlines and hotels, which can double the cost of your trip.

Whatever the season, Paris will charm you with her Old World elegance and beauty. There is so much to see and do. (See the "Paris Events Calendar" inset on pages 7 and 8.)

This chapter contains information on how to prepare for your romantic adventure. It includes sections on making airline reservations, choosing a hotel, obtaining a passport and travel insurance, exchanging money, studying the language and culture, asking friends for referrals, and packing.

Making Travel Reservations

Try to make your travel plans at least three months ahead, preferably even earlier, because many hotels and flights sell out well in advance. The best hotel deals are snapped up quickly, especially during peak travel times. Flights have become more costly during the last few years, so you want to give yourself plenty of time to check out your options.

Making Plane Reservations

Airline ticket prices vary considerably depending on the season. One option is to have your flight booked by a travel agent, who will charge a nominal fee. Or you can be adventurous and spend a few hours surfing various Internet sites. (See the inset on page 6.) Many of the sites offer package deals that include both the flight and the hotel. Just be aware that a good number of the hotels found in package deals are not in good locations, and choosing a hotel in the midst of all the sights is key to having an enjoyable trip.

Great Websites for Booking Flights

These days, specialized websites allow you to compare airline ticket prices and package deals, and then book the best flight you can find. I have found the following sites to be helpful.

AIR FRANCE

Air France offers nonstop flights to Paris from major US cities, and their prices are competitive. Traveling on this airline will get you in a "French" mood before you even land.
Website: www.airfrance.com

AMERICAN AIRLINES

Run by American Airlines, this site also lists the flights of other carriers.
Website: www.aa.com

EXPEDIA

This website offers package deals that include nice hotels in good locations at the top of the search results.
Website: www.expedia.com

KAYAK

This site searches for flight and hotel deals on other websites and lists the options by price.
Website: www.kayak.com

TRAVELZOO

This is a well-run site with lots of package deals—which can sell out quickly—and good prices from major airlines.
Website: www.travelzoo.com

Finding the Right Hotel

Even though Paris has become an expensive city to visit, there are still a number of charming, moderately priced hotels in great locations. This section focuses on affordable hotels, although I've included a handful of pricey options for a romantic splurge. Honeymoon, anyone?

As already mentioned, the key consideration is location. You want to be in the heart of the city where street life is bustling and Paris' historic sights and shops are within a short walk. Paris has twenty regions, called *arrondissements*. (To learn more about *arrondissements,* see page 9.) The *premier* (first), *sixième* (sixth), and *huitième* (eighth) *arrondissements* border the Seine River and one another in the center of the city (*centre de la ville*). Most of the hotels recommended in this chapter are concentrated in the *premier* and *sixième arrondissements*, but I've also suggest some in closely adjacent areas, such as the *quatrième arrondissement.*

Some hotel websites claim that they are "within a short walking distance" of major sights like the Louvre and Musée d'Orsay when they are actually located in *arrondissements* that are farther out. Their interpretation of a short walk is quite a stretch, because it would take well over half an hour to reach these places even if you moved at a brisk pace. If you're not absolutely sure, double-check the hotel's location. Many websites include a map with a hotel icon so you can see where the building is located in relation to key sights.

The Paris Events Calendar

Every year, Paris hosts special events that may be of interest to you and may even determine when you book your trip. You'll want to check the website www.paris.eventguide.com to verify when each event will be held the year of your visit. As you'll see below, every month brings another unique show, celebration, or holiday, but keep in mind that this is just a *sampling* of what's offered. Even more events can be found on the EventGuide website.

JANUARY

Salon du Mariage. Beginning with an event in January, and occurring throughout the year at places near Paris, the Salon du Mariage is a convention for those who want to purchase wedding attire and related items.

FEBRUARY

Festival of St. Valentine. Yes, Parisians celebrate Valentine's Day too. But they do it with flair. Anyone can purchase space to post a romantic message to their loved one on the public digital advertising boards operated by the city. The Paris mayor's office starts accepting love notes on February 1 on its website, www.paris.fr. Also, many hotels offer romantic Valentine's weekend package deals that include candlelight gourmet dinners and dancing.

MARCH

Poet's Springtime Festival. Starting on the second Monday in March, poetry readings and performances are held in locations around the city. For more information, visit the event website: http://www.printempsdespoetes.com/.

APRIL

Paris Marathon. If you're in shape for the twenty-six-mile tour, a great way to explore the city is to participate in the annual Paris Marathon. You are sure to be with Parisians—as well as people from many other countries in Europe—as you wind around the beautiful monuments and gardens.

MAY

May Day Holiday. On the first of May, most of the city closes for La Fête du Travail—what we call Labor Day. There is a large parade down the Avenue des Champs-Elysées, and some monuments remain open. On this day, it is also customary for men to give a bouquet of Lily of the Valley flowers to their beloved.

MAY TO JUNE

French Open Tennis Tournament. Starting in late May and running for two weeks into June, the French Open is held at Paris' famed Roland Garros Stadium adjacent to the Bois de Boulogne park. If you are a tennis fan, as I am, this world-class event is not to be missed. The crowd of spectators is elegant, the international tennis players are at the top of their game, and the venue is beautifully run. (See page 146 for more details.)

JUNE

Paris Air Show. Every two years in mid-June, nearby Le Bourget airport plays host to an amazing array of planes, large and small, that boast state-of-the-art gizmos and technology. One-day tickets are a reasonable 20 euros. For more information, check the show's website: www.paris-air-show.com.

JULY

Bastille Day. On July 14, Paris celebrates the start of the French Revolution with military parades and spectacular fireworks. This would be a good time to take an evening boat cruise, if you can get a reservation.

Paris Plage. Throughout the summer, a large area near the Seine River is transformed into a temporary beach—yes, the City of Paris trucks in the sand by the ton. There are impromptu concerts and many beach activities. (For more details, see page 143.)

AUGUST TO SEPTEMBER

Classical Music Festival. Hosted by Parc Floral in Bois de Vincennes, on the eastern edge of Paris, orchestras from several countries offer outside weekend performances at this Festival Classique du Vert.

OCTOBER

La Nuit Blanche. At the beginning of October, the City of Paris celebrates "White Night," and museums, galleries, city halls, and virtually hundreds of other cultural centers remain open *all night*. This custom started in 2002, and since then, it has become a major event.

NOVEMBER

Paris International Photo Fair. During the month of November, the art of photography is celebrated in various locations throughout Paris. A highlight is the four-day International Photo Fair exhibition at the Louvre. (For information on taking a professional photography tour/class, see page 178.)

DECEMBER

Ice Skating. Beginning in December and lasting until early March, ice skating rinks are set up by the city in front of Hôtel de Ville, Paris's City Hall, and the train/métro station at Montparnasse on the other side of the river. There is no charge to use the rinks, and you can rent skates for around 5 euros (for details, see page 148).

Understanding Arrondissements

Within this chapter, most of the hotels I recommend are found in the first and sixth *arrondissements,* because they are at the center of the action. But I also suggest some excellent choices in other districts. Before you select a hotel, it's a good idea to look at the following overview so that you understand what each of the key *arrondissements* has to offer.

Premier (First) *Arrondissement*

Located on the Right Bank—historically, the more affluent side of Paris—this district is at the hub of Parisian life. Staying here will place you in easy walking distance of the Louvre and Tuileries Garden, Le Palais Royal, and L'Orangerie, home of Monet's water lily murals. This area also has a major métro line that will take you to the Champs-Elysées, Arc de Triomphe, and Notre Dame.

Troisième (Third) *Arrondissement*

A bit off the beaten track for the major sights, this area nevertheless boasts some wonderful museums, including Musée Carnavalet and Musée Picasso. It also has many lively cafés.

Quatrième (Fourth) *Arrondissement*

The fourth *arrondissement* is one of the most picturesque because it features not only part of the historic Marais district, but also the two islands in the Seine River—Ile Saint-Louis and a portion of Ile de la Cité, which includes the famed Notre Dame Cathédrale. You'll also find many charming boutiques and cafés in this area.

Sixième (Sixth) *Arrondissement*

Located on the Left Bank, this area has an artistic feel and features winding streets, attractive hotels and shops, and plenty of street life after dark. Place Saint-Sulpice and the gorgeous Jardin du Luxembourg are in the southern part of this *arrondissement.*

Huitième (Eighth) *Arrondissement*

Situated on the Right Bank of Paris, this is one of the city's major business districts. Here you will find the Elysée Palace, the residence of the President of France; the Champs-Elysée; the Arc de Triomphe; and Place de la Concorde.

Seizième (Sixteenth) *Arrondissement*

This upscale residential area is a mecca for those who love the outdoors and sports. It features the fashionable Bois de Boulogne park, two race tracks (Auteuil and Longchamp), and the Roland Garros Stadium, home of the French Open.

Dix-Septième (Seventeenth) *Arrondissement*

Primarily a residential area, this district does include the Palais des Congrès de Paris—a concert venue and convention center. Its greatest advantage is that it borders the eighth *arrondissement,* which includes a number of famous Paris sights.

The Lay of the Land

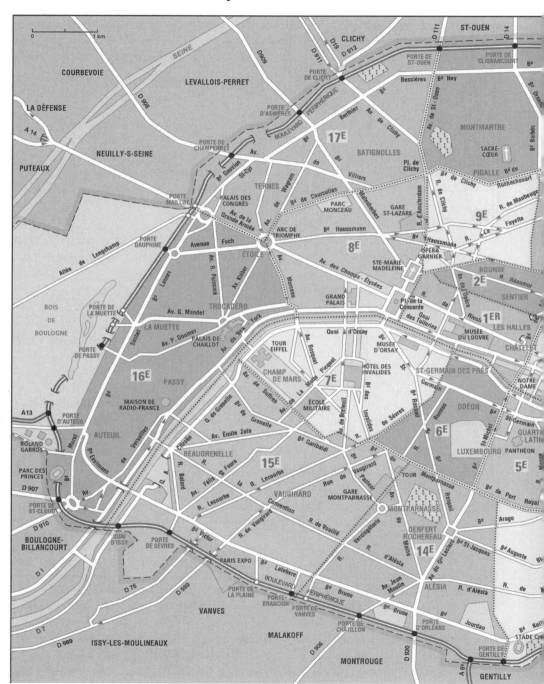

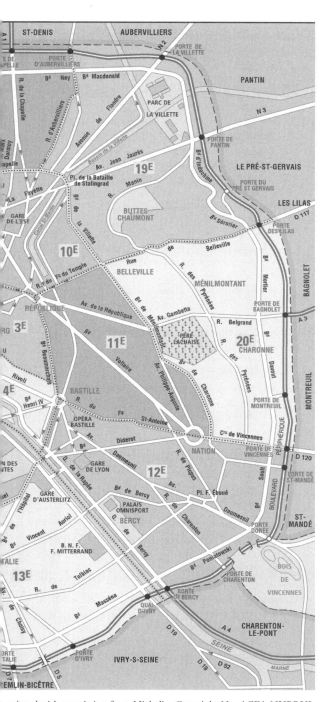

Paris is divided into twenty numbered neighborhoods, called *arrondissements*. They start in the center and spiral outward to the city limits. Each *arrondissement* has its own distinctive flavor and appeal. The Seine River divides Paris in half and is crisscrossed by more than thirty bridges, or *ponts*. The northern half of the city, referred to as the *Rive Droite,* or Right Bank, was long the stronghold of merchants and royalty. The Left Bank, or *Rive Gauche,* was first settled by intellectuals, writers, and artists, and it remains their home today.

Address numbers are determined by position relative to the Seine. Streets perpendicular to the Seine start their numbering at the river and move outward. Streets parallel to the Seine are numbered from east to west. One source of confusion is that addresses on opposite sides of the street do not necessarily correspond as they do in the States; for example, number 22 may be facing number 55 instead of number 23. For complete maps, get a copy of *Paris par Arrondissement,* a pocket-size mapbook that lists every street and address and is sold at many *tabacs* (newsstands) in Paris. This guide provides maps of the major *arrondissements* on pages 196 to 202.

Hotel Chains in Paris

If you want to use the frequent-traveler points you've accrued while staying at popular hotels in the United States and elsewhere, Paris offers some great choices, many of which are located in the hub of the city.

HOTEL LE PARC—TROCADERO PARIS (EXPENSIVE TO DELUXE)
55 Avenue Raymond-Poincaré
Phone: 01-44-05-66-66
Website:
http://www.marriott.com/hotels/travel/pars
p-hotel-le-parc-trocadero-paris/
16th *arrondissement*
Métro: Victor-Hugo and Trocadéro
Chain: Marriott-Renaissance Hotels
Cards: AE, MC, V

HOTEL PRINCE DE GALLES (EXPENSIVE TO DELUXE)
33 Avenue George V
Phone: 01-53-23-77-77
Website: www.princedegallesparis.com
8th *arrondissement*
Métro: George-V
Chain: Starwood Hotels and Resorts
Cards: AE, MC, V

HYATT REGENCY PARIS—MADELEINE (DELUXE AND BEYOND)
24 Boulevard Malesherbes
Phone: 01-55-27-12-34
Website: www.paris.madeleine.hyatt.com
8th *arrondissement*
Métro: Madeleine
Chain: Hyatt Regency Hotels
Cards: AE, MC, V

PARIS MARRIOTT CHAMPS-ELYSEES (DELUXE)
70 Avenue des Champs-Elysées
Phone: 01-53-93-55-00
Website: www.parismarriott.com
8th *arrondissement*
Métro: George-V and Charles-de-Gaulle-Etoile
Chain: Marriott-Renaissance Hotels
Cards: AE, MC, V

RADISSON BLU HOTEL, CHAMPS-ELYSEES (EXPENSIVE TO DELUXE)
78 bis Avenue Marceau
Phone: 01-53–23-43-43
Website: www.radissonblu.com
8th *arrondissement*
Métro: Charles-de-Gaulle-Etoile
Chain: Radisson Hotels and Resorts
Cards: AE, MC, V

WESTIN PARIS-VENDOME (EXPENSIVE TO DELUXE)
3 Rue de Castiglione
Phone: 01-44-77-11-11
Website: www.westin.com/paris
1st *arrondissement*
Métro: Tuileries and Concorde
Chain: Starwood Hotels and Resorts
Cards: AE, MC, V

$$$ SAVE SOME MONEY $$$

Although I usually recommend that you avoid booking hotels which have difficult cancellation policies, there is one big exception: Some very nice, rather expensive hotels offer a considerable discount on their websites (up to 20 percent) for *nonrefundable* bookings when you reserve early and pay the full amount in advance. So if you're keen on luxurious accommodations and are sure that you won't change your trip plans, look for this option on hotel websites when you make your reservations.

HOTELS

When compiling my list of recommended hotels, I looked for those in attractive surroundings with a charming ambience, good standards of cleanliness, and nice amenities. The differences in price reflect the levels of luxury, which includes the size of the room; the quality of the furnishings; hotel amenities like a spa, separate bar, or nice restaurant; and the soundproofing of the windows.

Generally, Paris hotel rooms are on the small side, as are the hotel elevators. I've read reviews on traveler feedback sites, and many tourists complain about the size of the hotel rooms and about the "matchbox" elevators. Real estate is at a premium in Paris, and many of the buildings are hundreds of years old, so it's best to appreciate the charm of your accommodations unless you want to spend a great deal of money on a deluxe hotel.

Like plane reservations, hotel reservations can be made through a travel agent or on your own. These days, many Paris hotels have their own websites where they post special rates and take reservations directly. In many cases, the website allows you to choose the language in which the information is printed. (Look for the flag of the United Kingdom or the word "English," and click on it.) In other words, you don't have to read French to navigate the website of a French hotel. If the website does not offer an English-language section, perform a search for the hotel using the Google search engine, and Google will give you a "translate this page" option. Click on the offered link, and you will find that the hotel website has been translated into English for you.

In addition to the websites of the individual hotels, there are several general sites that make it easy to secure reservations. See the inset on page 14 for hotel reservation sites.

Be wary of booking on a site that charges a cancellation fee. Some charge $25 and up even if you cancel more than a week ahead. If you do book through an Internet site, definitely call or email the hotel right away to confirm and verify the details. (Information on calling Paris can be found on page 58.) There is usually someone at the hotel who speaks English, so you shouldn't have a problem even if your French is rudimentary—or nonexistent. Some features you might want to request are a room that has been newly renovated (especially the bathroom), a room with a view, a room that is quiet, or amenities such as satellite TV and a hairdryer. You may also want to ask about the size of the bed, whether the bathroom has a shower or tub, if the hotel has an elevator (or "lift," as they call it), and if the room has air conditioning, or *climatisé*. If Internet access is important to you, ask if the hotel has WiFi or a computer hooked up to the Internet for use by guests. If it doesn't, don't despair. You can always check your email at a cybercafé. (See the inset on page 59 to learn more about cybercafés.) Don't worry about getting a nonsmoking room, as all hotels in France are nonsmoking as required by law. Finally, I recommend that you call a few days before your arrival and request the nicest room available in your category. That personal touch works like a charm.

In the following list, hotel costs have been indicated by the terms Deluxe, Expensive, Moderate, and Bargain, which are defined at right. When this guide went to print, the exchange rate was 1.4 US dollars to the euro, which means that you must multiply the euro price by 1.4 to get the dollar amount. Normally, the continental breakfast—coffee, juice, and pastries—is an additional charge.

Within each *arrondissement*, the hotels are arranged alphabetically, not in order of preference. The heart rating ♥ indicates my top suggestions, taking into consideration the charm and ambience of the hotel and the value for the cost. Some less expensive hotels aren't quite as luxurious as others, but nevertheless get the heart rating because they're well-located, comfortable, and very reasonably priced for the quality of the accommodations. You can spend the money you've saved on a great dinner—and *that's* romantic!

Key to Hotel Listings
Deluxe—$450 and over
Expensive—$250 to $450
Moderate—$125 to $250
Bargain—Some rooms
   under $125
(Prices are for double
   occupancy)

AE—American Express
MC—MasterCard
V—Visa

Great Websites for Hotel Reservations

Hotel websites provide a good deal of information about accommodations, and sometimes offer special deals and romantic getaways. But you can often find better prices on the following travel websites. Two of the sites also offer objective reviews by other tourists, providing a perspective that you are not going to get from any hotel.

DISCOUNT HOTEL RESERVATIONS
Discount Hotel Reservations recently purchased GTA Hotels, which used to be my favorite site for booking hotels. So far, I've found and used some good hotel deals with the new management. This site gives you a 20- to 30-percent discount off your stay. You pay in advance and must remember to present the Travel Voucher when you check in. You can usually cancel a few days before for full reimbursement.
Website: www.DHR.com

TRIPADVISOR
TripAdvisor is the go-to place to read other travelers' hotel reviews. You'll learn a lot, but be sure to take the criticism with a grain of salt, since the reviews aren't edited for accuracy. This website links you to other sites where you can make a reservation, but remember that while this is convenient, you may not get the best deals. Be sure to also visit the individual hotel sites and DHR.com.
Website: www.tripadvisor.com

VENERE.COM
Venere.com provides a huge selection of hotels in the center of Paris. To narrow down the choices, after pinpointing the city, use the toolbar to specify the area of Paris in which you're interested and your budget. Helpful reviews by other travelers are included.
Website: www.venere.com

The Premier (First) *Arrondissement*

The *premier arrondissement* is the hallmark of luxury and elegance and is very conducive to a romantic stay. One of the oldest areas of the city, this *arrondissement* was once the neighborhood of kings. Now it is home to the Louvre Museum, the Tuileries Garden, Palais Royal, and the start of Rue St.-Honoré—a famous street that is lined with designer shops. There are many renowned deluxe hotels in this area, but you can find moderately priced accommodations, as well. All the hotels in this section are in good locations, near famous sights and interesting shops and restaurants.

DUMINY-VENDOME (EXPENSIVE)

This clean, modern hotel is situated in a fashionable neighborhood near Place Vendôme, the Tuileries Garden, and great shopping on Rue St.-Honoré. The prices are reasonable for the *quartier* (area), but like many Parisian hotels, the rooms are small. There are other hotels in this neighborhood that are less costly, but this is a good choice if you want to be assured of a fairly luxurious room.

3 Rue du Mont-Thabor
Phone: 01-42-60-32-80
Website: www.hotel
   duminyvendome.com
1st *arrondissement*
Métro: Tuileries
Cards: AE, MC, V

HOTEL COSTES (DELUXE)

Reminiscent of a Renaissance palace, this trendy hotel combines one-of-a-kind antiques with sumptuous fabrics. From the moment you enter the courtyard, the people-watching and background music will give you the impression that you've stepped onto a film set. Both the rooms and the hotel restaurant are very expensive. If you don't want to pay the hefty prices, it's still worth a trip to have a drink at the bar and catch the "scene." For a similar experience at less cost, I recommend L'Hôtel in Saint-Germain-des-Prés. (See page 20.)

239 Rue St.-Honoré
Phone: 01-42-44-50-00
Website:
   www.hotelcostes.com
1st *arrondissement*
Métro: Tuileries and
   Concorde
Cards: AE, MC, V

HOTEL DE LA PLACE DU LOUVRE
(MODERATE TO EXPENSIVE)

Literally within a stone's throw of the Louvre on a side street near the Seine River, this nicely appointed artsy hotel has twenty rooms (some require stairs) with satellite TV, a mini-bar, air conditioning, and free WiFi access. I found the best rates on the hotel website, including an excellent weekend special. The website also conveniently lists nearby restaurants, spas, salons, and shops, and devotes a page to museums, sometimes listing current and upcoming Paris exhibitions.

21 Rue des Prêtres-St.-
   Germain l'Auxerrois
Phone: 01-42-33-78-68
Website: www.paris-hotel-
   place-du-louvre.com
1st *arrondissement*
Métro: Pont-Neuf and
   Palais-Royal-Musée-
   du-Louvre
Cards: AE, MC, V

HOTEL DU LION D'OR (BARGAIN TO MODERATE)

It's difficult to find inexpensive hotels in this desirable location, but Lion d'Or has good prices for the locale. The rooms are not luxurious, but are renovated and clean. If you'd like more space, the hotel offers studio apartments across the street that you can rent by the day. The relatively inexpensive breakfast includes coffee, fruit juice, pastries, and cereal.

5 Rue de la Sourdière
Phone: 01-42-60-79-04
Website: www.hotel-louvre-paris.com
1st *arrondissement*
Métro: Tuileries and Pyramide
Cards: AE, MC, V

HOTEL LONDRES SAINT-HONORE (MODERATE)

This is in another great location, facing the Eglise Saint-Roch, a historic Paris church that chimes on the hour, providing a lovely ambience. The rooms are small but clean and contain all the amenities, including satellite TV, direct phone, and a mini-bar. Upon entering the hotel, you walk upstairs to the lobby, where an elevator provides access to most rooms. The hotel has a five-day cancellation policy, which provides less leeway than you have with most other hotels.

13 Rue St.-Roch
Phone: 01-42-60-15-62
Website: www.hotellondressthonore-paris.com
1st *arrondissement*
Métro: Tuileries
Cards: AE, MC, V

HOTEL MAYFAIR (DELUXE) ♥

A member of Exclusive Hotels, which emphasizes "Charm and Character," Hôtel Mayfair is ideally located on a side street off the Tuileries Garden. Sumptuously appointed rooms are impeccable and include all the amenities. The hotel staff is attentive, and a comfortable lounge offers drinks and snacks. Although the price is steep, you can get a 25-percent discount on the website in exchange for a nonrefundable deposit. Go through the booking process and click on "Best Internet Rate Conditions."

3 Rue Rouget de Lisle
Phone: 01-42-60-38-14
Website: www.paris-hotel-mayfair.com
1st *arrondissement*
Métro: Place-de-la-Concorde
Cards: AE, MC, V

HOTEL MOLIERE (EXPENSIVE)

Hôtel Molière is a bit more expensive than some of the other listings in this great neighborhood, but the rooms have all the amenities as well as attractive furnishings. The other benefit is that the Molière is small and located on a charming side street, just off Avenue de l'Opéra and not far from the Louvre. The hotel's three-night Internet rate falls just under the "Moderate" rating.

21 Rue Molière
Phone: 01-42-96-22-01
Website: www.hotel-moliere.fr
1st *arrondissement*
Métro: Palais-Royal-Musée-du-Louvre
Cards: AE, MC, V

HOTEL MONTPENSIER (MODERATE)

Adjacent to Palais Royal and a few blocks from the Louvre, the Montpensier is listed because it charges reasonable prices for the area and features charming old-fashioned French décor. The least expensive double rooms share a shower down the hall. Rue de Richelieu is a noisy street, so request a quiet room.

12 Rue de Richelieu
Phone: 01-42-96-28-50
Website: www.montpensierparis.com
1st *arrondissement*
Métro: Palais-Royal-Musée-du-Louvre
Cards: AE, MC, V

HOTEL PRINCE ALBERT LOUVRE (MODERATE) ♥

Many rooms of this hotel have been recently renovated, and this is a great bargain for the upscale neighborhood. The rooms are small but have most amenities. Not all rooms have air conditioning, so be sure to request it if you're visiting in the summer. The lobby offers a comfortable sitting area, where you can relax while reviewing your guidebooks, and a small fee gets you access to the Internet. Be sure to check out the shops on neighboring Rue Marché St.-Honoré and the trendy cafés in Place du Marché St.-Honoré.

5 Rue St.-Hyacinthe
Phone: 01-42-61-58-36
Website: www.hotel
  princealbert.com (click
  on Louvre)
1st *arrondissement*
Métro: Tuileries and
  Pyramide
Cards: AE, MC, V

HOTEL REGINA (DELUXE) ♥

Although this is listed as Deluxe, the hotel website does offer specials that fall into the Expensive category. Under "Reservations and Packages," scroll down to "Best Available Rate" and you'll find a good discount. This is a grand old formal Parisian hotel with a courteous staff, intimate bar, gourmet restaurant with garden, and beautifully appointed rooms. Ask for a room that faces the Tuileries Garden with the Eiffel Tower in the distance. It's a spectacular view!

2 Place des Pyramides
Phone: 01-42-60-31-10
Website: www.regina-
  hotel.com
1st *arrondissement*
Métro: Tuileries and
  Palais-Royal-Musée-
  du-Louvre
Cards: AE, MC, V

HOTEL ROYAL SAINT-HONORE
(EXPENSIVE TO DELUXE) ♥

Luxurious with a beautiful lobby, this is fast becoming one of my favorite hotels in this great location. The rooms, which are nicely decorated with colorful fabrics, have all the amenities, including marble bathrooms and good soundproofing. Best of all, the hotel's website offers an Internet rate that is a third off the normal rate if you pay for your room in advance (nonrefundable).

221 Rue St.-Honoré
Phone: 01-42-60-32-79
Website: www.royal-st-
  honore.com
1st *arrondissement*
Métro: Tuileries
Cards: AE, MC, V

HOTEL SAINT-ROCH (MODERATE)

A good option for this wonderful neighborhood, Hôtel Saint-Roch is on a charming street only two blocks from the Tuileries Garden, surrounded by lovely shops. The prices are very reasonable for the location and the amenities, which include satellite TV, a mini-bar, and a hairdryer. Most rooms also have air conditioning. In some instances, you can get a slightly better price by calling or emailing the hotel directly, rather than reserving on the website.

25 Rue St.-Roch
Phone: 01-42-60-17-91
Website: www.hotelsaint
  roch-paris.com
1st *arrondissement*
Métro: Tuileries
Cards: AE, MC, V

LE RELAIS SAINT-HONORE (EXPENSIVE) ♥

For a romantic splurge, you can't beat this hotel. Within this chic area, there are many Deluxe hotels that I have chosen not to include. At about half the price for a double room, Le Relais Saint-Honoré has gorgeous design touches and luxurious accommodations, including high-quality bedding and beautifully appointed bathrooms.

308 Rue St.-Honoré
Phone: 01-42-96-06-06
Website: www.relaissaint
  honore.com
1st *arrondissement*
Métro: Tuileries
Cards: AE, MC, V

The Troisième (Third) *Arrondissement*

The *troisième arrondissement* is part of the historic Marais district. The surrounding area is rich in history, and some medieval streets still remain. As part of the renovation begun in 1962, landmark buildings have been converted to museums, including Musée Carnavalet, which charts the history of Paris, and Musée Picasso. This area also includes Paris' oldest square, Place des Vosges, built in 1605 by King Henry IV of France and encircled by ancient arcades and stately "apartment" buildings that formerly housed aristocrats. One of Paris' most acclaimed restaurants, L'Ambroisie, is at one end of the square, and the elegant Hôtel Pavillon de la Reine is at another corner.

HOTEL PAVILLON DE LA REINE
(EXPENSIVE TO DELUXE) ♥

This is a wonderful choice for a romantic interlude in Paris. The décor is beyond sumptuous, with beautiful fabrics, textures, and one-of-kind design touches. And for the quality of the rooms, the price is reasonable by Paris standards. When you enter an inner courtyard to reach the hotel lobby, it's like stepping into a peaceful oasis. The hotel website offers very good package deals, some of which include a full breakfast, a spa treatment, and free parking.

28 Place des Vosges
Phone: 01-40-29-19-19
Website: www.pavillon-de-la-reine.com
3rd *arrondissement*
Métro: St.-Paul
Cards: AE, MC, V

HOTEL SEVIGNE (BARGAIN)

This is one of the rare "bargain" hotels in Paris. The Hôtel Sévigné is located in a good neighborhood and has renovated rooms with all the basic amenities, including air conditioning, satellite TV, WiFi, and a hairdryer.

2 Rue Malher
Phone: 01-42-72-76-17
Website: www.le-sevigne.com
4th *arrondissement*
Métro: St.-Paul
Cards: AE, MC, V

The Quatrième (Fourth) *Arrondissement*

The *quatrième arrondissement* includes a portion of one of Paris' oldest districts, the Marais, and also embraces two islands in the middle of the Seine—Ile Saint-Louis and Ile de la Cité. Most (but not all) of the hotels I recommend in this *arrondissement* are found on Ile Saint-Louis, a tiny picturesque island that exudes romantic ambience and charm. The main street, Rue St.-Louis-en-l'Ile, is lined with interesting boutiques, intimate cafés, and the famous Berthillon ice cream shop. Notre Dame, the impressive Gothic cathedral, towers only a short distance away on the adjoining island. Generally, Paris hotel rooms are small, but on Ile Saint-Louis, the rooms are *très petite* because space is at a premium.

GRAND HOTEL MALHER (MODERATE)

This hotel is officially in the fourth *arrondissement,* but is only a few blocks from Place des Vosges, which is in the third *arrondissement.* This makes it a less-expensive option if you want easy access to the Marais *quartier.* Each of the thirty-one rooms has recently been renovated and is equipped with satellite TV, a mini-bar, and a hairdryer. Enjoy breakfast (9 euros) in the hotel's seventeenth-century wine cellar, or try one of the area's charming cafés.

5 Rue Malher
Phone: 01-42-72-60-92
Website: www.grand hotelmalher.com
4th *arrondissement*
Métro: St.-Paul
Cards: AE, MC, V

HOTEL DES DEUX-ILES (MODERATE TO EXPENSIVE) ♥

Depending on the euro rate at the time of your trip, Hôtel des Deux-Iles could fall into the Moderate or Expensive category. I recommend the splurge. The island feels like a very small, picturesque "city within a city" and is a lovely respite after a day of sightseeing. With only seventeen rooms, this hotel is always *complet* (booked), and has been known to overbook, so be sure to reconfirm your reservation. Recently renovated, each room has air conditioning, a TV, a hairdryer, and an in-room safe.

59 Rue St.-Louis-en-l'Ile
Phone: 01-43-26-13-35
Website: www.deuxiles-paris-hotel.com
4th *arrondissement*
Métro: Pont-Marie
Cards: AE, MC, V

HOTEL DU JEU DE PAUME
(MODERATE TO EXPENSIVE) ♥

The most elegant hotel on Ile Saint-Louis is also the most pricey, but the website offers some less-expensive options as well as excellent package deals. The name of the hotel recalls the days when members of King Louis XIII's court used this location as a clubhouse when they played *jeu de paume*—a game similar to tennis. Design aficionados are drawn to the well-executed contemporary style within the seventeenth-century building. Staying here is an "experience within an experience." Just be prepared for small spaces.

54 Rue St.-Louis-en-l'Ile
Phone: 01-43-26-14-18
Website: www.jeude paumehotel.com
4th *arrondissement*
Métro: Pont-Marie
Cards: AE, MC, V

HOTEL SAINT-LOUIS (MODERATE)

Cleverly priced less than Hôtel des Deux-Iles down the street (see the second listing on this page), this hotel is a great value for the money and provides a friendly welcome and clean rooms with all the usual amenities—TV, mini-bar, hairdryer, and in-room safe. On confirmation of your reservation, your credit card will be billed for the first night—an amount that is refundable up to seventy-two hours before your arrival. I don't recommend paying 12 euros for the breakfast; instead, try a nearby café such as Le Flore en l'Isle.

75 Rue St.-Louis-en-l'Ile
Phone: 01-46-34-04-80
Website: www.hotelsaint louis.com
4th *arrondissement*
Métro: Pont-Marie
Cards: MC, V

The Sixième (Sixth) Arrondissement

The *sixième arrondissement,* also known as Saint-Germain-des-Prés, is on the Left Bank, just across the River Seine from the first *arrondissement.* Since the 1920s, this area has been renowned for the writers and artists who frequented the local cafés, discussing art, religion, and politics late into the night. Visitors are reminded of that legacy while enjoying the same cafés, browsing through art galleries and antique shops, viewing the latest fashions in trendy boutiques, and bargaining with the aspiring artists who sell their sketches on Boulevard St.-Germain. Hotels in the *sixième* reflect this creative, artistic ambience.

ARTUS HOTEL (MODERATE TO EXPENSIVE) ♥

Located in an ideal spot amid the art galleries and shops near Boulevard St.-Germain, the Artus Hôtel offers luxurious rooms that are sleek, modern, and beautifully appointed. It's a bit costly, but if you shop the website, you can usually find a few rooms in the Moderate category as well as special offers that include use of the sauna. The quality is excellent, and the lounge is great for curling up with a glass of champagne. This is a romantic hotel!

34 Rue de Buci
Phone: 01-43-29-07-20
Website:
www.artushotel.com
6th *arrondissement*
Métro: St.-Germain-des-Prés
Cards: AE, MC, V

CRYSTAL HOTEL (MODERATE)

Just off Boulevard St.-Germain, this hotel offers decent prices at an excellent location. The rooms are small, as is the elevator. Ask for one of the recently renovated rooms; they are fresher and have much nicer bathrooms. Amenities include an in-room safe, a hairdryer, and satellite TV. Continental breakfast is served in the stone cellar.

24 Rue St.-Benoît
Phone: 01-45-48-85-14
Website: www.hotelcrystal saintgermainparis.com
6th *arrondissement*
Métro: St.-Germain-des-Prés
Cards: AE, MC, V

L'HOTEL (DELUXE AND BEYOND) ♥

I love this hotel! In addition to being on a quiet street adjacent to the prestigious Ecole des Beaux-Arts (the art and architecture university), L'Hôtel was recently remodelled by famed designer Jacques Garcia, and the décor is yummy. The twenty rooms are small (this is an old building), yet sumptuously decorated with beautiful fabrics and antiques, and the well-appointed bathrooms have all the amenities. There is also an intimate gourmet restaurant off the lobby, a cozy bar area, and a private swimming pool and steam room for two. Prices are commensurately high.

13 Rue des Beaux-Arts
Phone: 01-44-41-99-00
Website: www.l-hotel.com
6th *arrondissement*
Métro: St.-Germain-des-Prés
Cards: AE, MC, V

HOTEL BONAPARTE (MODERATE)

For four generations, the same family has owned and run this lovely hotel near Place Saint-Sulpice. The rooms are simple and the elevator is small, but Hôtel Bonaparte has good prices for the location. Rooms are air-conditioned and contain a small refrigerator, a hairdryer, an in-room safe, and satellite TV, and the 6-euro breakfast is a real bargain.

61 Rue Bonaparte
Phone: 01-43-26-97-37
Website:
www.hotelbonaparte.fr
6th *arrondissement*
Métro: St.-Sulpice
Cards: AE, MC, V

HOTEL D'AUBUSSON (EXPENSIVE TO DELUXE) ♥

This opulent hotel in a converted seventeenth-century mansion is worth the price if your checkbook can afford it. You'll find a convenient location near the Seine; a pampering staff; spacious, beautifully designed rooms; and *all* the amenities. To add to the romance, the hotel's Café Laurent hosts live jazz in the evenings—a wonderful way to unwind at the end of the day. The website offers a romance package, which includes a superior room, transportation from the airport, a daily breakfast, a champagne lunch, tickets to the Louvre, and a concert.

33 Rue Dauphine
Phone: 01-43-29-43-43
Website: www.hotel
daubusson.com
6th *arrondissement*
Métro: Odéon and
Mabillon
Cards: AE, MC, V

HOTEL DE FLEURIE (MODERATE) ♥

Boasting a great location in Saint-Germain-des-Prés, Hôtel de Fleurie has nicely decorated rooms with double-glazed windows, air conditioning, and all the amenities. Bathrooms are well appointed and include heated towel racks. The prices are good for the luxury level of the rooms, and the website offers special double rates. But the cancellation policy is harsh; you can cancel up to three days before arrival, but you will be billed a 40-euro cancellation charge.

32 Rue Grégoire de
Tours
Phone: 01-53-73-70-00
Website: www.fleurie-
hotel-paris.com
6th *arrondissement*
Métro: St.-Germain-des-
Prés and Odéon
Cards: AE, MC, V

HOTEL DE L'ABBAYE (EXPENSIVE) ♥

Set off from the street behind a courtyard, Hôtel de L'Abbaye near Place Saint-Sulpice and the Luxembourg Garden is one of my top recommendations and receives rave reviews for its romantic ambience. The décor is exquisite, with nice antiques and colorful fabrics. The rooms are small but well appointed with all the amenities, including air conditioning. Afternoon tea is served in the lovely garden terrace or cozy sitting room.

10 Rue Cassette
Phone: 01-45-44-38-11
Website: www.hotel
abbayeparis.com
6th *arrondissement*
Métro: St.-Sulpice
Cards: AE, MC, V

HOTEL DES MARRONNIERS (MODERATE)

Situated in the midst of the Left Bank art galleries, Hôtel des Marronniers is reasonably priced for this high-rent district. The rooms are small but nicely decorated, and all of them have air conditioning. Be certain to request a "garden side" room if you're concerned about street noise.

21 Rue Jacob
Phone: 01-43-25-30-60
Website: www.paris-hotel-
marronniers.com
6th *arrondissement*
Métro: St.-Germain-des-
Prés
Cards: AE, MC, V

HOTEL LE CLEMENT (MODERATE)

This is a charming hotel in the heart of Saint-Germain. The rooms are very small but nicely decorated and have air conditioning and satellite TV. The best part, though, is the reasonable prices.

6 Rue Clément
Phone: 01-43-26-53-60
Website: www.hotel-
clement.fr
6th *arrondissement*
Métro: Mabillon
Cards: AE, MC, V

HOTEL LUXEMBOURG PARC (EXPENSIVE)

Hôtel Luxembourg Parc is a bit farther from the heart of the Left Bank shops and sights than many other hotels in this district. On the plus side, this elegant hotel faces the lovely Luxembourg Garden and offers great service and beautiful rooms with all the amenities, including luxurious marble bathrooms. Visit the hotel's website for special rates. The lowest rates are prepaid and nonrefundable; the next level requires cancellation forty-eight hours before arrival.

42 Rue de Vaugirard
Phone: 01-53-10-36-50
Website:
    www.luxembourg-paris-hotel.com
6th *arrondissement*
Métro: St.-Sulpice
Cards: AE, MC, V

HOTEL PRINCE DE CONDE (MODERATE TO EXPENSIVE) ♥

Situated between Boulevard St.-Germain and the Seine River, on a street lined with art galleries, this small renovated hotel has charming English décor. All twelve rooms include air conditioning, a mini-bar, an in-room safe, double-glazed windows, satellite TV, and a hairdryer.

39 Rue de Seine
Phone: 01-43-26-71-56
Website: www.prince-de-conde.com
6th *arrondissement*
Métro: St.-Germain-des-Prés
Cards: AE, MC, V

HOTEL RECAMIER (EXPENSIVE)

Hôtel Récamier is ideally located on Place Saint-Sulpice. What was once a bargain-priced hotel for the area is now a fully renovated, highly elegant twenty-four-room oasis, and the room prices are commensurate.

3 bis Place St.-Sulpice
Phone: 01-43-26-04-89
Website: www.hotel recamier.com
6th *arrondissement*
Métro: St.-Sulpice
Cards: AE, MC, V

HOTEL RELAIS CHRISTINE (EXPENSIVE TO DELUXE) ♥

Formerly a sixteenth-century cloister, the elegant Hôtel Relais Christine is popular with well-heeled tourists who can afford the high prices. Beautiful fabric-covered walls, one-of-a-kind antiques, and luxurious marble baths with all the amenities draw visitors back time and time again. Rooms are on the small side, so request a large room and/or one overlooking the garden. The website includes romantic specials and discounted rates that require nonrefundable prepayment.

3 Rue Christine
Phone: 01-40-51-60-80
Website: www.relais-christine.com
6th *arrondissement*
Métro: Odéon
Cards: AE, MC, V

LA VILLA (MODERATE TO EXPENSIVE)

If you're looking for contemporary décor, you'll love La Villa. Again, it's in a great location between Boulevard St.-Germain and the River Seine, surrounded by lovely shops. It's more expensive than many hotels in the area, reflecting the quality of the rooms with all the amenities, including luxurious bathrooms with fluffy towels, bathrobes, and nice toiletries. Windows are double-glazed, but it's a busy street, so request a quiet room. Breakfast is overpriced, so either venture into the charming neighborhood or go to L'Hotel for a deluxe breakfast (see page 20). Check the website for moderate-priced specials.

29 Rue Jacob
Phone: 01-43-26-60-00
Website: www.villa-saintgermain.com
6th *arrondissement*
Métro: St.-Germain-des-Prés
Cards: AE, MC, V

WELCOME HOTEL (MODERATE)

One of the less expensive options in the trendy Saint-Germain area, this hotel does provide a nice welcome. The thirty rooms are small but quite comfortable. Some have only bathtubs with a shower attachment, though, so specify a standing shower if that's important to you. The one thing this hotel can't guarantee is a quiet stay. Located on a busy intersection, rooms are noisy on the weekends despite the double-glazed windows. There is no air conditioning, so it's best not to book this hotel for a July or August stay.

66 Rue de Seine
Phone: 01-46-34-24-80
Website: www.welcome
  hotel-paris.com
6th *arrondissement*
Métro: St.-Germain-des-
  Prés and Odéon
Cards: AE, MC, V

The Huitième (Eighth) *Arrondissement*

The *huitième arrondissement,* the business hub of Paris, is divided by Avenue des Champs-Elysées. The French President's office, in the Elysée Palace, and the American Embassy are located at one end of the avenue, near Place de la Concorde. The Arc de Triomphe, surrounded by the circular Place Charles de Gaulle Etoile, is at the other end. Lots of expensive stores, cafés, clubs, and theaters line this grand avenue, but I prefer the adjoining side streets, where you'll find more intimacy and charm. Due to the expensive surroundings, accommodations are costly. If you have an abundance of hotel points, you can use them for chain hotels, several of which are found in the eighth *arrondissement.* (See the inset on page 12.) If your budget is unlimited, see the inset on page 24 for four eighth *arrondissement* choices that are the height of luxury.

HOTEL ASTOR SAINT-HONORE

(MODERATE TO EXPENSIVE)

Tucked away on a quiet street a few blocks from the fashionable Rue du Faubourg-St.-Honoré, the Astor was built in 1907. The 130 rooms have lovely furnishings, tapestry accents, and modern bathrooms. The public areas include a library, an English bar, and a gourmet restaurant that occasionally has live jazz at night. The least expensive rooms in the Early Bird category fall into the Moderate range, but you must book a few months ahead and the deposit is nonrefundable.

11 Rue d'Astorg
Phone: 01-53-05-05-05
Website: www.astorsaint
  honore.com
8th *arrondissement*
Métro: St.-Augustin and
  Miromesnil
Cards: AE, MC, V

HOTEL SAN REGIS (EXPENSIVE TO DELUXE) ♥

A member of the Small Luxury Hotels of the World, the San Régis was recently ranked fifth of all hotels in Paris on the Condé Nast Traveler's Gold List. The four hotels above it— George V, Ritz, Meurice, and Bristol—are all much more expensive, if not double the cost. So for the location, quality of the rooms, excellence of the restaurant, and attentive service, this is a great deal.

12 Rue Jean-Goujon
Phone: 01-44-95-16-16
Website: www.hotel-
  sanregis.com
8th *arrondissement*
Métro: Champs-Elysées-
  Clemenceau
Cards: AE, MC, V

The Height of Luxury

If money is no object, you may want to consider staying at one of the top luxury hotels in Paris. The Five Star Alliance presents a good selection, including some hotels that are recommended elsewhere in this chapter. Their website provides one-stop shopping so you can check out Paris' luxury hotels and compare their services. (Visit www.fivestaralliance.com, then click on the Paris icon.) This site's prices are competitive, although you're not going to get any bargains. After narrowing down your choice, you might want to check each hotel's individual website for specials, as well as sites like www.lhw.com (Leading Hotels of the World), just to make sure you're getting the best deal.

The following hotels are the eight biggest-name hotels in the Five Star Alliance. They are all located in the center of Paris, and are the height of luxury, pampering, and, of course, expense.

FOUR SEASONS HOTEL
GEORGE V PARIS
31 Avenue George V
Phone: 01-49-52-70-00
Website: www.fourseasons.com/paris
8th *arrondissement*
Métro: Alma-Marceau and George-V
Cards: AE, MC, V

HOTEL DE CRILLON PARIS
10 Place de la Concorde
Phone: 01-44-71-15-00
Website: www.crillon.com
8th *arrondissement*
Métro: Concorde
Cards: AE, MC, V

HOTEL LE BRISTOL PARIS
112 Rue du Fauboug St.-Honoré
Phone: 01-53-43-43-00
Website: www.lebristolparis.com
8th *arrondissement*
Métro: Miromesnil and Champs-Elysées-
Clemenceau
Cards: AE, MC, V

HOTEL LE MEURICE
228 Rue de Rivoli
Phone: 01-44-58-10-10
Website: www.lemeurice.com
1st *arrondissement*
Métro: Tuileries and Concorde
Cards: AE, MC, V

HOTEL PLAZA ATHENEE PARIS
25 Avenue Montaigne
Phone: 01-53-67-66-65
Website: www.plaza-athenee-paris.com
8th *arrondissement*
Métro: Alma-Marceau and Franklin-D.-
Roosevelt
Cards: AE, MC, V

HOTEL RITZ PARIS
15 Place Vendôme
Phone: 01-43-16-30-30
Website: www.ritz.com
1st *arrondissement*
Métro: Tuileries and Opéra
Cards: AE, MC, V

RAPHAEL PARIS
17 Avenue Kléber
Phone: 01-53-64-32-00
Website: www.raphael-hotel.com
16th *arrondissement*
Métro: Charles-de-Gaulle-Etoile
Cards: AE, MC, V

SHANGRI-LA HOTEL
10 Avenue d'Iéna
Phone: 01-53-67-19-98
Website: www.shangri-la.com
16th *arrondissement*
Métro: Iéna and Trocadéro
Cards: AE, MC, V

The Seizième (Sixteenth) *Arrondissement*

The *seizième arrondissement* is not in the heart of Paris, but a short distance away. As the other areas have become more congested with traffic and tourists, this upscale *quartier* has maintained its serenity and beauty. Because this is a bit off the beaten track, you're more likely to be among Parisians strolling with their pets and enjoying neighborhood cafés and boutiques.

HOTEL ELYSEES REGENCIA (EXPENSIVE) ♥
Many couples choose to spend a special romantic occasion at Hôtel Elysées Régencia, which receives raves for the location, friendly staff, and wonderful accommodations. The forty-three rooms in the converted townhouse are beautifully decorated in vibrant colors, and they feature all the amenities, including air conditioning, satellite TV, and "a hospitality tray with tea and coffee." Check the website for specials such as their Romance Packages.

41 Avenue Marceau
Phone: 01-47-20-42-65
Website:
  www.regencia.com
16th *arrondissement*
Métro: George-V and
  Alma-Marceau
Cards: AE, MC, V

SAINT JAMES PARIS (DELUXE) ♥
Billed as the "only château hotel in Paris," the Saint James has lovely grounds and is in a beautiful, quiet neighborhood, yet still within walking distance of the Arc de Triomphe and the Champs-Elysées. Currently being renovated, the forty-eight rooms and suites are spacious and the height of luxury, in keeping with the rates. The Saint James also has a first-class spa, a "clubby" Library Bar, and an excellent restaurant with outdoor patio.

43 Avenue Bugeaud
Phone: 01-44-05-81-81
Website: www.saint-james-paris.com
16th *arrondissement*
Métro: Victor-Hugo
Cards: AE, MC, V

The Dix-Septième (Seventeenth) *Arrondissement*

The *dix-septième arrondissement* is largely a residential and business area, so if you stay here, you will be among Parisians going about their daily activities. Since this area is just north of the eighth *arrondissement*, you can find accommodations that are close to some of Paris' most fascinating sights but a bit less pricey. The area also offers some gourmet restaurants and interesting shops.

HOTEL SPLENDID ETOILE (EXPENSIVE)
Talk about being in the center of the action! Hôtel Splendid Etoile is a few steps from the Arc de Triomphe, and some rooms have balconies facing the Arc—definitely request one of those. All fifty-seven rooms have beautiful furnishings, antiques, marble baths, and every convenience and amenity. And the Air France bus from the airport stops across the street. Check the website for specials.

1 Avenue Carnot
Phone: 01-45-72-72-00
Website:
  www.hsplendid.com
17th *arrondissement*
Métro: Charles-de-
  Gaulle-Etoile
Cards: AE, MC, V

APARTMENT RENTALS

If you're lucky enough to be in Paris for more than a few days, you may prefer to rent a furnished apartment so that you will have a kitchen, more living space, and a more homey atmosphere. Fortunately, there are several agencies that can find a rental in the area of your choice with the amenities that you prefer. Here are a few suggestions:

HAVEN IN PARIS
Phone: 617-395-4243 (in US)
Website: www.haveninparis.com
Cards: AE, MC, V

PARIS PERFECT
Phone: 888-520-2087 (in US)
Website: www.parisperfect.com
Cards: AE, MC, V

PARIS VACATION APARTMENTS
Phone: 06-09-65-94-55 or 06-42-00-82-07 (in Paris)
Website: www.parisvacationapartments.com
Cards: MC, V

YELLOWSTAY
Phone: 01-43-25-54-87 (in Paris)
Website: www.yellowstay.com
Cards: MC, V

Applying for Your Passport

As the form says, "Avoid the last minute rush." If you don't have a passport, apply for it at least six months prior to departure. Passports are obtained through the United States Department of State Passport Agency, which has offices in most major cities and posts all the information you need, including forms, on their website: http://travel.state.gov/passport.

To obtain a passport for the first time, you need to go in person to one of over 9,000 passport acceptance facilities (http://iafdb.travel.state.gov/) located throughout the United States. Bring with you two photographs of yourself in the specified format; proof of US citizenship, such as a birth certificate that bears a stamped seal; and a valid form of photo identification, such as a driver's license.

If you already have a passport, check the expiration date to make sure it will be current at least six months after your trip's return date. Some airlines will not allow passengers to board flights departing the United States if their passport is set to expire shortly.

For more information on French regulations for entry and extended stays, see the list of French tourist offices in the inset on page 27.

Travel Insurance

Hopefully, your trip to Paris will be memorable for its excitement and romance—not because of illness or theft. To minimize the inconvenience of an unforeseen problem during your trip, there are a couple of precautionary steps to take.

First, check your medical insurance policy for coverage abroad. If your current healthcare policy will not provide coverage during your stay in Paris, obtain travel insurance with medical protection. The best program is offered by MedjetAssist (www.medjetassist.com). In the event of accident or illness, this company will fly you back to the medical facility and doctor of your choice.

AMERICAN HOSPITAL
63 Boulevard Victor-Hugo
92200 Neuilly-sur-Seine
Phone: 01 46-41-25-25
Website: www.american-
hospital.org

The American Hospital in Paris has full services, and the staff speaks English. Normally, ambulances will take you to the closest hospital, so you need to specify the American Hospital in Neuilly. The hospital requests immediate payment, but the staff will fill out the proper forms for reimbursement on U.S. health insurance policies, so make sure to take along your health insurance card or a copy of your policy number.

It's also important to have coverage for luggage and other belongings. Purse snatching and lost luggage are all too common when traveling. I have spoken to women who had purses grabbed from their hands, and I had a suitcase stolen from under my bed on a train while I slept! Fortunately, theft insurance is included in most renters' and homeowners' policies. Check to see if your possessions are covered while you're traveling. Also, many credit card companies offer some travel insurance if you book the trip on their card.

Should you purchase trip cancellation insurance? I don't think so. This insurance makes sense for travelers who are going on a pricey exotic cruise, but if you're simply flying to Paris, the cost to change your ticket would be around $250—about the same as the cost of the insurance itself.

French Tourist Offices

The French government provides several tourist offices that are set up to provide detailed information for people who are planning trips to France. For example, if you want to stay in Paris longer than the ninety-day guest visit allowed, the tourist office will explain the application procedure. There are four offices in the United States, which you'll find listed below. A central website—www.franceguide.com— also offers information, including brochures in PDF form. If you wish to find tourist offices in France, visit http://www.towd.com/search.php?country=France.

Chicago
French Government Tourist Office
John Hancock Center, Suite 3214
875 North Michigan Avenue
Chicago, IL 60611
Phone: 312-751-7800
Email: info.chicago@franceguide.com

Miami
French Government Tourist Office
1 Biscayne Tower, Suite 1750
2 South Biscayne Boulevard
Miami, FL 33131
Phone: 305-373-8177
Email: info.miami@franceguide.com

Los Angeles
French Government Tourist Office
9454 Wilshire Boulevard, Suite 715
Beverly Hills, CA 90212
Phone: 310-271-6665
Email: info.losangeles@franceguide.com

New York
French Government Tourist Office
444 Madison Avenue
New York, NY 10022
Phone: 212-838-7800
Email: info.us@franceguide.com

Exchanging Money and Using Credit Cards

In the not-too-distant past, you had to stock up on travelers checks before you left for France, and then you had to stand in long lines in Paris to have them exchanged for French francs. These days it's as simple as going to the nearest ATM (automated teller machine) and taking out euros, which have been France's currency since 2002. (For more detailed information, see page 41.)

Before you leave for Paris, remember to call your bank and credit card companies to inform them of the dates of your trip. If you don't, they are likely to refuse to honor your cards while you're traveling, since they're concerned about identity fraud. Also make sure that both your ATM and credit cards will work in Paris. Credit card machines in Paris are being revamped to read a different type of magnetic strip—one that is not used on many US credit cards. This means that a card that worked in the past in Paris may not work on your next trip. The safest option is to have a few cards from different companies (Visa and American Express, for instance) and to always have a supply of euros on hand.

It is advisable to buy at least $75 worth of euros before departing (I usually get $150) so you'll have money for small expenses upon arrival–taxi, snacks, and phone calls, for instance. I don't recommend changing money or using ATMs at the airport, where they tack on a much higher handling fee. Wait until you're in the city to get more euros.

Most businesses in Paris accept credit cards, except for purchases that total less than 10 euros and a few small hotels that require you to pay cash. Some restaurants and stores do not accept American Express because the company charges businesses a higher transaction fee. In any case, for nearly every credit card transaction you make, you will be charged a small handling fee for converting euros into US dollars.

Studying the Language and Culture

You will find it much easier to navigate in Paris if you take the time to familiarize yourself with the French language. This doesn't mean that you need a degree in French literature, but it will make a world of difference if you are able to speak rudimentary French phrases—especially, *s'il vous plaît* (if you please) and *merci* (thank you).

Contrary to popular belief, the French will not be critical of your accent when you speak their language. In fact, they will appreciate the effort you're making and the respect you're showing for their culture. The French take great pride in their language and have an institution called the Academie Française that acts as a watchdog to preserve the integrity of the language.

There are numerous options for beginning your French studies. The easiest route is to get a CD course that you can play in your car or at home. Many adult education programs offer French courses in the evening, and Alliance Française has branches in many cities. An advantage of taking a French class is that most courses include lessons in the history and modern-day traditions of France. I have also included a Suggested Readings list on page 203 with wonderful books on the history of Paris and fascinating stories about French culture. When you arrive in Paris, the sights and sounds will be more familiar. Whatever your level of knowledge, Paris' charm and historical richness will intrigue you and instill the desire to learn more.

Many French phrases and their translations are included throughout this guide. In addition, a glossary is provided on page 185.

The Importance of Referrals

This is an invaluable step you can take to prepare for your trip. Cast a wide net to your friends and business associates and try to get names of people you can contact when you arrive in Paris. The city comes alive when you are welcomed by Parisians who show you their favorite Paris sights. The charm and romance of intimate neighborhood restaurants and local points of interest will be the highlight of your trip. You may end up forming long-term friendships, especially with the ease of communicating via email. Some of my dearest friends are French people I met through introductions.

Packing

Just as important as what you take is what you leave behind! The experts aren't kidding when they advise to "pack light." If you don't, you'll wish you had. Ways to lighten the load include using lightweight luggage on wheels, mailing items home as you buy them, and leaving an outfit in your closet if you think you'll wear it only once.

But I'm not of the school of thought that says, "All you need are comfortable, practical clothes." Paris is one of the most elegant cities in the world, and the men and women dress very smartly. You will receive better service and be treated with more respect if you are dressed for the part. When I choose the pieces that I am going to bring with me, I keep in mind a few goals that may prove helpful to you:

- Choose separates that can be mixed and matched for casual sightseeing and dressier evening outings.

- Select a variety of tops that can be hand-washed when necessary.

- Be adaptable to changes in weather that may occur during your visit.

- Take along comfortable shoes that are attractive and stylish.

- Choose items that you will wear at least a few times; otherwise, they won't be worth the space they take up in your luggage.

The season will dictate your packing choices. Temperatures vary drastically from summer to winter, and umbrellas are de rigueur much of the year. Dress in layers—a camisole, nice shirt, and sweater, for instance—and you'll be ready for most moderate-weather seasons. In wintertime, you will definitely need a warm coat and boots. Paris gets very cold in November and stays cold through February and March.

Packing experts recommend using a two- or three-color scheme and picking separates that match and don't wrinkle too much. A couple of scarves will add a splash of color.

Shoes and an attractive traveling purse are also important to your overall look. Many young Americans make the mistake of traveling in running shoes and wearing a backpack—not a glamorous sight. I wear comfortable walking shoes when I plan to be on my feet for hours at a time, usually with other tourists at sightseeing spots like Versailles or the Louvre. When I'm among Parisians strolling elegant avenues, shopping in boutiques, or enjoying lunch at a popular bistro, I wear attractive flats and carry a large purse that holds a guidebook, camera, and other essentials.

At least a week before your departure, decide what you will pack and make up a list. You may need to have that special dress dry-cleaned or your favorite shoes polished, so plan early. The "Sample Packing Checklist" presented in the inset on pages 31 to 32 is designed to help you make smart choices. Also refer to "Caroline's Flying Tips" on page 38 for items you'll want to carry with you on the plane.

Luggage

Your luggage should be lightweight, but sturdy, and preferably have wheels or shoulder straps for easier transport. Avoid taking one huge bag. Instead, break up the weight among two pieces that are easier to carry. If you're traveling as light as I recommend, you should be able to take one piece of rolling luggage and a smaller shoulder bag on the plane as your two items. (Your purse may have to go into the shoulder bag when you board.) If your rolling bag is too big to stow in the overhead compartment or too heavy for you to lift, check that in with the airline, but make sure you keep your traveling papers, sundries, and one change of clothes in the bag with you in case the checked luggage is temporarily lost. (In most cases, airlines find lost luggage within a few days.) Label each bag inside and out with your name and the phone number where you can be reached. It's a good idea to bring an extra collapsible bag for purchases.

How to Pack

These days, it's no small task to pack so that you conform to airline regulations but still have everything you need. The following tips should help.

❑ Put everything in a staging area.

❑ Pack your small carry-on bag with essentials—money, passport, documents, medication, some sundries (see the following tip), and a change of clothes (in case your luggage ends up in another city).

❑ When taking liquids and gels such as lotion and toothpaste in a carry-on bag, be sure to conform with new airline regulations. Pack each substance in an individual container that holds 3.4 ounces (100 milliliters) or less, and place all the containers in one quart-size clear zip-top bag. (You are limited to one quart-size bag only.) This rule does not apply to sundries that you pack in checked luggage; those amounts are unlimited. For more information on these regulations, visit the website of the Transportation Security Administration (TSA) at http://www.tsa.gov/travelers/airtravel/prohibited/permitted-prohibited-items.shtm.

❑ Stuff shoes with socks and stockings so they will hold their shape, and place them in bags (cloth shoe bags are best).

Sample Packing Checklist

You'll feel more confident in Paris if you pack with an eye to both comfort and style. Below, you'll find the list that I use when packing for my Paris trips. I choose mostly black clothes and use jackets and scarves to add color. By using this list as a guide and adapting it to fit your needs and tastes, you'll be able to dress well and avoid the burden of excess baggage.

When packing liquids and gels in your carry-on luggage, be sure to follow the TSA regulations found on page 30. Despite these regulations, which are challenging, I recommend that you carry makeup and other "necessities" on board so that you won't be without them if your luggage is misplaced by the airline.

Finally, before packing electronic devices and/or appliances, be sure to read the "Phones, Electronics, and Appliances" discussion on page 33.

Clothes

❑ two pairs jeans or slacks, preferably black

❑ one pair dressy pants (microfiber or wool)

❑ one skirt or dress

❑ three blouses

❑ one cardigan sweater

❑ one pullover sweater (in colder months)

❑ one black pashmina shawl

❑ one versatile jacket in complementary color

Lingerie *(enough for four days, then hand-wash)*

❑ underwear and bras

❑ socks

❑ t-shirts

❑ pajamas

Accessories and Coats

❑ flats and/or sandals

❑ comfortable walking shoes

❑ one pair dressier shoes or boots

❑ one large daytime purse

❑ one small evening purse (optional)

❑ belts

❑ scarves

❑ inexpensive jewelry

❑ warm coat (in winter) or rain jacket

❑ gloves (in winter)

Makeup

❑ foundation

❑ blush or bronzer

❑ eye pencil, liner, shadow, concealer

❑ mascara

❑ lipstick

❑ perfume bottle/sample

Medical

❑ aspirin or equivalent

❑ Band-Aid adhesive bandages

❑ prescription medications

❑ sanitary needs

❑ eye care products and extra eyeglasses or contact lenses

Sundries

- hand/body lotion
- body wash
- hand sanitizer
- face cleanser
- face moisturizers
- sunscreen
- shampoo, conditioner, and styling products
- mouthwash
- toothbrush, toothpaste, and floss
- breath mints

- deodorant
- washcloth
- cotton swabs and rounds
- tweezers and small pair scissors (maximum 3-inch-long blade)
- shaving needs
- pocket tissues
- small container of mild detergent for washing lingerie
- nail polish and emery boards (don't pack polish remover, as it can spill; buy in Paris if needed)

Appliances/Miscellaneous

- cell phone
- camera
- batteries (see page 35 for details)
- battery-powered travel alarm clock (optional)

- calculator (for converting currency) (optional)
- small sewing kit and safety pins (optional)
- small umbrella

Don't Forget

- passport
- euros for use on arrival
- itinerary (see page 35 for details)

- ATM card
- credit cards
- driver's license (if you're renting a car)

- Roll up as many articles of clothing as you can; they take up much less space this way and you can pack them around fragile items. This tactic will come in especially handy on your return trip, when you may be toting breakable souvenirs.

- If you're taking an item of clothing that tends to wrinkle, such as a silk blouse or knit dress, place the item on a lightweight hanger from a dry cleaner. Place a plastic dry-cleaning bag over the top, as this will trap air around the item. Lay the bottom half of the plastic bag on the bottom of the suitcase, place other items (such as sweaters) in the middle, and fold the top half of the item over the "filling." This will cushion the item and help prevent fold marks.

- Set aside what you will wear on the flight. Dress comfortably, but not at the expense of style. I suggest wearing a nice jacket, so it won't take up room in your luggage or get wrinkled in transit, and an attractive shawl to use as a wrap or blanket. Your romantic adventure starts at the airport, and if there are any last-minute upgrades to be had, airline attendants are much more likely to put well-dressed passengers in business or first class.

Phones, Electronics, and Appliances

If you're like most people, you use a number of electronic items and personal appliances on a daily basis—cell phones, computers, and more. While you're on vacation, these gadgets can help you stay in touch with friends back home, make reservations, calculate currency conversions, translate French phrases into English, record your trip, and otherwise enhance your vacation.

Phones and Apps

I recommend using your cell phone in Paris rather than using hotel or other public phones, but you first need to make sure that your phone will work in France. Usually, this is indicated by a phone description that includes the terms "global roaming," "tri-band," or "quad-band." Contact your service provider to see if any action is needed to make your phone Paris-ready. In most cases, you will have to sign up for "international roaming" for the duration of your trip to get a better rate per minute. In some cases, you may need to get a different phone. Skype is another option. This service is free if you call from your laptop computer to another computer, but there is a small charge per call if you load it onto your cell phone. At this point, Skype works only on iPhone and Android.

One advantage of "smartphones"—mobile phones with an integrated computer—is that they can also serve as a video camcorder and camera, and through apps (applications), can translate French into English, convert currency, and do much more. On my last few trips to Paris, I used a Blackberry, which nicely replaced both my digital camera and camcorder and also allowed me to calculate currency exchanges. If your phone doesn't have these applications, consider taking a small calculator, a travel alarm clock, and, of course, a lightweight camera. (See page 178 about choosing a camera for your trip.)

The range of services available on various smartphones is astounding and growing all the time. A quick search of the Internet will inform you of the many apps that may be compatible with your phone. Below, I recommend several that have proven useful over time. In all these cases, you will be connecting to the Internet, so international roaming charges for Internet use will apply. These rates are usually lower than those charged for making calls.

- **FlightBoard.** Don't ask me how they were able to design this app, which shows you "in real time" what the arrival and departure boards at the airports are showing. This is especially useful when flights are being cancelled or postponed due to bad weather. The cost is $3.99, and currently, the service is available for iPhone and Android.
  Website: http://www.mobiata.com/apps/flightboard-iphone

- **Google Translate.** The most popular language translation app, Google Translate will not only translate English into French and French into English, but also speak the French words and phrases so you that you hear the actual pronunciation. This program is free, and is currently available for iPhone and Android.
  Website: http://www.google.com/support/mobile/bin/answer.py?hl=en&answer =1075927

- **XE Currency.** Using the current exchange rate, this site converts euros into US dollars so that you will have an accurate idea of what you're spending on that trendy outfit—*before* you hand over your credit card. This service is free, and you can access the site from any mobile phone.
Website: http://www.xe.com/tools.php (go down page to Mobile section)

- **Paris Metro Interactive Map.** The Paris Transportation Authority provides this interactive map of métro lines. When you click on a specific line, it shows all the stops. Another feature is the "Recherche sur le plan" tab on the toolbar on top; the pull-down menu lists all the métro stops, and when you click on a certain stop, it shows the métro lines on which that stop is found. This is a free service that can be accessed from any mobile phone.
Website: http://www.ratp.fr/plan-interactif/

- **Google Maps.** When you go to Google Maps and type in "Paris, France," it shows an overview of the city. You can zoom in to certain sections and streets and even click on the icon under "More" to get a "street view" of what the buildings and streets look like, taken from satellite photos. This service is free and can be accessed from any mobile phone.
Website: http://maps.google.com/ (then type in Paris, France)

Computers

Although a laptop will allow you to use the Skype software application, I don't recommend taking one unless you usually travel with one or need it for business. It's another thing to carry and potentially get lost or stolen. I *do* recommend taking advantage of hotel computers that are provided for guest use and/or neighborhood cybercafés. In some cases, hotels charge for use; in other cases, use is free. The inset on page 59 of Chapter 2 provides a list of cybercafés and directions for using the Internet during your stay in Paris.

Powering Your Electronics

Most, if not all, current electronic gizmos come with a power cord that has a small converter box attached to the cord. On this box, if you get out a magnifying glass to read it, you will see that it lists both the US and French volts (110 and 220 respectively) and the two Hertz (Hz) frequencies (60 for the US and 50 for France). Make sure that both these sets of numbers are on the converter box. That means you're good to go—all you need is a small adapter plug that enables you to plug the cord into a French wall socket. If there is no converter box on the cord, you'll need to get that, too, but do some research to make sure it is appropriate for your appliance.

Usually, the French socket takes a two-prong plug with round prongs, but some French sockets also have a round prong that comes out of the socket. For this reason, it is best to get an adapter that has a hole plus two prongs on the side that couples with the French outlet, and three holes on the side that couples with the plug on your appliance, which may have two or three prongs. These adapter plugs aren't the easiest to find. Your best bet is a specialty travel store that carries all kinds of travel accessories.

If you must take along extra batteries to power your devices, keep them with you in your carry-on luggage. Make sure that they are wrapped individually, so that they will not accidentally cause sparks or set a fire, and then stored in a protective case or plastic bag.

A Final Note

Finally, I want to address the topic of portable hairdryers. In the "old days," many hotels did not provide them in the rooms. Now, most automatically include them as an amenity or are able to provide them upon request. So unless you need a specific kind of dryer, I recommend that you don't bring your own.

Your Pre-Trip Checklist

The last few weeks before your trip to Paris can be hectic as you make final arrangements. In the rush, don't overlook the following tasks, which can make the difference between a dream vacation and a travel nightmare.

❑ Reconfirm your flight reservations, double-check your seat booking, and determine if you need to buy meals at the airport before you board. Also learn which airport terminal you will need to go to for your return flight. (Terminals at Charles De Gaulle are very far apart.)

❑ Reconfirm your Paris hotel reservations.

❑ Type up an itinerary that includes confirmation numbers, departure times, airport terminals, and your hotel address and phone number. As a backup, you can put the itinerary into an email you send to yourself. You'll then be able to pick it up from the guest computer at your hotel if needed.

❑ Photocopy your credit cards (front and back), your ATM card, and your passport. Keep the copies separate from the cards themselves—in the inside pocket of a jacket, for instance.

❑ Call credit card companies and your bank to let them know that you'll be using your credit cards and bank ATM card out of the country. (See page 28 for details.)

❑ Take out at least $75 in euros. (See page 28 for details.)

❑ Make sure that your cell phone will work in Europe. (See page 33 for details.)

❑ Place a "vacation hold" on your newspaper and mail deliveries.

The time you take to prepare for this adventure will help ensure its success. Travel in itself is unpredictable enough without worrying about finding a hotel room or buying a French phrase book after you arrive. Anticipation and preparation are part of the fun: You'll realize that Paris is no longer a faraway dream, but instead, a reality. And your romance with Paris will begin long before you step on the plane—and last long after you return.

Bon voyage!

2. C'est La Belle Vie

You Arrive! How to Adapt

No matter how much time you have allotted for your stay in Paris, it won't be enough. *C'est la belle vie* means "It's the good life," and you will soon realize why this phrase is so popular. The French savor the simple things in life to the fullest—sipping an espresso at a sidewalk café while observing the passing scene, window-shopping on elegant boulevards, enjoying world-class art in an intimate setting, or strolling through one of the many colorful *jardins* (gardens).

This chapter will take you from your departure to your arrival in Paris and through the first day or two of adapting to French customs and your glorious new surroundings.

The Flight

Airlines recommend that you arrive at the airport two to three hours before your flight departs, depending on the passenger load at that airport. They do this for a reason. You can plan on encountering long lines, particularly on international flights, which involve increased security. Some airlines will allow you to check in online twenty-four hours before the flight is due to depart, which will cut down on some of your wait time at the airport.

After the long flight, your body will feel the effects of arriving in a distant time zone. There are a number of ways to cope with "jet lag"—the term used to explain why you feel as though you've just been run over by a truck and want to sleep for twenty-four hours. Most experts advise that you resist the temptation to nap when you arrive. Instead, it's best to put your body right into the time frame of the city. For example, if you arrive in the morning, eat a hearty breakfast and start exploring your surroundings. Studies indicate that exposure to sunlight can help reduce the effects of jet lag. If you nap during the day, your sleep is likely to be fitful that night. If you generally have trouble sleeping when you travel from time zone to time zone, consider talking to your doctor about using an over-the-counter or prescription sleep aid the first few nights you are in Paris. This can help your body make the adjustment.

I try to book a nonstop flight that leaves at the end of the day. That way, I arrive in the afternoon and have a relatively short day ahead of me. I have also developed some simple strategies that make the flight more pleasant and reduce the hours of jet lag. The tips below also include pointers about airline security regulations that should be kept in mind.

Caroline's Flying Tips

❑ Dress in layers so that you can pull clothing on or off to adjust to the temperature. A soft shawl works great as a blanket or pillow.

❑ Bring snacks to munch on and gum if you have ear-pressure problems. Buy bottled water after you pass through security.

❑ To help pass the time, bring a novel in the genre you love.

❑ Bring small containers of hand lotion and lip gloss to help minimize the dehydrating effects of cabin pressure. Carry a small container of mouthwash, as well. Remember that carry-on liquids and lotions must be restricted to 3.4 ounces each. (See page 30 of Chapter 1 for a more complete discussion of the Transportation Security Administration's regulations.)

❑ Every few hours, walk around and stretch to increase your circulation. This may not seem necessary at the time, but it will make a difference in your overall sense of well-being after you arrive.

❑ If you want to sleep on the plane, two items will help—an inflatable neck rest that holds your head in a comfortable position, and shades that go over your eyes and fasten with an elastic band. Both can be purchased in stores that carry travel accessories.

❑ If you are traveling with a cell phone, remember that you will not be allowed to turn it on until the plane has landed in France and has stopped at the terminal. Wait for the flight crew to give you the "all-clear."

❑ When you get into the terminal, freshen up by brushing your teeth (use your mouthwash or pack a small tube of toothpaste), rinsing your face, and applying lotion or sunscreen. Add a light spritz of perfume to give your spirits a lift and increase your allure.

Taking Precautions

There is much less crime in Paris than in many other big cities, and there is a robust police presence on the streets as well as security cameras in most public areas, including the métro system. Just the same, it's important to remember that as a tourist, you're more susceptible to being accosted by pickpockets, especially in popular areas like those near the Eiffel Tower, the Avenue des Champs-Elysées, and the Louvre. It's all too easy to be distracted by the inspiring sights of the city and by crowds of other tourists. Since nothing can ruin your trip more quickly than having a purse or wallet snatched, be alert at all times and keep your handbag or wallet securely within your grasp.

The Paris Visitors Bureau

The Paris Visitors Bureau was designed to assist visitors during their stay in Paris. The office is open Monday through Saturday from 10:00 AM to 7:00 PM, and can help you make last-minute hotel reservations, book tickets for a show, or answer general questions. It has long lines, so be prepared to wait. Use the bureau's website to find information on hotels, museums, transportation, special exhibitions, shopping, and practical advice for enjoying the city.

25 Rue des Pyramides (just below Avenue de l'Opéra)
Website: http://en.paris info.com/
1st *arrondissement*
Métro: Pyramides

Finding Transportation to Your Hotel

Both airports serving Paris—Orly and Charles de Gaulle (CDG), which is farthest from Paris—have excellent transportation services that run on a frequent basis. My top recommendation is the convenient bus service run by Air France. If this doesn't appeal to you, there are other options. (For information on transportation within the city, see page 45.)

Buses

I highly recommend taking one of the Air France buses (called Les Cars Air France), which leave the CDG airport terminals about every fifteen minutes from 6:00 AM to 11:00 PM. The cost is about 24 euros roundtrip or 15 euros one way. The bus stops at Porte Maillot (at La Defense) and

AIR FRANCE BUS TRANSPORTATION
Website: http://videocdn. airfrance.com/cars-airfrance/index_en.html

then Charles de Gaulle Etoile (at the Arc de Triomphe on Avenue Carnot). The Les Cars Air France website has up-to-date information on routes and fares in English.

Les Cars Air France also has regular buses leaving from the other major Paris airport, Orly, every twenty minutes from 6:00 AM to 11:00 PM. The buses make three stops in Paris—at Gare Montparnasse, Invalides, and Charles de Gaulle Etoile (at the Arc de Triomphe on Avenue Carnot). Since this airport is closer to the city than CDG, the cost is a bit less: 19 euros roundtrip or 12 euros one way. From the bus stop, you can catch a cab to your hotel, which will still be pricey. (On my last trip, I paid 10 euros to go less than three miles.) Another option is to take the métro (subway), which stops near most of the bus debarkation points.

There is also a Paris "regional transport authority"—the RATP bus, also referred to as the Roissy bus—which runs every fifteen to twenty minutes and makes one stop at the Opéra Garnier on Rue Scribe, near the American Express office. This bus, though, is not nearly as comfortable as those supplied by Air France.

Whichever bus you take, you'll want to have euros on hand to pay for your tickets. Sometimes credit cards are accepted, depending on whether there is an Air France ticket window nearby or a working credit card machine on the Roissy bus, but this is not guaranteed.

Taxis

Although cabs are easy to use, you'll end up spending a small fortune (around 60 euros, which translates into $85) to get to your hotel. If you don't speak French, it's a good idea to have your hotel name, address, and *arrondissement* (region of Paris) written on a piece of paper to show the driver. Many drivers don't speak much English. When you catch a cab from a taxi station, the meter starts at around 2.5 euros. There is an additional charge of a few euros to carry luggage.

Trains and Subway

A less expensive but more complicated option for getting to your hotel is the RER (regional train). You catch a shuttle at the airport that takes you to the nearby train station, which has service into Paris and connects with the métro system. (See page 45 for a detailed discussion of the métro.) For more information on getting back and forth from Paris airports, visit the Paris for Visitors website.

PARIS FOR VISITORS TRANSPORTATION INFORMATION
Website: http://europefor visitors.com/paris/articles /paris-cdg-ground-transportation.htm

Arriving at Your Hotel

When you arrive at your Paris hotel, make sure the room is what you reserved. Sometimes the bed size is different from what you requested, and in some cases, it may be possible to move to a quieter room or one with a better view. Tipping is the same as in the States—tip the bellhop for bringing up your luggage, and leave a tip for the maid before you check out.

Befriend the concierge and desk personnel. They can be very helpful in answering questions and giving you advice about the week's events, sights of interest, and nearby shopping and dining. Pick up a few of the hotel's business cards, so you will have the address and phone number handy when you're out.

Understanding Euros and Using ATMs

In Chapter 1, I advised you to change some United States currency into euros before leaving home to cover your initial expenses after landing in Paris. Once you get to Paris, of course, you'll want to have a working knowledge of the currency and be able to obtain additional cash as needed from ATMs.

Since 2002, as a member of the European Union (EU), France has used euros instead of its old system of francs. The new currency includes seven different bills and eight different coins. The bills are available in denominations of 5, 10, 20, 50, 100, 200, and 500 euros. Like the US dollar, the euro dollar is divided into 100 cents. The coins are available in 1, 2, 5, 10, 20, and 50 cents, as well as 1- and 2-euro pieces. The coins have a common side and a national side. The national side indicates the issuing country.

At the time of this writing, the strength of the euro dollar is at an all-time high—about 1.4 US dollars to 1 euro dollar. This means that you must multiply the euro price by 1.4 to get the US dollar amount. A pocket calculator or a smartphone with a currency conversion application is a big help in making fast and accurate conversions.

When you need to obtain cash through an ATM, you'll find these machines are all over Paris. In fact, there's one on almost every block in the center of the city. Try to choose one that is not in a major tourist spot, though, so you'll be less likely to run into pickpockets.

The procedure for using a French ATM is basically the same as that for using a US machine:

1. Insert your card in the slot.

2. Hit the "English" button.

3. Type in your PIN code and then the amount of euros you want to withdraw.

4. To complete the transaction, hit "Valid," which means "Enter." (If you hit "Annul," you will cancel the procedure.)

Be aware that there will be a small service charge for using the ATM and another charge (1 to 2 percent) for converting your withdrawn US dollars into euros.

French Signs in Buildings

The floor numbers in French buildings are different from those in most buildings in the United States. The ground floor is called the *rez-de-chaussée,* and the first floor is what we call the second level.

Part of the culture shock you experience will be adapting to French terms in buildings. Here are some translations to enable you to open doors and find exits:

Dames	Ladies (for restroom)	*Poussez*	Push
Messieurs	Men (for restroom)	*Tirez*	Pull
Ascenseur	Elevator	*Entrée*	Entrance
Escaliers	Stairs	*Sortie*	Exit
Escalier Roulant	Escalator	*Sortie de Secours*	Emergency Exit
Caisse	Cashier	*Interdit*	Do Not Enter

Getting to Know Your Neighborhood

As you prepare to explore the neighborhood around your hotel, it's best to have a good map. I use a fold-out laminated map of Paris that I bought in a travel accessory store. There are maps of the key *arrondissements* in this guide on pages 196 to 202, and the hotel's front desk normally has a good one-page map of major boulevards. If you need detailed directions, though, you'll want to pick up a copy of *Paris par Arrondissement*. A complete guide that covers every street, this is available at many newsstands (*kiosks* or *tabacs*) in Paris.

The first day will feel a bit overwhelming. You'll be not only coping with travel fatigue but also adjusting to a foreign language! These days, more French people speak some English, but there are still many that don't, so brush up on those travel phrases and start soaking up that romantic ambience. On my first day in Paris, I usually buy a small bunch of flowers to brighten up my hotel room and find the closest stores where I can grab snacks.

One way to immerse yourself in Paris life is to frequent a local café. If you stop by each day for your morning or afternoon *café crème,* you will become accustomed to the rhythms of the café, start to be treated as a regular, and feel much more at home. This spot will become a fond memory. (Standout cafés are listed on page 93.)

An excellent way to acquaint yourself with the layout and major landmarks of Paris is to take a tour of the city. My top recommendation is L'Open Tour, which offers yellow double-decker buses that stop at all the major sights in Paris. This and other bus tours are discussed in greater detail in the "Paris Bus Tours" inset found at the bottom of this page. If bus tours don't appeal to you, other great options are available. If you love to walk—and Paris is a *great* city for walking—see the inset "Cultural Walking Tours" on page 79 to learn about Context's scholar-led tours. If you'd prefer to explore Paris by bike, see page 147 to learn about Fat Tire Bike Tours and Bike About Tours, both of which will take you around the city and fill you in on its neighborhoods and landmarks. (For information on other cultural tours in Paris, see Chapter 4. For information on tours of the surrounding countryside, turn to Chapter 10.)

Paris Bus Tours

There are two major tour operators in Paris—Cityrama and Paris Vision—both of which have locations in the first *arrondissement*. They offer a wide range of bus and walking tours, from a few hours in Paris to day-long trips that stop at châteaux in the countryside. You can check out the companies' websites to find a tour of interest—an evening at the Louvre Museum, an afternoon at Versailles to view the fountain display, or a full-day tour of the city, for instance. These services make it convenient to get around, especially if you'd like to plan trips out of town that would be harder to arrange on your own. Both Cityrama and Paris Vision also take all major credit cards.

As discussed on page 42, my favorite bus tour service is L'Open Tour, which is part of Cityrama. (Visit the Cityrama website and click first on "Paris by Day," then on "Hop on Hop off Tours.") You catch the double-decker yellow bus at any location on the route, and hop off to explore an area of interest. Then, when you're finished seeing the sights, you can catch another bus at the same stop. Begin your trip at any of L'Open's stops; your hotel will guide you to the one that's closest. L'Open provides recorded commentary in English accompanied by lively French music. Don't lose your ticket or the small earpiece through which you will hear the commentary; you'll need both each time you board the bus. The main L'Open route is the "Paris Grand Tour" on the green line. The same ticket also covers the orange line to Montparnasse/Saint-Germain, the red line to Montmartre, and the blue line to Bastille. The cost for one day is approximately 29 euros, and a ticket for two consecutive days costs about 32 euros, which is an excellent value. L'Open Tour takes all major credit cards.

CITYRAMA
2 Rue des Pyramides
Phone: 01-44-55-61-00
Website: www.pariscityrama.com
1st *arrondissement*
Métro: Palais-Royal-Museé-du-Louvre,
    Tuileries, and Pyramides
Cards: Accepted

PARIS VISION
214 Rue de Rivoli
Phone: 01-42-60-30-01
Website: http://en.parisvision.com/
1st *arrondissement*
Métro: Tuileries
Cards: Accepted

Emergency Information

We all hope our trips will be trouble free, but if you do encounter an emergency situation while visiting Paris, you will find some helpful phone numbers and addresses listed below. In most cases, the person who answers the phone will be able to connect you with someone who speaks English. Be aware, too, that your hotel's concierge should be able to directly contact or guide you to emergency services. You need to dial 01 and then the eight-digit number.

AMERICAN HOSPITAL   Phone: 01-46-41-25-25

63 Boulevard Victor-Hugo in Neuilly
Website: www.american-hospital.org

This hospital has full services, and the staff speaks English. Should you find yourself in an emergency medical situation, be sure to request transfer to the American Hospital because it may be difficult to communicate with the staff at other facilities. Since this is on the outskirts of Paris, you'll probably want to catch a cab.

PARIS VISITORS BUREAU

25 Rue des Pyramides
Website: http://en.parisinfo.com/
1st *arrondissement*
Métro: Pyramides

This bureau was designed to assist visitors during their stay in Paris. For more information, see page 39.

PHARMACIE (DRUGSTORE)   Phone: 01-45-62-02-41

84 Avenue des Champs-Elysées
8th *arrondissement*
Cards: Accepted

This pharmacy is centrally located on the Champs-Elysées and is open twenty-four hours a day, seven days a week.

UNITED STATES EMBASSY Phone: 01-43-12-22-22 (after-hours emergency)

Consular Section/American Citizen Services
4 Avenue Gabriel
Website: http://france.usembassy.gov
8th *arrondissement*

Part of the embassy's mission is to protect and assist US citizens traveling abroad. The embassy suggests that for nonemergency situations, you make an appointment through the website. In an emergency situation, dial the emergency number above, hit 0, and you will hear an automated greeting followed by connection to a live attendant. Ask to speak to the Embassy Duty Officer.

Using Transportation in Paris

Paris boasts one of the most efficient public transportation systems in the world. You have your choice of the métro or buses, which are more comfortable but a little harder to figure out. If you have money to burn, you can always grab a taxi. And if you're interested in getting a little exercise, you can rent a bicycle and pedal your way across Paris.

The Métro

Paris has a wonderful subway system called the métro, which is the fastest way to travel around the city. Métro trains run every few minutes, and many major lines have signs hanging near the track indicating the time the next car will arrive and the direction in which it will be going.

In central Paris, there are métro stops every few blocks. (See the map on page 46.) They are connected at major intersections, called *correspondances,* which can require walking a fair distance underground and up stairs to catch connecting trains.

If you're going to be using the métro more than a few times, it's cheaper to buy a *carnet,* ten tickets for a discounted rate (around 12 euros), rather than buying separate tickets (*billets*) for about 1.7 euros apiece. Many métro stations have ticket machines rather than a person at a ticket window, and these machines take euros but sometimes have trouble reading American credit cards. If your Visa card doesn't work, try using an American Express card. To play it safe, be sure to take euros with you if you plan to use public transportation. While you're at the ticket counter, ask for the large fold-out map of the métro lines and bus routes. It's free and will make the systems much easier to navigate.

Métro trains run from 5:30 AM until 1:30 AM, seven days a week. It's safe to catch the métro until around 11:00 PM; after that, you might be better off using a taxi. When traveling, be sure to hang onto your métro ticket until you exit the station. Also keep a close watch on your belongings, especially at peak times, when cars are packed.

Buses

Paris buses are slower than the métro, but you're aboveground and get a great view of streets, sights, and shops you might want to revisit. Buses take the same tickets you use for the métro. You can buy a single ticket on the bus, but if you want the cheaper ten-ticket *carnet,* you'll have to go to a métro station. During one stay in Paris, I hopped on a bus by the Opéra Garnier, euros in hand, planning to buy one ticket. The Parisians around me were scandalized that I was paying full price. An elegantly dressed Frenchwoman insisted on giving me one of her tickets, and politely refused to accept any money from me. Who says the French aren't friendly?

The Paris system of bus routes is divided into five zones. One ticket is valid for travel through two zones covering the center of the city. If you travel a greater distance, you will need additional tickets. Maps of the system are posted on the backs of the bus shelters, and each line has a beginning and end point, similar to the métro. Be sure to note the direction of the route, indicated by arrows, to avoid going the wrong way.

The Paris Métro System

The Paris métro system includes sixteen lines (*lignes*), each of which is identified by a line number, a specific color, and a name that indicates the stops at each end point. For example, the métro line that runs along the Rue de Rivoli and Avenue des Champs-Elysées is called *M1. Château de Vincennes—Grand Arche de La Defense. M1* is the number of the metro line, *Château de Vincennes* is the farthest stop on the eastern end, and *Grande Arche de La Defense* is the farthest stop on the western end. Make sure that the train you catch is going in the right direction. The end point will be posted on the wall signs directing you to that track. The following translations will help you navigate in the métro stations:

Poussez. Push (on door)

Tirez. Pull (on door)

Billet. One ticket

Carnet. Ten tickets

Sortie. Exit

Correspondances. Connecting métro lines

RER. Special express métro lines that go into the suburbs and make only a few stops in Paris. (One of these trains will take you to Versailles.)

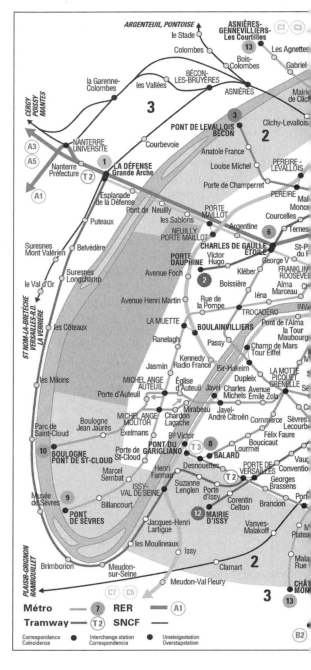

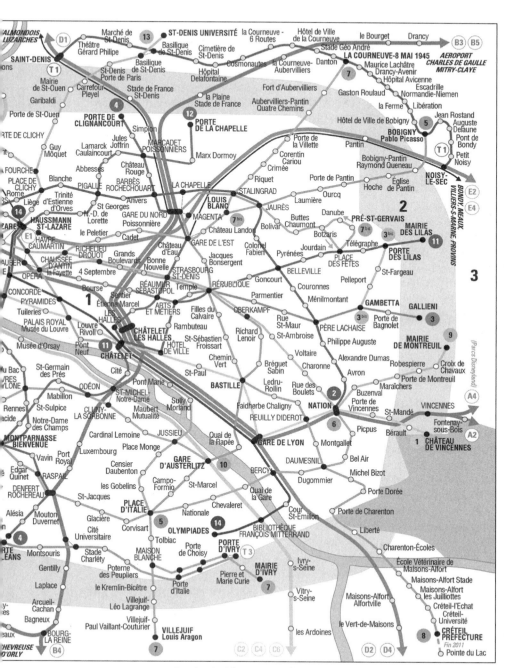

Sightseeing Via the Métro

The following charts show places of interest found along three métro lines that run through the heart of Paris. For each of these lines, I have highlighted my top picks in the following categories: Museums & Sights, Points of Interest, Restaurants (or Restaurants & Cafés, when applicable), and Shopping (or, in some cases, Shopping & Salons). I did not include every restaurant, museum, etc. discussed in the book— just the ones I feel are most noteworthy. You'll notice, too, that not every stop includes suggested sights. This is because the best places tend to be located in the "middle" of each line, as this portion of the line is in the center of the city, where the action is. I have nevertheless included all the stations so that you will have a better sense of what you will see as you travel each line. You'll find the line number and the end-point stops posted at each entrance on the way to the platform.

For each place of interest, I provide a general idea of whether it is "right there"

LINE 1 — La Défense · Esplanade de La Défense · Pont de Neuilly · Les Sablons · Porte Maillot · Argentine · Charles de Gaulle Etoile · George V · Franklin D. Roosevelt · Champs Elysées Clemenceau · Concorde · Tuileries

Getting off at Charles de Gaulle Etoile

Museums & Sights:
■ Arc de Triomphe (right there) (see page 78)
Points of Interest:
■ Air France bus drop-off (right there, on Avenue Carnot) (see page 39)
■ Drugstore Complex (shops, 24-hour pharmacy) (a few blocks away) (see page 44)
Restaurants:
■ Guy Savoy (a few blocks away) (see page 102)
■ L'Angle du Faubourg (a few blocks away) (see page 108)
■ L'Arc (right there) (see page 110)

Getting off at George V

Restaurants:
■ Le Fouquet's (a few blocks away) (see page 94)

Getting off at Franklin D. Roosevelt

Points of Interest:
■ Métro ticket window offers free fold-out maps of bus and métro lines (right there) (see page 45)
■ Movie theaters (a few blocks away) (see page 157)
Restaurants:
■ Spoon (a few blocks away) (see page 109)
Shopping & Salons:
■ Guerlain salon (a few blocks away) (see page 65)
■ Louis Vuitton (a few blocks away) (see page 128)
■ Near start of Avenue Montaigne (with haute couture and top designer shops) (a few blocks away) (see the inset on page 127)

(adjacent to the stop) or a few blocks away. In some cases, like Sacré-Coeur, you can get to the sight more quickly by taking another métro line. The best métro stop for each sight is listed on the page of the book that provides a full description of that location. Page numbers are included throughout the charts so that you can easily learn more about any sight that piques your curiosity.

You will discover that certain stops, like Cité, Saint-Germain-des-Prés, and Palais Royal Musée du Louvre, are treasure troves of cultural sights, wonderful stores, and great restaurants. For instance, the Palais Royal Musée du Louvre station—found on both Line #1 and Line #7—will bring you to the Louvre Museum, the Palais Royal Garden, the Louvre des Antiquaires art galleries, Le Grand Véfour restaurant, and much more. You can't go wrong by spending time in these Parisian neighborhoods.

The following charts were created as straight lines to make it easier to understand the succession of stops and the many sights that you can enjoy along the way. Naturally, the actual métro lines are not straight, but follow the topography of the city.

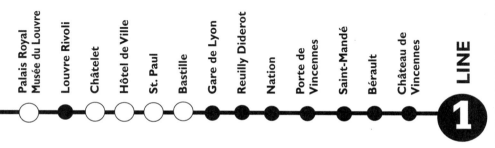

Getting off at Champs Elysées Clemenceau

Restaurants:
■ MiniPalais (a few blocks away) (see page 109)

Getting off at Concorde

Museum & Sights:
■ Musée de l'Orangerie (right there) (see page 84)
■ Place de la Concorde (right there) (see page 81)
Points of Interest:
■ Tuileries Garden (right there) (see page 142)
Restaurants:
■ Bar 228 du Meurice (a few blocks away) (see page 153)
■ Senderens (half-mile away) (see page 101)
■ Tante Louise (a few blocks away) (see page 109)

Getting off at Concorde (cont.)

Shopping:
■ Fauchon gourmet foods (at Place Madeline, half mile away) (see page 114)
■ WH Smith bookstore (a few blocks away) (see page 86)

Getting off at Tuileries

Points of Interest:
■ Tuileries Garden (right there) (see page 142)
Restaurants:
■ Angelina tea salon (a few blocks away) (see page 74)
■ Le Rubis wine bar (a few blocks away) (see page 111)
Shopping:
■ Colette (a few blocks away) (see page 122)

Getting off at **Tuileries (cont.)**

Shopping:
■ Place Vêndome (high-end jewelry) (half-mile away)
■ Rue St.-Honoré with many designer stores (a few blocks away) (see inset on page 127)
■ Tourist shops on Rue de Rivoli (right there)

Getting off at
Palais Royal Musée du Louvre

Museum & Sights:
■ Musée des Arts Decoratifs (right there) (see page 134)
■ Musée du Louvre (right there) (see page 84)

Points of Interest:
■ Palais Royal Garden (a few blocks away) (see page 143)

Getting off at **Palais Royal Musée du Louvre (cont.)**

Restaurants & Cafés:
■ Café Le Nemours (right there) (see page 94)
■ Le Grand Colbert (half-mile away) (see page 104)
■ Le Grand Véfour (a few blocks away) (see page 97)
■ Macéo (half-mile away) (see page 103)
■ Willi's wine bar (half-mile away) (see page 112)

Shopping:
■ Louvre des Antiquaires (right there) (see page 135)

Getting off at **Châtelet**

Points of Interest:
■ Jazz clubs (a few blocks away) (see page 154)

LINE

4

Porte de Clignancourt · Simplon · Marcadet Poissonniers · Château Rouge · Barbès Rochechouart · Gare du Nord · Gare de l'Est · Château d'Eau · Strasbourg Saint-Denis · Réaumur Sébastopol · Etienne Marcel · Les Halles

Getting off at **Porte de Clignancourt**

Points of Interest:
■ Puces de Saint-Ouen (Clignancourt) flea market (few blocks away) (see page 139)

Getting off at **Château Rouge**

Museum & Sights:
■ Place du Tertre (half-mile away) (see page 79)
■ Sacré-Coeur (half-mile away) (see page 78)

Points of Interest:
■ Cook'n With Class (a few blocks away) (see page 115)

Getting off at **Châtelet**

Points of Interest:
■ Jazz clubs (a few blocks away) (see page 154)

Getting off at **Cité**

Museums & Sights:
■ Notre Dame (a few blocks away) (see page 79)
■ Sainte-Chapelle (right there) (see page 89)
■ Bateaux Vedettes du Pont-Neuf boat tour (a few blocks away) (see page 80)

Getting off at **Hôtel de Ville**

Points of Interest:
■ Bateaux Vedettes du Pont-Neuf boat tour (a few blocks away) (see page 80)
■ Hôtel de Ville (ice skating and flea markets) (right there) (see pages 148 and 138)
Museums & Sights:
■ Notre Dame (a few blocks away) (see page 79)
■ Sainte-Chapelle (a few blocks away) (see page 89)
Restaurants:
■ Le Flore en l'Ile (a few blocks away) (see page 95)

Getting off at **St. Paul**

Museums & Sights:
■ Musée Carnavalet (a few blocks away) (see page 83)
■ Musée Picasso (a few blocks away) (see page 85)

Getting off at **Bastille**

Museums & Sights:
■ Opéra de Paris Bastille (right there) (see page 87)
Points of Interest:
■ Place des Vosges (a few blocks away)
Restaurants:
■ Bofinger (right there) (see page 105)

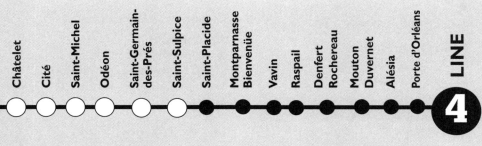

Getting off at **Cité (cont.)**

Points of Interest:
■ Hôtel de Ville (ice skating and flea markets) (a few blocks away) (see pages 148 and 138)
Restaurants:
■ Le Flore en l'Ile (half-mile away) (see page 95)

Getting off at **Saint-Michel**

Museums & Sights:
■ Eglise Saint-Julien-Le-Pauvre (a few blocks away) (see page 88)

Getting off at **Saint-Michel (cont.)**

Museums & Sights:
■ Eglise Saint-Severin (a few blocks away) (see page 88)
Shopping:
■ Shakespeare and Company bookstore (a few blocks away) (see page 86)

Getting off at **Odéon**

Museums & Sights:
■ Musée de Cluny (a few blocks away) (see page 84)
Points of Interest:
■ Movie theaters (right there) (see page 157)

Getting off at Odéon (cont.)

Restaurants:
■ La Rôtisserie d'en Face (a few blocks away) (see page 108)
■ Les Editeurs (right there) (see page 106)

Getting off at Saint-Germain-des-Prés

Museums & Sights:
■ Eglise Saint-Germain-des-Prés (right there) (see page 88)

Getting off at Saint-Germain-des-Prés (cont.)

Restaurants & Cafés:
■ Café de Flore (right there) (see page 93)
■ Fish La Boissonnerie (a few blocks away) (see page 107)
■ La Boussole (a few blocks away) (see page 106)
■ La Palette (a few blocks away) (see page 95)

LINE 7

La Courneuve — Fort d'Aubervilliers — Aubervilliers-Pantin Quatre Chemins — Porte de la Villette — Corentin Cariou — Crimée — Riquet — Stalingrad — Louis Blanc — Château Landon — Gare de l'Est — Poissonnière — Cadet — Le Peletier — Chaussée d'Antin La Fayette — Opéra — Pyramides

Getting off at Porte de la Villette

Points of Interest:
■ Parc de la Villette's free outdoor summer movies (a few blocks away) (see page 157)

Getting off at Chaussée d'Antin La Fayette

Shopping:
■ Galeries Lafayette department store (right there) (see page 114)

Getting off at Opéra

Museums & Sights:
■ Opéra Garnier (right there) (see page 87)
Points of Interest:
■ Roissy bus to CDG airport (right there) (see page 39)
Restaurants & Cafés:
■ Café de la Paix (right there) (see page 93)
■ Harry's Bar (a few blocks away) (see page 152)

Getting off at Opéra (cont.)

Shopping:
■ Lavinia wine store and restaurant (a few blocks away) (see page 111)
■ Printemps department store (a few blocks away) (see page 123)

Getting off at Pyramides

Points of Interest:
■ Paris Visitors Bureau (right there) (see page 39)
Restaurants:
■ Le Grand Colbert (a few blocks away) (see page 104)
■ Le Grand Véfour (a few blocks away) (see page 97)
■ Macéo (a few blocks away) (see page 103)
■ Verlet tea and coffee salon (a few blocks away) (see page 75)
■ Willi's wine bar (a few blocks away) (see page 112)

Getting off at
Saint-Germain-des-Prés (cont.)

Restaurants & Cafés:
■ Les Deux Magots (right there) (see page 94)
Shopping:
■ Great area for boutiques and art galleries (few blocks away) (see pages 20 and 127)

Getting off at Saint-Sulpice

Shopping:
■ Bon Marché department store (half-mile away) (see page 122)
■ Robert Clergerie shoe store (a few blocks away) (see page 126)
■ Yves Saint Laurent (right there) (see page 120)

Palais Royal Musée du Louvre · Pont Neuf · Châtelet · Pont Marie · Sully Morland · Jussieu · Place Monge · Censier Daubenton · Les Gobelins · Place d'Italie · Tolbiac · Maison Blanche · Porte d'Italie · Porte de Choisy · Porte d'Ivry · Pierre et Marie Curie · Mairie d'Ivry

LINE 7

Getting off at Pyramides (cont.)

Shopping & Salons:
■ Colette (a few blocks away) (see page 122)
■ Rue St.-Honoré with many designer stores (a few blocks away) (see page 127)
■ Saint Honoré Coiffure (a few blocks away) (see page 64)
■ Tourist shops on Rue de Rivoli (a few blocks away)

Getting off at
Palais Royal Musée du Louvre

Museums & Sights:
■ Musée des Arts Decoratifs (right there) (see page 134)
■ Musée du Louvre (right there) (see page 84)
Points of Interest:
■ Palais Royal Garden (a few blocks away) (see page 143)
Restaurants & Cafés:
■ Café Le Nemours (right there) (see page 94)

Getting off at
Palais Royal Musée du Louvre (cont.)

Shopping:
■ Louvre des Antiquaires (right there) (see page 135)

Getting off at Pont Neuf

Museums & Sights:
■ Notre Dame (half-mile away) (see page 79)
■ Sainte-Chapelle (a few blocks away) (see page 89)
Points of Interest:
■ Bateaux Vedettes du Pont-Neuf boat tour (a few blocks away) (see page 80)

Getting off at Châtelet

Points of Interest:
■ Jazz clubs (a few blocks away) (see page 154)

Paris City Bus in Front of Opéra Garnier.

When you enter the bus, you punch (*oblitérer*) the ticket in the machine near the driver. You then hang onto your ticket for the duration of the ride. There are bus stops every few blocks. Just push the red button near the seat to notify the driver that you need to get off at the next stop.

I strongly recommend that you be adventurous and use buses to get around Paris. Once you get the hang of it, the bus system is actually very convenient and covers all the major streets. Even during rush hour, buses move fairly

MAP OF BUS ROUTES
Website: http://www.ratp.fr/
plan-interactif/

quickly because there are now designated bus lanes. The link found at right provides an excellent map of the routes. If you go to a métro ticket counter to buy a ten-ticket *carnet*, ask for the large fold-out map of the bus routes, as this will make travel far easier.

$ $ $ SAVE SOME MONEY $ $ $

While the bus tours described in the inset on page 43 are great, they are definitely pricey—around 29 euros for one day. But for under 2 euros, you can hop on a Paris city bus and explore the city on your own. You won't be traveling directly to all the major landmarks and you won't get a recorded tour, but you will be among Parisians and will be able to discover the city for yourself. A link to the bus map is found above. Here are a few highly recommended routes:

❏ Route #21 starts at Gare St.-Lazare behind the Opéra Garnier, passes Palais Royal and the Louvre, and stays on the Right Bank until it reaches Ile de la Cité. It then crosses the island in front of Notre Dame Cathedral and continues onto the Left Bank past the Cluny Museum and Luxembourg Garden.

❏ Route #29 starts at Gare St.-Lazare behind the Opéra Garnier and continues east through the Marais, past Place des Vosges.

❏ Route #95 starts in the north at Montmartre (above Sacré-Coeur), and travels past the Opéra Garnier and down Avenue de l'Opéra to Palais Royal. It then goes past the Louvre, across the Seine River, and over to the Left Bank.

When taking most bus routes, you will want to get off before the final stop, which is farther out from the center of the city. You can make your return trip on the same line, or you can try a different route to see different sights.

Taxis

Paris taxis are pricey and you have to pay in euros, as most cabs don't accept credit cards. You can find taxi stands, *tête de station*, throughout the city—especially at major tourist locations like Notre Dame and the Eiffel Tower—and at airports and train stations, where prospective passengers line up and wait their turn. Your hotel can also call a cab for you, but the meter starts running as soon as the driver begins heading toward your location to pick you up. Since Paris' streets are congested, the time and cost can climb before you reach your final destination. *Service* (a gratuity) is included in the price, but you should add a few more euros, depending on the fare. I use taxis when I'm traveling with luggage and late at night, and otherwise enjoy the adventure of figuring out the public transportation system.

Keep in mind that there are times when it is virtually impossible to catch a cab—at evening rush hour or during a heavy rain, for instance. So even if you're willing to pay the high price of a taxi, it's important to be familiar with other forms of city transportation.

Bicycles

In a groundbreaking attempt to deal with car congestion and pollution, Paris has installed Vélib, a system of self-service bicycle rental stations found every few blocks throughout the center of the city. The first half-hour is free; the second half-hour costs one euro; the third half-hour, 2

VELIB BICYCLE RENTALS
Website: www.velib.paris.fr
Cards: Accepted

Making Your Trip Memorable

Studies have shown that travelers have more enjoyable and memorable trips when they immerse themselves in at least one activity that provides a "peak moment." With that in mind, I have compiled a list of top ten picks that are guaranteed to be the highlights of your stay in Paris. Hopefully, you'll have time for more than one of these special activities. In some cases, you will want to make your reservations a few weeks before your departure to ensure that your "peak moment" actually happens.

1. Take a Cooking Class. Cooking classes are not only a great way to spend an afternoon or evening in Paris—especially in inclement weather—but also a wonderful way to make memories that will come alive whenever you recreate the dishes at home. See page 115 to learn more about Paris cooking classes.

2. Attend a Live Fashion Show. Galeries Lafayette department store hosts a live fashion show on Friday afternoons (see page 123). This is a chance to experience French high fashion up close and personal, and it is available exclusively to tourists visiting France. You might even come home with a trendy new outfit!

3. Go on a Photography Tour. To experience Paris in a unique way, take a half-day guided photography tour that includes instruction in camera techniques. In addition to improving your shutterbug skills, you'll take home beautiful photos that will be enjoyed for years to come. To further explore these tours, see page 178.

4. Splurge on a Romantic Dinner With Entertainment. Nothing is more romantic or exciting than Paris nightlife. Two fabulous choices are dinner at an intimate jazz club, such as Duc des Lombards (see page 155), and a Bateaux Parisiens dinner cruise (see page 159).

5. Indulge in Tea at an Elegant Hotel. Paris' top hotels are elegant, refined, and *très cher* (very expensive), charging upwards of $500 for a room. For far less money, you can experience these settings while savoring delectable desserts and a pot of

euros; and additional half-hours, 4 euros. You must use a credit card, and there is a refundable deposit of around $200. Again, the Visa credit card is not working at these stations, but American Express is. Before you leave with your rented bike, make sure that it is in good working order—that you can adjust the seat height and that the tires are in decent condition.

The only catch so far in using Vélib is that although you can theoretically return your bicycle to any other station, sometimes all the docking areas are full and you're left scrambling to find a place to turn in your bike. (They're working on this.) There are many new bicycle lanes on the streets, but you'll still want to be wary of fast Parisian drivers who might not see you. Also keep in mind that they expect you to observe the traffic rules, and there is a 90-euro penalty to ride a bicycle through a red light. For more information, visit the Vélib website and click on the British flag "download" icon to get two pages of instructions in English. For information on renting and using other bicycles in the city, see page 147 in Chapter 8.

---

tea. Two lavish afternoon tea options include the Hôtel Ritz (page 74) and the Plaza Athénée (page 74).

6. Revel in a Light and Fireworks Display at Versailles. On summer nights, the beautifully landscaped grounds adjacent to the Château de Versailles are home to *Les Grandes Eaux Nocturnes*—an illuminated water fountain display followed by fireworks. Details about Versailles can be found on page 175.

7. Spend a Day in Champagne Country. Reims, the capital of Champagne, is an hour-long scenic train ride east of Paris. Once there, you can visit the historic Reims cathedral before touring champagne houses and sampling world-class *cuvées* (blends). Suggestions for restaurants and hotels start on page 167.

8. Take a Bike Tour of Special Hideaways and Major Sights. To experience Paris' beauty while learning about its past, take a half-day guided bike tour. Bike About Tours start at Notre Dame and include secret passageways in addition to monuments (see page 147). Fat Bike Tours meet at the Eiffel Tower and offer several sightseeing options (see page 147).

9. Enjoy a Concert at Sainte-Chapelle. For a night you'll never forget, attend a chamber music concert at this lovely and intimate church on Ile de la Cité. Sainte-Chapelle is renowned for its awesome stained glass windows and beautiful setting. For information on upcoming performances, see page 89.

10. Savor Wines at a Popular Paris Hangout. A trip to Paris wouldn't be complete without joining the locals in one of their favorite pastimes, sampling good French wines. Two elegant venues that serve a great variety of wines by the glass are Lavinia (see page 111) and Legrande Filles et Fils (see page 111.)

These special activities are guaranteed to introduce you to fascinating aspects of French culture while providing memories that will last a lifetime. I highly recommend that you choose at least one of them to enjoy on your trip. You'll be glad you did!

Using the Telephone in Paris

There are many options for placing calls from Paris, depending on the electronics you are bringing with you and how much time you plan to spend on the phone. For most of us, the easiest option is to use a cell phone that has the capacity for international roaming. This costs about a dollar a minute. (See page 33 for more information.) Calling from your hotel room is good for emergencies, but you'll pay a premium for the convenience—especially on long-distance calls.

SKYPE PHONE SERVICE
Website: www.skype.com

Many of my friends like to keep in close touch with family back home and prefer to have the luxury of unlimited calling, so they use Skype on their iPhone or iPad, or they bring a netbook or small laptop and make calls using another voice-over-Internet service provider.

Télécartes (pre-paid phone cards) are another way to make local and long-distance calls from public phones or, for a fee, from your hotel phone. They can be purchased at major newsstands. Be sure to get one that connects to an English recording for calling instructions.

Placing a Call

When making calls within Paris, from Paris to home, or from home to Paris, you'll want to keep certain things in mind:

❏ Phone numbers in Paris are composed of eight digits, preceded by the region code 01. When you are calling within the Paris area, dial all ten digits.

❏ When you are calling Paris from the United States, dial 011-33-1- followed by the eight-digit Paris number. Do not dial the 01 region code that precedes the Paris numbers listed throughout this book.

❏ To call the United States from France, dial 00-1 followed by the US area code and phone number.

French Phone Phrases

Even if you don't speak French, mastering a few simple phrases should help you place your calls. The following are translations of those French phrases most commonly used over the phone:

You say,	*"Je voudrais parler à"* and give the name of the person. (I would like to speak to . . .)
They respond,	*"De la part de qui?"* (Who is calling?)
You give your name.	
They respond,	*"Ne quittez pas"* or *"Un instant."* (Hold on) or (Just a minute)
Other phrases:	*"Entendu"* (Heard/Understood) *"Il/elle est en ligne"* (He/she is on the line) *"Voulez-vous attendre?"* (Do you want to wait?)

Internet Cybercafés

Many hotels have a computer available in their lobby so that guests can access the Internet and check their email. These computers can usually be rented by the quarter-hour. I find it easier, though, to open an account at a nearby cybercafé and use it periodically during my stay. The price isn't bad—5 to 7 euros for about two hours.

Regardless of the computer you end up using, you will probably find it a little challenging to get started. Here's how to do it:

1. Type in your user name, called the *Nom D'Utilisateur.* Then enter your password, or *Mot de Passé.* (These words will be given to you by the desk clerk when you pay for the service.)

2. Some computers have a box that asks you if you want to start: *Demarrer?* Click on that box or the box that says *Oui* (Yes).

3. Hit the *Connexion* button to start your connection.

4. Hit the *Internet Explorer* button.

5. Place the cursor at the top of the page and type in the website you want to access, such as www.aol.com.

6. Click on the *Mail* button and then *Your Account.* Hit *Se Connector* to connect. *Never* check the box that says *Keep Me Signed In,* as this will allow others to access your account after you've left.

7. If you want to print out a message or page, click on *Fichier* (Edit). Then hit *Imprimer* (Print). If you want to delete anything, hit *Supprimer* (Delete).

8. When you're finished, *always* click on the *Sign Out* button to make sure that your password has been deleted.

9. Hit *Deconnecter* (Disconnect). When it asks you if you are sure, hit *Oui Me Deconnecter* (Yes, Disconnect Me).

Check with your hotel to find the nearest cybercafé. Be sure to request a keyboard in English because the French keyboard has the letters in different positions, which will slow you down. Below are a few good options. As you'll see, one cybercafé is found near the Opéra Garnier, the second is offered by a bike tour business near the Eiffel Tower, and the third is on the Left Bank near the Luxembourg Garden.

FAT TIRE BIKE TOURS
24 Rue Edgar Faure
Phone: 01-56-58-10-54 (Paris)
1-866-614-6218 (toll free
   from US)
Website: www.fattirebike
   toursparis.com
15th *arrondissement*
Métro: Dupleix and La-Motte-
   Picquet-Grenelle
Cards: Not Accepted

LUXEMBOURG MICRO
81 Boulevard Saint Michel
Phone: 01-46-33-27-98
Website: www.luxembourg-
   micro.com
5th *arrondissement*
Métro: Luxembourg
Cards: Not Accepted

**MILK OPERA
INTERNET HALL**
28 Rue du Quatre-Septembre
Phone: 01-40-06-00-70
Website:
   www.milklub.com/wp/
2nd *arrondissement*
Métro: Opéra and Quatre-
   Septembre
Cards: Not Accepted

Understanding French Customs

The French are very polite and show a great deal of respect and formality when addressing each other. Their language reflects this custom. For example, the French have two methods of addressing people, the formal and the informal. While we say "you" in every situation, the same word in French can be spoken in two different ways—*vous* in the formal, and *tu* in the informal. Corresponding verbs have different endings, depending on the formality used.

When French people are introduced, they speak in the formal until they become better acquainted—which can take years. Then they ask permission to speak in the informal. Young people address their elders in the formal, and some couples use the formal address their entire lives. Similarly, the French are less likely to use first names with new acquaintances. When you're speaking to Parisians, it is respectful to address them by *monsieur* (sir) or *madame* (ma'am), and to begin a request with *s'il vous plaît* (if you please).

The French emphasis on politeness carries over into the most casual of daily interactions. When Parisians enter a boutique, for instance, they say "bonjour" to the salesgirl, which is a nice way to acknowledge her presence. You will get better service and feel more at home if you follow this practice. We Americans tend to be more informal in our communications, which can appear rude to the French. The best approach is to be friendly, courteous, and respectful, and to smile a lot. Your French hosts will respond in kind and make you feel welcome.

Here are a few French customs to keep in mind:

❑ In most parks, it is *interdit* (forbidden) to sit on the grass. Many parks have chairs and benches for visitors.

❑ When buying fresh fruit at an outdoor street *marché* (market), it is customary to show the vendor what you want so that he or she can bag it for you. Don't touch the fruit yourself.

❑ Cell phone use in restaurants and on public transportation is frowned upon. Use your phone when you're strolling on the street or in your hotel room.

❑ Dogs are allowed inside casual coffee houses and even formal tearooms, like Angelina, and they always seem well-behaved.

For all the differences between our two cultures, there are many similarities. If you are friendly and show an interest, you will be rewarded with a warm response. A shoe salesman in Galeries Lafayette spent an hour giving me and a girlfriend valuable advice about ways of discerning top-quality merchandise. Another time, I went into a store to ask where I could buy a cat poster like the one in the window, and the saleswoman took it down and gave it to me.

You are bound to return from Paris with your own wonderful examples of French *gentillesse* (kindness).

3. Les Fantaisies

Spoil Yourself and Discover the Secrets of French Femininity

Paris is a wonderful city for female travelers for many reasons. One of them is the opportunity to observe Frenchwomen and learn about their fashion, their style, and their *savoir vivre* (knowing how to live).

A great way to recuperate from the transatlantic flight and "recharge your batteries" is to spend a day among Frenchwomen exploring their secrets of femininity. There are many wonderful options, including:

- A visit to an elegant French hair salon for a shampoo and blow-dry (*brushing*), which is an ideal way to give yourself a lift as well as a sexy new look to kick off your trip.

- A manicure at one of the nearby beauty salons that offer treatments to nourish, beautify, and rejuvenate your body in a luxurious and restful setting.

- A relaxing, revitalizing afternoon spent at one of Paris' many Arab-style steam baths, or *hammams*.

- A trip to a lingerie store, where you'll be enticed with a wide array of lacy, silky undergarments, many of them handmade.

- Choosing your scent (*griffe*) at a French perfume boutique, and indulging in a matching lotion to "layer" the scents.

Armed with all this knowledge and allure, you should wear a badge warning that you're a *femme dangereuse!*

If you're traveling with an amour, while you are off pampering yourself, he can take a walking or photography tour on the streets of Paris and report back to you on his adventures. (See page 79 in Chapter 4 for information on walking tours and page 178 of Chapter 11 for information on photography tours.) Plan a fitting finale to your day of indulgence by enjoying afternoon tea accompanied with finger sandwiches and delectable desserts.

In this chapter, the heart rating ♥ indicates my favorite choices.

Hair Salons

You'll observe that Frenchwomen strive for a natural, feminine look that requires minimal effort. They wear their hair in classic styles—clean cuts at chin or shoulder length, pulled back and tied with an attractive clasp, or worn short to frame the face. Hair accessories are used to add flair and personal style. Like many other aspects of appearance, this is something that's passed on from mother to daughter.

French hair salons differ widely from elite, expensive establishments to smaller, less costly neighborhood shops. Passing a few hours in one of the top salons will give you the opportunity to rub shoulders with and observe a rare breed of Frenchwomen in a glamorous setting. If you are on a budget, the neighborhood salons will do a very good job at half the price, and because Frenchwomen take great care in their appearance, you'll find one on almost every block.

I suggest that you don't get carried away with a drastic new cut in the latest style. I made that mistake once and lived to regret it for months until it grew out. A *shampooing and brushing*—equivalent to our shampoo and blow-dry—is a great way to pamper yourself at a cost of 20 to 28 euros ($30 to $40) at a neighborhood salon, depending on the length of your hair. The "high end" salons cost much more. Even though service is included in the price, I recommend adding a few euros—about 10 percent—as a tip. Most hair salons are closed on Sundays and Mondays.

On the next few pages, you will find a selection of chic French hairdressers. They are all in the pricey category—upwards of 42 euros ($60) for a shampoo and blow-

Hair Accessories as Art Pieces

No matter what your hair length, a beautiful headband, hair clip, barrette, or hair comb will add polish and glamour to your look. I thought I'd seen it all until I stepped into the Alexandre de Paris Accessoires boutique on Rue St.-Honoré. Beautifully displayed on shelves, each piece looked like a carefully crafted jewel. There is a widely varied selection, and prices start at a jaw-dropping 50 euros (about $70). A less expensive option is to get ideas from these one-of-a-kind pieces and look for lower-priced versions at the department stores. (See also the "Save Some Money" inset on page 65.)

ALEXANDRE DE PARIS ACCESSOIRES
235 Rue St.-Honoré
Phone: 01-42-61-41-34
Website: www.alexandredeparis-accessories.com
1st *arrondissement*
Métro: Tuileries and Concorde
Cards: Accepted

Hair Salon Terms and Costs

While you don't have to be fluent in French to enjoy an afternoon in a French hair (*cheveaux*) salon, it is important to be able to request the procedure you want. The following basic terms should help. Although I have included the word for "color," I recommend steering clear of color treatments, because the French methods are often different from those used in the States. If asked what kind of shampoo process you want, I suggest that you choose the *normal* instead of the pricier version, which includes special conditioners.

The approximate costs printed below are what you would pay in one of the top salons. If you go to a less-expensive neighborhood salon, you'll pay *half* the price.

ENGLISH	FRENCH	APPROXIMATE COST
Blow-dry	*Brushing* or *Coiffage**	62 euros
Color	*Couleur**	60–100 euros
Cut	*Coupe†*	135–175 euros
Hair Conditioning	*L'Essentiel Cheveux**	50 euros

* *Shampooing* (known as a *normal shampoo*) is included in this procedure.

† A shampoo, cut, and blow-dry are included in this procedure.

dry—except for Saint Honoré Coiffure, a great neighborhood salon on the Right Bank, and Coiff1rst, which is on the Left Bank. These lower-priced establishments start at around 30 euros ($42) for a shampoo and blow-dry. Translations of hair salon terms can be found in the inset above.

CARITA

Carita is a French "institution" catering to well-heeled Parisians and visitors alike. This flagship store on trendy Faubourg St.-Honoré is elegance personified and faces a lovely patio. The hairdressers are known for their stylish hairstyles. Carita is a *Maison de Beauté*, meaning that it offers many other beauty treatments, including facials and makeup applications.

11 Rue du Faubourg St.-
  Honoré
Phone: 01-44-94-11-11
Website: www.carita.com
8th *arrondissement*
Métro: Madeleine and
  Concorde
Cards: Accepted

COIFF1RST

Set back from the street, this Left Bank salon makes you feel as if you're stepping into another world as you pass a courtyard and enter a chic modern salon. Despite the elegant décor, prices are reasonable.

44 Rue du Four
Phone: 01-45-44-84-39
Website: www.coiffirst.com
6th *arrondissement*
Métro: Mabillon and St.-
  Germain-des-Prés
Cards: Accepted

DESSANGE
This small boutique salon is independently owned and very well located off Rue St.-Honoré, near Place de la Madeleine. It's open on Mondays, when many salons are closed.

6 Rue du Chevalier de St.-George
Phone: 01-42-60-17-72
1st *arrondissement*
Métro: Madeleine
Cards: Accepted

SAINT HONORE COIFFURE ♥
This is my favorite small neighborhood hair salon, located near the Louvre on fashionable Rue St.-Honoré. It is a few doors away from the excellent Parisian tearoom Verlet (see page 75 for details).

270 Rue St.-Honoré
Phone: 01-42-60-65-36
1st *arrondissement*
Métro: Tuileries and Pyramides
Cards: Accepted

SALON DESSANGE
Famed hairstylist Jacques Dessange created an upscale chain of hair salons that is recommended by my Parisian girlfriends. This boutique is in the high-priced Champs-Elysées area.

39 Avenue Franklin D. Roosevelt
Phone: 01-43-59-31-31
Website: www.dessange.com
8th *arrondissement*
Métro: Franklin-D.-Roosevelt
Cards: Accepted

BEAUTY SALONS

French beauty salons offer a wide variety of treatments, including different kinds of facials, waxing, manicure and pedicure, eyebrow and lash tint, makeup application, and more. If this is your first salon experience, a manicure is a good choice. A professional makeup application is another way to add a sparkle to your look and give you fresh ideas for practice later. Most salons sell the products they use, so you can pick up a souvenir that will bring a smile to your face every time you use it. (See the inset on page 65 for translations of beauty salon terms.)

Guerlain's Institute de Beauté is one of the oldest and most elegant salons in Paris. Completed in 1828, Guerlain is located on the Champs-Elysées and is renowned for its classic methods, high-quality products, and discreet service. This salon enjoys a stream of American clients, but the vast majority of its customers are well-to-do Frenchwomen, sometimes many generations from the same family. The motto at Guerlain is *"La perfection de la tradition"* (the perfection of the tradition), and the salon emphasizes "luxury, calm, and voluptuousness."

The listing that begins on the next page includes some of Paris' top beauty salons. All offer a wide variety of treatments in beautiful settings amid a parade of elegant Frenchwomen. It is best to make your reservation well in advance, either by calling from the United States or by asking your hotel concierge to book the appointment before your arrival. Costs vary from about 50 euros ($70) for a manicure to about 100 euros ($140) for a facial, and a small tip—about 10 percent—is appreciated on top of the modest service charge included in the cost.

$ $ $ SAVE SOME MONEY $ $ $

If the prices in Paris' top stores give you sticker shock, find a nearby Monoprix or Prisunic discount department store and check out their counters for beauty accessories and products. Located throughout the city, these stores are similar to a Target store in the US, but their offerings have unmistakable French flair. I'm always finding good deals on stylish hair accessories (a lovely hair twist for only 4 euros), nail polish in beautiful colors (again, 4 euros for a small bottle that's perfect for travel), and interesting makeup sets.

INSTITUT DE BEAUTE GUERLAIN ♥
Guerlain has opened other salons in Paris, but this is the original and most elaborate; the atmosphere and luxurious décor are well worth a visit. You can also choose from a wonderful selection of their signature perfumes.

68 Avenue des Champs-Elysées
Phone: 01-45-62-11-21
Website: www.guerlain.com
8th *arrondissement*
Métro: Franklin-D.-Roosevelt
Cards: Accepted

L'INSTITUT LANCOME
Built in 1936, this venerable salon is world-renowned. Products are sold on the ground floor, and the beauty institute is on the second floor. This street is great for strolling; don't miss the other glamorous boutiques in the area.

29 Rue du Faubourg St.-Honoré
Phone: 01-42-65-30-74
Website: www.lancome.com
8th *arrondissement*
Métro: Madeleine and Concorde
Cards: Accepted

Beauty Salon Terms and Costs

If, like me, you've experienced the frustration of trying to communicate in another language by waving your arms around and pointing, this list should simplify matters. The cost stated below should give you an idea of what you can expect to pay for each treatment in one of the better salons. If you have the same treatment in a small neighborhood salon, you will probably pay only half this price.

ENGLISH	FRENCH	APPROXIMATE COST
Body massage	*Modelage esthetique relaxant*	100 euros
Facial	*Beauté complete du visage*	100 euros
Makeup application	*Maquillage*	60 euros
Manicure	*Manucure*	50 euros
Pedicure	*Beauté des pieds**	70 euros

*This is the straight pedicure, not the *medicale,* which is more elaborate.

PRINTEMPS DE LA BEAUTE

Part of the large Printemps department store located near the Opéra Garnier, this upstairs salon offers practically every treatment that you can imagine. You can also choose from among three hundred brands of beauty products. Turn to the Chapter 6 discussion "Applying for Sales Tax Reimbursement" (found on page 131) to see if you should combine all your purchases at this store to qualify for tax reimbursement.

64 Boulevard Haussmann
Phone: 01-42-82-50-00
Website:
    www.printemps.com
9th *arrondissement*
Métro: Havre-Caumartin
Cards: Accepted

Spas and Hammams

One of the best ways to pamper yourself while in Paris is to indulge in a few hours at a spa or that increasingly popular establishment, the hammam. Either way, you are sure to emerge relaxed and rejuvenated.

Most of the big-name Paris hotels offer their guests state-of-the-art spa facilities, and many of the more intimate boutique hotels also have first-class spas. Some standouts include the Right Bank's lavish Hôtel Costes (page 15), which offers a spa with an atmospheric indoor pool, and the Left Bank's stylish L'Hôtel (page 20), which has a private swimming pool and steam bath for two in a stunning converted wine cellar.

If you're staying in a hotel that doesn't have a spa, or you simply want to take a more exotic route, you can join Parisians in one of their favorite pastimes, a trip to a nearby hammam. An Arab-style "collective" steam bath, a hammam charges anywhere from a reasonable 35 euros to over 200 euros for special massages and a half-day of treatments. Many (but not all) hammams adhere to the Arabic tradition of having separate days for men and women, since they use one room for bathing. Be sure to check the available options in advance and ask if there's anything you should bring in addition to your bathing suit. Be aware that most Frenchwomen wear bikini bottoms and walk around topless. Another adventurous aspect of a hammam is that the staff might not speak much English; this will truly be an "immersion" experience.

On the next page, you'll find listings of several good hammams and one spa, but many more options are available. You can locate other facilities by flipping through the weekly *Pariscope* guide, which is available at *tabacs* (newsstands) throughout the city. Look under *Paris Pratique* and the subhead *Bien-Etre* (well-being).

"Hammams, as they are called, have mosaic-tile steam rooms where you slather yourself in olive oil-based soap, sweat, rinse, have your skin buffed with a scratchy mitt, then get a massage. Afterward, you retreat to a darkened room, lounge around in a cotton robe, drink mint tea from a silver pot and fall in and out of sleep."
—Angela Doland, Associated Press

LES BAINS DU MARAIS ♥

Les Bains du Marais provides a more elegant setting than the Hammam de la Mosquée de Paris, described below. It has days reserved for men or women exclusively, but it also offers days when men and women can enjoy the facilities at the same time. Check the website for the schedule and choose the option that suits you best. Prices start at 35 euros for the hammam, sauna, and *salle de repos* (resting room). Another possibilitiy is the hammam steam bath followed by a *gommage* (exfoliating body scrub) and a twenty-minute massage for 70 euros.

31-33 Rue des Blancs Manteaux
Phone: 01-44-61-02-02
Website: www.lesbains dumarais.com
4th *arrondissement*
Métro: Hôtel-de-Ville
Cards: Accepted

HAMMAM DE LA MOSQUEE DE PARIS

This traditional hammam has separate days for men and women. It's less expensive than the other options but tends to get pretty crowded. The setting is very authentic, and there is a lovely adjoining tearoom. Prices start at 38 euros for the steam bath and a *gommage* (exfoliating body scrub). A ten-minute massage costs an additional 10 euros, and for another 4 euros, you get "soft soap" and mint tea.

39 Rue Geoffrey St.-Hilaire
Phone: 01-43-31-38-20
Website: www.la-mosquee.com
5th *arrondissement*
Métro: Place-Monge
Cards: Accepted

HAMMAM PACHA PARIS

This beautiful hammam is only a few years old, so the facilities are new and luxurious. (The original Hammam Pacha is on the outskirts of the city.) Prices are a bit steep, starting at 60 euros for a basic package that includes use of the showers and steam room; black soap and glove; and an exfoliating body rub.

17 Rue Mayet
Phone: 01-43-06-55-55
Website: http://www.hammamp acha.com/en/plan.htm
6th *arrondissement*
Métro: Duroc
Cards: Accepted

HARNN & THANN

If you are traveling with a significant other, this Thai spa near the Louvre would be an excellent choice, as men and women are welcome on the same day. It even offers a "Formule Saveurs et Bien Etre" for couples, which includes steam, massage, and dinner afterwards at a nearby Thai restaurant. The cost for two, with everything included, is 250 euros.

11 Rue Molière
Phone: 01-40-15-02-20
Website: www.harnn-spa.fr
1st *arrondissement*
Métro: Pyramides
Cards: Accepted

Hammam Pacha Paris.

LINGERIE STORES

Frenchwomen are notoriously seductive and spend almost as much energy choosing what's underneath their clothes as they do on their outward appearance. They are also inventive and playful, as you'll see from the numerous lingerie store window displays—obviously a popular shopping detour in Paris!

According to French legend, it was enterprising Hermine Cadolle who invented the brassiere in 1890 and liberated her fashionable clients from the corset. Ever since then, Frenchwomen have been setting lingerie trends for the world. Cadolle's *maison de lingerie* is still a Paris institution and is run by Hermine's great-great granddaughter, Poupie. The prestigious international clientele chooses among luxurious hand-sewn items that range from a custom-fitted bra to a full-length fitted nightgown, all for astronomical prices (we're talking upwards of $600). I took the corset liberation one step further by purchasing an ivory silk camisole, which is *très confortable* (very comfortable).

One way to indulge in intimate apparel without spending a fortune is to buy silky sheer French stockings. Chantal Thomass (listed below) has a great selection of sexy stockings in a variety of colors and attractive patterns. The following list includes some of the top lingerie and hosiery stores in Paris. You will run across many others as you stroll Paris' elegant streets.

CADOLLE BOUTIQUE
Cadolle has two stores—this boutique, which sells ready-to-wear silky lingerie, and the flagship store, Cadolle Couture (listed below), which offers individually sewn lacy bras and other sexy undergarments.

4 Rue Cambon
Phone: 01-42-60-94-22
Website: www.cadolle.com
1st *arrondissement*
Métro: Concorde
Cards: Accepted

CADOLLE COUTURE
The house of Cadolle is one of the original couturiers, sewing each garment to the client's exact measurements. The final result—a perfectly fitted bra, for instance—is seen by only a few eyes, but the value is priceless and the cost is high. Cadolle Couture is open by appointment only.

255 Rue St.-Honoré
Phone: 01-42-60-94-94
Website: www.cadolle.com
1st *arrondissement*
Métro: Concorde and
  Madeleine
Cards: Accepted

CHANTAL THOMASS ♥
This boutique offers lingerie, wonderful hosiery, and a very good selection of less-expensive gifts, including sexy parasol-type umbrellas, journals and small notepads, and candles. If you want an item gift-wrapped, ask for a *paquet cadeau*.

211 Rue St.-Honoré
Phone: 01-42-60-40-56
Website:
  www.chantalthomass.fr
1st *arrondissement*
Métro: Tuileries and
  Pyramides
Cards: Accepted

FOGAL

The small Fogal boutique, which is found near Place de la Madeleine, specializes in silky sheer stockings fastened with garter belts, and carries some pantyhose as well. The selection of colors and designs is one of the best in Paris.

380 Rue St.-Honoré
Phone: 01-42-96-81-47
Website: www.fogal.com
1st *arrondissement*
Métro: Madeleine
Cards: Accepted

GALERIES LAFAYETTE

Galeries Lafayette is a large department store that includes a big selection of lingerie and hosiery. The atmosphere is not as intimate as that of most boutiques, but you get the choice of many top labels. (See the discussion on page 122 to learn more about Galeries Lafayette.)

40 Boulevard Haussmann
Phone: 01-42-82-36-40
Website: www.galeries
   lafayette.com
9th *arrondissement*
Métro: Opéra and
   Chaussée-d'Antin-La-
   Fayette
Cards: Accepted

SABBIA ROSA

In the heart of the Left Bank, near Boulevard St.-Germain, Sabbia Rosa is a Parisian institution catering to young and old, to famous models and even American tourists who want to bring back a sliver of French femininity in the form of a lacy undergarment.

71-73 Rue des St.-Pères
Phone: 01-45-48-88-37
6th *arrondissement*
Métro: St.-Germain-des-
   Prés and Sèvres-
   Babylone
Cards: Accepted

Perfume Shops

Perfume is a multibillion-dollar industry in France, steeped in mystique and rich in history. Catherine de Medici is credited with founding the first perfume factory in Grasse, France in the sixteenth century. Grasse is still considered the perfume capital of the world, and students flock to this tiny town in the southern countryside to learn how to identify over 3,000 scents.

Coco Chanel was the first *couturière* to use her own name on a perfume when she launched Chanel No. 5 in 1923. It was so successful that many other designers followed suit. Considered a classic, Chanel No. 5 remains in big demand and is regarded as one of the best-selling perfumes of all time.

The renowned Guerlain line of perfumes has been in existence since the nineteenth century, when Pierre-François Guerlain created custom fragrances for members of European royalty. Today, at the boutiques on Place Vendôme and the Champs-Elysées, you are invited to select the perfume that best suits your personality. Each of the scents has distinctive characteristics and ascribed traits. Shalimar, which was created by Jacques Guerlain in 1925, is one of Guerlain's most popular fragrances. I chose L'Heure Bleue, developed in 1912, for "women who are romantic, sensitive, refined, and feminine," all qualities I'm aspiring to—at $140 for a small flacon of eau de parfum.

Perfumes are sold in many boutiques throughout Paris. Galeries Lafayette (see page 122) is the best place to find every scent—almost—under one roof. Most of the ground floor is devoted to perfumes and beauty products. The salespeople speak English, and United States citizens can get a 10-percent discount card at the Welcome Desk by showing a passport. Perfumes and soaps are also sold at airport duty-free shops. This is fine for last-minute purchases of popular brands—assuming that you have time and don't get stuck in a long security line—but airport shops don't have the selection that you'll find in Paris stores.

On the next few pages, you will find the listings for Chanel and Guerlain, as well as stores in busy areas that offer a good selection of perfumes, cosmetics, and small gift items that you can have wrapped. I have included one discount store, Benlux, which offers a wide range of perfumes at great prices.

"Frenchwomen are faithful to their fragrance and use their personal scent as a signature, one with which they are associated and by which they are remembered. . . . Frenchwomen never drench themselves with perfume. They apply it in layers, so that the scent is gently released with their natural body movements. And they stick to the same scent for every form of fragrance used.

"They begin with scented soap and bubble bath or bath oil, followed by matching body lotion. They finish with eau de toilette for day, or perfume for night. They carry a small flacon in their handbags to refresh their fragrance every few hours."
—Susan Sommers, French Chic

BENLUX PARIS DUTY FREE

Conveniently located across the street from the Louvre, Benlux offers a long list of perfumes, beauty products, and handbags, and its great deals pack in the shoppers. The usual 12-percent tax is taken off the price even if you spend under the 175-euro requirement to get "duty free." If you spend over that amount, the discount is even higher, up to 20 percent. You will still need to process the *détaxe* papers at the airport desk when you go home. (See page 131 for details.)

174 Rue de Rivoli
Phone: 01-47-03-66-63
1st *arrondissement*
Métro: Palais-Royal-
    Musée-du-Louvre
Cards: Accepted

CHANEL

There are two Chanel boutiques where you can purchase classic perfumes as well as other Chanel products. The flagship store—Coco Chanel's first and oldest boutique—is the one on Rue Cambon.

31 Rue Cambon
Phone: 01-42-86-26-00
Website: www.chanel.com
1st *arrondissement*
Métro: Concorde and Madeleine
Cards: Accepted

42 Avenue Montaigne
Phone: 01-47-23-74-12
Website: www.chanel.com
8th *arrondissement*
Métro: Franklin-D.-Roosevelt
    and Alma-Marceau
Cards: Accepted

GUERLAIN

Both the Place Vendôme boutique and the flagship store on the Champs-Elysées offer the company's legendary fragrances as well as its newest scents and other Guerlain products.

2 Place Vendôme
Phone: 01-42-60-68-61
Website: www.guerlain.com
1st *arrondissement*
Métro: Tuileries
Cards: Accepted

68 Avenue des Champs-Elysées
Phone: 01-45-62-11-21
Website: www.guerlain.com
8th *arrondissement*
Métro: Franklin-D.-Roosevelt
Cards: Accepted

MARIONNAUD

Located just off Avenue de l'Opéra, Marionnaud offers beautiful bath products by many different companies, including Le Couvent des Minimes in Provence. The boutique's complimentary gift-wrap is very classy, and they have boutiques in other parts of the city, as well.

59 Rue des Petits Champs
Phone: 01-42-96-00-24
Website:
   www.marionnaud.fr
1st *arrondissement*
Métro: Pyramides and
   Opéra
Cards: Accepted

PARFUMERIE NOCIBE

As the name indicates, this store specializes in perfumes. It also carries makeup kits, bath products, and many items on sale (*soldes*).

187 Rue St.-Honoré
Phone: 01-40-15-91-73
Website: www.nocibe.fr
1st *arrondissement*
Métro: Tuileries and
   Pyramides
Cards: Accepted

SEPHORA

If you live in or near a major American city, you may already be familiar with this French-owned cosmetics superstore, which stocks a huge variety of perfumes, cosmetics, and other beauty-related items. Here are a couple of Sephora's Paris boutiques—one on the Left Bank in the sixth *arrondissement,* and one on the Right Bank in the first *arrondissement.*

79 Boulevard St.-Germain
Phone: 01-55-42-62-90
Website: www.sephora.com
6th *arrondissement*
Métro: Cluny-La-Sorbonne and Odéon
Cards: Accepted

75 Rue de Rivoli
Phone: 01-40-13-16-50
Website: www.sephora.com
1st *arrondissement*
Métro: Pont-Neuf and Châtelet
Cards: Accepted

Learning More About Perfumes

If you enjoy fragrance and want to know more about it, you'll find some great opportunities during your stay in Paris.

A visit to the Parfumerie Fragonard, located in an elegant townhouse from the period of Napolean III, will help you "understand and appreciate the role of perfume in history and our society." Perfume has its origins in the burning of incense during funerary rites; only later was scent applied to the body. The museum's collection of objects dates from 3000 BC up through modern times. The range of exhibited perfume bottles shows the evolution of taste and fashion, as well as the development of ceramic art.

The Parfumerie Fragonard is open Monday through Saturday, and admission is free. The gift shop offers a selection of scents and soaps.

If you are curious about the art of perfume making, consider taking a three-hour workshop on the history and composition of perfume. Held at L'Artisan Parfumeur, a perfume house created by Jean Laporte, the workshop begins by having you smell and identify a range of natural raw materials. You then learn about different methods of capturing natural fragrances and creating perfumes. There is also a *pause gourmande* (gourmet break), where you savor different types of teas and other food specialties. The cost is 95 euros per person. A workshop in which you create your own fragrance—and take it home with you—is offered for 170 euros. Email the company to make a reservation for a course in English or to receive more information. The scheduling depends on demand.

PARFUMERIE FRAGONARD
9 Rue Scribe
Phone: 01-47-42-04-56
Website: www.fragonard.com
9th *arrondissement*
Métro: Opéra
Cards: Accepted

L'ARTISAN PARFUMEUR
2 Rue de l'Amiral de Coligny
Phone: 01-44-88-27-50
Website: www.laboutiquedelartisan
  parfumeur.com
Email: atelier@artisan-parfumeur.com
1st *arrondissement*
Métro: Louvre-Rivoli
Cards: Accepted

Perfume Pointers

Shopping for a Scent

The French know that because fragrance is affected by body chemistry, a particular scent will not smell the same on any two people. They also know that scent in the bottle does not smell the same as it does on the skin, and that it must be tried on and worn for a while before making a decision about buying it.

- Shop for scent late in the day, when the sense of smell is sharpest.

- Wait at least ten minutes before checking the scent to give it time to develop.

- Try on a maximum of three scents at one session; the nose cannot differentiate between more than this.

Where to Apply

Both *eau de toilette* and perfume are applied at the pulse points so that the body's heat will help bring out the fragrance:

- between the knees
- between the thighs
- the décolletage
- base of the throat

- insides of the wrists
- at the elbows
- behind the ears

From *French Chic* by Susan Sommers. Copyright @ by Susan Sommers. www.dresszing.com

TEA SALONS

The perfect finale to your day of luxury and rejuvenation is a break for tea at one of the popular tea salons. This is one of those customs the French have elevated to a fine art. They love to spend an afternoon visiting over a cup of tea while devouring a *pâtisserie*. It is a pastime you will warm to immediately and probably try to recreate the moment you return from your trip. I know I have!

Afternoon tea is also an excellent way to enjoy the most luxurious, expensive hotels in Paris. My top picks in this category are the Hôtel Ritz on Place Vendôme and the Plaza Athénée on Avenue Montaigne. They are more costly than the tearooms, but are well worth the extra euros for a romantic rendezvous with your *amour* or an afternoon splurge with friends.

ANGELINA ♥

One of the most famous tearooms in Paris, Angelina has always been popular among models, young couples, and older Frenchwomen, who bring their well-behaved poodles along with them. The Belle Epoque décor sets the perfect mood to indulge, the renowned *L'Africain* hot chocolate (*chocolat chaud*) is delicious, the desserts are decadent. and the presentation is elegant. There is often a line to be seated, especially on weekends.

226 Rue de Rivoli
Phone: 01-42-60-82-00
Website: www.angelina-paris.fr
1st *arrondissement*
Métro: Tuileries and Concorde
Cards: Accepted

HOTEL PLAZA ATHENEE ♥

Every afternoon from 3:00 to 7:00 PM, coffee, tea, and dessert are served in the hotel's luxurious La Galerie des Gobelins. This is not a formal three-course high-tea; you order *à la carte,* and coffee and dessert run around 23 euros. La Galerie does not take reservations, and it's very busy on weekends.

25 Avenue Montaigne
Phone: 01-53-67-66-65
Website: www.plaza-athenee-paris.com
8th *arrondissement*
Métro: Franklin-D.-Roosevelt and Alma-Marceau
Cards: Accepted

HOTEL RITZ PARIS ♥

Formal afternoon tea is served in the Bar Vendôme from 4:00 to 6:00 PM, seven days a week, except Saturdays, when it moves to the Salon d'Eté. The cost is 55 euros for a choice of special-blend and organic teas, mini sandwiches, and a "buffet" of mouthwatering *petit* desserts prepared by the Ritz pastry chef. In summertime, tea is served on the outdoor terrace. The bar takes reservations, and weekends are very busy.

15 Place Vendôme
Phone: 01-43-16-33-63
Website: www.ritzparis.com
1st *arrondissement*
Métro: Concorde and Tuileries
Cards: Accepted

MARIAGE FRERES ♥

Founded in 1854 to promote "l'art Français du thé," Mariage Frères is *the* place that tea connoisseurs frequent for its selection of more than 400 gourmet tea blends and its expert tea preparation. The company now has three locations in Paris, each of which is open seven days a week and sells a huge variety of teas and accessories. The price of a large pot of tea is hefty—around 9 euros. The price of a small bag of tea to take home is around 7 euros.

30 Rue du Bourg-Tibourg
Phone: 01-42-72-28-11
4th *arrondissement*
Métro: Hôtel-de-Ville
Cards: Accepted

13 Rue des Grands Augustins
Phone: 01-40-51-82-50
Website:
www.mariagefreres.com
6th *arrondissement*
Métro: Saint-Michel
Cards: Accepted

260 Rue du Faubourg
St.-Honoré
Phone: 01-46-22-18-54
8th *arrondissement*
Métro: Ternes
Cards: Accepted

VERLET ♥

Verlet was established in 1880 and has been my favorite neighborhood haunt for the past two decades. The upstairs room is attractive, but I prefer the hubbub of the ground floor, which offers a huge selection of teas, coffee beans, and dried fruits for sale. You can order a pot of tea from the pages-long menu or get a gourmet coffee—along with a wonderful dessert, of course. This is a great place to purchase loose tea or coffee beans and have them ground to your specifications.

256 Rue St.-Honoré
Phone: 01-42-60-67-39
Website:
www.cafesverlet.com
1st *arrondissement*
Métro: Palais-Royal-
Musée-du-Louvre and
Pyramides
Cards: Accepted

Your Day Of Indulgence Awaits

The salons, boutiques, and tearooms I've shared with you in this chapter are an important part of what makes Paris a special city for women. I know that these wonderful places have enhanced my appreciation of life's feminine pleasures, and I hope they will do the same for you.

Sainte-Chapelle.

4. La Culture

Learn About History and Art Firsthand

Learning about Parisian culture is a wonderfully participatory experience. All you need do is step outside your hotel and start walking. The *centre de la ville* (center of the city) is a special world unto itself with new discoveries at every turn.

You will come across many monuments that seem like old friends because you've seen them so many times before in movies, on television, and in photos—the Eiffel Tower piercing the sky, Place de la Concorde with its fountains illuminated at night, and the Arc de Triomphe standing watch over the Champs-Elysées. No, you're not in a dream. This is the real thing!

I used to subscribe to the school of serendipity, exploring without a set timetable and allowing the city to unveil herself at my feet. That philosophy has changed as I've learned that it pays to plan ahead (at least a bit) to make sure the sights I want to see are open and to research special exhibitions and places of interest nearby.

Depending on whether this is your first trip (and you want to view the major sights) or a return visit, you will be thrilled by the variety and quality of your options. Paris is a city rich in history and culture that has been well preserved and is very accessible to visitors. This chapter highlights key historic sights, museums, bookstores, and venues for concerts, ballet, and opera. Palaces and other historic sights found on the periphery of Paris and in the surrounding countryside—for example, Versailles and Giverny—are discussed in Chapter 10. The heart rating ♥ indicates my top recommendations.

HISTORIC SIGHTS

Paris is steeped in fascinating history, and many monuments have been constructed to celebrate past glories. Over the centuries, each ruler has left his mark by commissioning the leading architect of the time to design yet another palace or square or garden, and that tradition continues today.

One of the best ways to catch a glimpse of the major historic sights is to take one of the L'Open Tour yellow double-decker buses, which provide recorded commentary and allow you to hop on and hop off at will. (See page 43 for details.) Another way to view the spectacular architecture of the city from a scenic vantage point is to take a boat tour along the Seine River. (See the inset on page 80 for details.) If you want to get some exercise while you're exploring Paris, consider scholar-led walking tours (see the inset on page 79) or guided bicycle tours (page 147).

The following are a handful of Paris' most famous landmarks. You will see many other monuments and statues during your trip, since they're on almost every corner. Parisians are very proud of their achievements. These sights are open year-round; the listed websites provide more background information.

ARC DE TRIOMPHE

Standing majestically at the foot of the Champs-Elysées, the Arc de Triomphe was commissioned by Napoleon in 1806 to commemorate his victories. It houses the tomb of France's unknown soldier and is at the center of the busiest traffic hub in Paris—the Place Charles de Gaulle Etoile (*étoile* means star), from which twelve avenues radiate. The safest way to enter this monument is the underground walkway from the Champs-Elysées. On the observation deck, accessible by stairs or an elevator, you'll find an excellent view of the Eiffel Tower, the Champs-Elysées, and the Louvre beyond.

Website: http://arc-de-triomphe.monuments-nationaux.fr/en/
8th *arrondissement*
Métro: Charles-de-Gaulle-Etoile

LA BASILIQUE DU SACRE-COEUR

Located at the top of Butte Montmartre, the highest point in Paris, the white-domed church of Sacré-Coeur can be seen from miles away and offers a great view of Paris—especially if you climb the dome. Designed in the Roman-Byzantine style and completed in the early twentieth century, the church is immense in size and built of travertine stone, which bleaches over time, making the structure a stunning white. Sacré-Coeur is also notable for a garden of meditation, a fine pipe organ, and one of the largest mosaics in the world.

This historic site is a bit off the beaten track and requires a long métro ride followed by either a walk up the steep hill

34 Rue du Chevalier-de-la-Barre
Phone: 01-53-41-89-00
Website: www.sacre-coeur-montmartre.com
18th *arrondissement*
Métro: Abbesses and Anvers

The Paris-Story Cultural Slide Show

A nice way to get a small dose of history is to view the Paris-Story ninety-minute slide show on "the development of the monuments and culture that have become the Paris of today." It starts with the early Celtic invasions; continues through the twelfth-century construction of Notre Dame Cathedral, the seventeenth-century design of the first royal squares (such as Place des Vosges), and the French Revolution; and concludes with the outstanding architecture of modern times. I wouldn't go out of my way to view this show, but if it's raining or you're near the Opéra Garnier, this is worth a stop. Tickets cost 10 euros, and it's open 365 days a year. The shows start on the hour from 10:00 AM to 6:00 PM.

PARIS-STORY
11 bis Rue Scribe
Phone: 01-42-66-62-06
Website: www.paris-story.com
9th *arrondissement*
Métro: Opéra
Cards: Accepted

Cultural Walking Tours

If you have a genuine interest in the culture, art, and architecture of Paris, you may want more than the average tour, which provides only general information about the city's sights. Context can be a great choice. This company offers a fascinating variety of intimate walking tours led by experts in the fields of architecture, art, archaeology, cuisine, history, and urban planning. Options include "Origins of Paris" at 64 euros a person, "Louvre French Masters" at 65 euros, "Baguette to Bistro—Culinary Traditions of Paris" at 75 euros, and much more. Groups are limited to six people at most, and private customized tours can be arranged (for a hefty price). If Context's tours are too costly for your budget, check the website for ideas on sights and activities that you can pursue on your own.

CONTEXT
14 Rue Charles V
Phone: 800-691-6036 (in US)
01-72-81-36-35 (in Paris)
Website: www.context travel.com/city/Paris
4th *arrondissement*
Métro: St.-Paul
Cards: Accepted

or use of a convenient motorized tram. (Just follow the signs for the "Funiculaire.") It's worth the trip, though. While you're in the neighborhood, visit nearby Place du Tertre, a square known for the dozens of artists who set up easels there, many of whom are eager to paint your portrait. The square is very touristy and "kitschy," but still entertaining, and you'll find plenty of cafés and *créperies* nearby.

CATHEDRALE DE NOTRE DAME ♥

One of the great Gothic cathedrals of Europe, Notre Dame is located on Ile de la Cité, one of the small islands in the Seine River. This sight has a tumultuous history. Construction began in 1163 and took almost two centuries to complete. During the French Revolution, Notre Dame was pillaged and damaged. In the nineteenth century, the stained glass and spire were restored, returning the cathedral to its former glory.

Place du Parvis de Notre Dame
Phone: 01-42-34-56-10
Website: http://www.notredame deparis.fr/-English
4th *arrondissement*
Métro: Cité, Hôtel-de-Ville, and St.-Michel

Check local listings (see page 87 to learn about *Pariscope*) for not-to-be-missed organ recitals and concerts held in this memorable cathedral. Or visit during Sunday morning services, when the church is crowded but likely to have wonderful organ music. Tours of the cathedral towers—which involve climbing 402 steps—begin at the foot of the North Tower, on the left as you're facing the main entrance. The line is normally long.

While you're visiting Notre Dame, enjoy the rest of the island. In nice weather, the lovely park behind the cathedral is a great spot for a picnic lunch. The nearby area has wonderful examples of Renaissance architecture and is one of the most exclusive districts in Paris. The Conciergerie (a former royal palace and prison) and Sainte-Chapelle (see page 89) are within walking distance.

Boat Tours: A Different Vantage Point

Boat tours along the Seine River provide a wonderful way to get out into the fresh air, soak up some sun, and enjoy a scenic view of Paris' striking monuments. Some tours include interesting commentary about the history of the buildings you pass and the bridges you ride beneath.

BATEAUX VEDETTES DU PONT-NEUF ♥

Square du Vert Galant
Phone: 01-46-33-98-38
Website: www.vedettes dupontneuf.com/
1st *arrondissement*
Métro: Pont-Neuf and Cité
Cards: Not Accepted

For many reasons, this is my top recommendation for a charming boat tour. It starts from a picturesque locale on the tip of Ile de la Cité, near Notre Dame, so there's plenty to see before and after your cruise. Another big plus is that alongside the boat entrance, the tour company provides a clean *toilette* and small gift shop, and has an attractive bar that serves drinks or a good, strong espresso. In other words, it's comfortable and civilized. Once on the boat, the commentary in English and French is informative and entertaining; our guide pointed out a bridge where couples' wishes come true. I call that romantic!

To get to the tour, go down the stairs to the Vert Galant park, and follow the signs to the entrance. The tour lasts about an hour and costs 12 euros. The company doesn't accept credit cards. To save a little money, visit the website and print a coupon that will give you a 2-euro discount off each ticket. Be sure to bring it with you when you buy your ticket. There is no need to pay or reserve a specific time in advance.

BATOBUS

Email: Batobus.reservation @Batobus.com
Website: http://www.batobus.com /english/index.htm
Cards: Accepted

Batobus is a hop-on-hop-off boat service that will allow you to board or disembark at eight major sights, including the Eiffel Tower, Musée d'Orsay, Notre Dame, and the Louvre. Signs on the riverbank point to the locations where the boat stops. Tickets, which are good for an entire day, are 13 euros each and can be purchased at any of the eight locations. This tour does not include commentary.

VEDETTES DE PARIS

Port de Suffren
Phone: 01-44–18-19-50
Website: http://www .vedettesdeparis.com/
7th *arrondissement*
Métro: Champ-de-Mars-Tour-Eiffel and Trocadéro
Cards: Accepted

Vedettes de Paris boats depart below the Eiffel Tower, on the Left Bank of the city. The one-hour cruise, called the Sightseeing Cruise, includes recorded commentary and costs 11 euros. Some of the Vedettes de Paris boats have bars, so you can enjoy a glass of champagne while taking in the sights.

LE CIMETIERE DU PERE-LACHAISE

The Cimetière du Père-Lachaise (Father Lachaise Cemetery) is the most famous cemetery in Paris, and possibly all of Europe. Located on the eastern edge of the city, it includes 118 acres of tree-lined paths, providing a peaceful and surprisingly romantic setting for a stroll despite the more than 70,000 nineteenth-century funeral monuments that cover the grounds. Among the French and foreign individuals who rest here are novelist Honoré de Balzac, composer Frederic Chopin, musician Jim Morrison, singer Edith Piaf, and playwright Oscar Wilde. Special monuments honor those Frenchmen who died in the resistance during the Second World War. Even a short visit to Père-Lachaise will deepen your appreciation of France's history and cultural heritage while providing a serene break from city life.

16 Rue de Repos
Phone: 01-55-25-82-10
Website:
http://www.sacred-destinations.com/france/paris-pere-lachaise
20th *arrondissement*
Métro: Pére-Lachaise

PLACE DE LA CONCORDE

Located on the eastern end of the Champs-Elysées, Place de la Concorde is a busy thoroughfare adjacent to the Tuileries Garden. Complete with a 3,000-year-old Egyptian obelisk and fountains adorned with mermaids and sea nymphs, the square is especially lovely when floodlit at night. It will remind you of a suspenseful movie chase scene, and many have been shot here—most recently, one for *The Da Vinci Code*. To add to the intrigue, remind yourself that this was the setting for the Reign of Terror during the French Revolution. Thousands of people died here under the blade of the guillotine, including King Louis XVI and his queen, Marie Antoinette.

Website:
http://www.paris.org/Monuments/Concorde/
8th *arrondissement*
Métro: Concorde

LA TOUR EIFFEL

Built as an entrance to the 1889 World's Fair—the *Exposition Universelle*—the Eiffel Tower was very controversial during its construction. The tallest structure in the world at that time, it was labeled "useless and monstrous" and was scheduled to be torn down after twenty years. Thankfully, it has endured to become a symbol of Paris. You won't be thankful about the long lines to take an elevator up to the observation deck, but if you're feeling ambitious, you can always take the 1,655-step staircase, which has shorter lines and goes up to the second level. (From there, you'll still need to catch an elevator to the top of the tower.) The Jules Verne restaurant on the second level offers a spectacular view, gourmet cuisine created by celebrated chef Alain Ducasse, and a very romantic (if a bit touristy) ambience. (See page 100 for more information about the restaurant.)

Website:
http://www.tour-eiffel.fr/teiffel/uk/
7th *arrondissement*
Métro: Trocadéro, Bir-Hakeim, and Ecole-Militaire
Cards: Accepted

One great way to approach the tower is by taking the métro to Trocadéro. The side of Trocadéro facing the Eiffel Tower has a platform between Palais de Chaillot and Musée de l'Homme that offers a breathtaking view of the Seine and Eiffel Tower. Go down the stairs on the river side and walk across the Pont d'léna bridge. This will give you a wonderful sense of perspective.

The Eiffel Tower is said to be the most visited sight in Paris. I think it's worth a look—the size is awesome when you stand beneath it—but if you're going to be in Paris for just a few days, I don't recommend spending hours in line. One way to cut down your wait time is to buy your ticket online on the tower website and bring your e-ticket (with barcodes) to the waiting area for *visitors with tickets*. Try to schedule your visit first thing in the morning on a weekday to beat the crowds. If you decide to skip the ride to the top, you can view the city from other sights, such as the Arc de Triomphe (page 78) and Sacré-Coeur (page 78).

MUSEUMS

There are so many world-class museums in Paris that it could take months to visit them all. The Louvre and Musée d'Orsay are the most popular with first-time visitors and have beautiful collections, but they are large and usually crowded, so you want to go at non-peak times and have a clear idea of what you want to observe. I don't recommend trying to see it all; plan two- to three-hour visits and leave time for other pursuits in the area.

For a more intimate experience, the smaller museums are my preference. Musée Rodin is surrounded by beautiful gardens, with Rodin's sculptures interspersed throughout. Musée de l'Orangerie showcases Claude Monet's gorgeous large wall murals. And Musée Jacquemart-André houses a small collection of Italian and French paintings that were purchased by the couple who lived in this charming "mansion." The former salon is now a café that serves lunch and afternoon tea.

If you want to learn about current exhibitions before you select museums of interest, check the website Réunion des Musée Nationaux (RMN). Click on the United Kingdom flag graphic to translate the site into English, and you'll be able to see if your favorite artist is being featured in a special show.

REUNION DES MUSEE NATIONAUX (RMN)
Website: www.rmn.fr

Museum admission costs range from about 8 to 10 euros ($11 to $14). If you're an art buff planning to see a lot of museums, you can purchase a *Carte Musées et Monuments*—a museum and monument pass that is valid for two, four, or six consecutive days. This pass allows you to bypass the long lines and walk in right away at designated entrances. You can also use the shorter museum pass line when purchasing tickets for special exhibits. And the pass allows you to visit the same museum several times, with breaks in between for lunch or sightseeing. It is sold at museums and in major métro stations, and while it doesn't apply to every museum and monument—for instance, you can't use it to get into the Eiffel Tower—it covers more than sixty-five in all, including most of the major ones.

PARIS MUSEUM PASS
Website: http://en.paris museumpass.com/
Cards: Accepted

Security is tight in all public buildings, so guards at most museums will ask to check your bags. Some museums also have metal detectors, similar to those found in airports. Museums are generally closed on Mondays or Tuesdays. Most are open from 10:00 AM to 6:00 PM, although hours vary and some have evening hours on specific days. Here are my top recommendations among the museums that are devoted to French artists and French history.

Museum Restaurants
With Views of the Eiffel Tower

Within my list of museum recommendations, I mention several noteworthy museum cafés. The two restaurants listed below are also worth visiting. In fact, they are destination points in themselves for both their greatly admired views of the Eiffel Tower and their excellent cuisine. Both are pricey options, so consider stopping by for a light lunch or, in the case of Les Ombres, afternoon tea.

CAFE DE L'HOMME AT MUSEE DE L'HOMME
17 Place du Trocadéro
Phone: 01-44-05-30-15
Website: http://www.restaurant-cafedelhomme.com/en/
16th *arrondissement*
Metro: Trocadéro
Cards: Accepted

LES OMBRES AT MUSEE DU QUAI BRANLY
17 Quai Branly
Phone: 01-47-53-68-00
Website: http://www.lesombres-restaurant.com/
7th *arrondissement*
Métro: Alma–Marceau and Iéna
Cards: Accepted

MUSEE CARNAVALET ♥

23 Rue de Sévigné
Phone: 01-44-59-58-58
Website: www.carnavalet.paris.fr
3rd *arrondissement*
Métro: St.-Paul and Chemin-Vert
Cards: Accepted

The Carnavalet's stated purpose is to illustrate the history of Paris, from its most distant origins to the present day. Formerly the famous *Hôtel* (meaning "residence") of the Marquise de Sévigné, it is now owned by the City of Paris. This 400-year-old mansion is crammed with furniture, paintings, clothes, and *objets d'art*. The section devoted to the French Revolution offers one of the most complete and provocative documentations of this difficult period, including furnishings used by the royal family during their imprisonment and several small-scale models of the deadly guillotine. Admission to the museum is free.

While you are in the Marais district, it is well worth your while to stroll a few blocks to Place des Vosges, the oldest square in Paris and one of the most beautiful. Created for Henri IV in 1605, it was at one time the major dueling ground of Europe. Now, Place des Vosges boasts a lovely public park surrounded on four sides by arcades that house shops, cafés, and art galleries.

$$$ SAVE SOME MONEY $$$

If you're planning to visit a number of museums and monuments during your stay in Paris, the costs can mount up. Instead of paying a separate entrance fee for each place of interest, purchase a *Carte Musées et Monuments*. This pass is valid for two, four, or six consecutive days, and will enable you to get into over sixty-five museums and monuments for a single fee, saving you lots of euros. Plus, it will allow you to skip the long lines and enter immediately at special entrances. Purchase this card in museums and most major métro stations.

MUSEE DE CLUNY

Many people consider the Cluny the most attractive museum in Paris. Officially known as Musée National du Moyen Age (National Museum of the Middle Ages), it is housed in one of the few medieval buildings still in existence and devoted mainly to the French arts and crafts of the Middle Ages. The famous medieval tapestries of *La Dame à la Licorne* (*The Lady and the Unicorn*) are among the Cluny's prized collections, and ruins of Roman baths are on exhibit in the garden.

6 Place Paul Painlevé
Phone: 01-53-73-78-00
Website:
http://www.musee-moyenage.fr/ang/index.html
5th *arrondissement*
Métro: Cluny-La-Sorbonne, St.-Michel, and Odéon
Cards: Accepted

MUSEE DE L'ORANGERIE ♥

Located at the west end of the Tuileries Garden, adjacent to Place de la Concorde, this former citrus nursery offers one of the most sensational art experiences in Paris—two rooms of Claude Monet's giant water lily murals. Each mural takes up a full wall, so that's eight murals in total. We're talking *large*. The museum also displays art by Pierre-Auguste Renoir, Paul Cézanne, Pablo Picasso, Henri Matisse, and Amedeo Modigliani.

Jardin des Tuileries
Phone: 01-44-77-80-07
Website:
http://www.musee-orangerie.fr/
1st *arrondissement*
Métro: Concorde
Cards: Accepted

MUSEE D'ORSAY ♥

A converted train station along the River Seine, Musée d'Orsay was designed by a woman, Gae Aulenti. With wonderful natural light streaming in from the arched glass roof, it houses art from the nineteenth and twentieth centuries on three levels, with sculpture scattered throughout. The large collection of Impressionist works is a big draw and includes paintings by Edouard Manet, Claude Monet, Paul Cézanne, Vincent Van Gogh, and Pierre-Auguste Renoir.

1 Rue de Bellechasse
Phone: 01-40-49-48-14
Website:
http://www.musee-orsay.fr/en/home.html
7th *arrondissement*
Métro: Solférino
Cards: Accepted

The museum's roof-top café offers casual snacks, and an outdoor terrace provides a great view of the Seine and Notre Dame. The Restaurant of the Musée d'Orsay is an art experience unto itself. Belle Epoque décor and a frescoed ceiling give you the impression of stepping back in time, and the traditional dishes are very good, if a bit pricey.

MUSEE DU LOUVRE ♥

The Louvre is the largest building in Paris and the most well-known museum in Europe. In 1993, the Louvre received much attention (some of it derogatory) for the new glass pyramids, designed by famed architect I.M. Pei, which greatly facilitate the large crowds of people entering the museum. Personally, I'm a fan of this somewhat high-tech look juxtaposed with the traditional lines of the former palace. The new entrance is one of the most modern and well-organized in the world and is a good example of France's emphasis on preserving and enhancing national monuments.

Main Entrance, Cour Napoléon
Phone: 01-40-20-53-17
Website:
http://www.louvre.fr/llv/commun/home.jsp?bmLocale=en
1st *arrondissement*
Métro: Palais-Royal-Musée-du-Louvre
Cards: Accepted

The Louvre houses over 400,000 works of art, and its sheer size and grandeur are a bit intimidating. I don't normally recommend guided tours, but in this instance it will give you the opportunity to see the highlights, learn about the building's fascinating history, and avoid getting lost in the maze of 224 halls. And you won't accidentally miss seeing the Mona Lisa. (A ninety-minute English language tour is conducted twice a day, and costs 9 euros, in addition to the entrance fee.)

The Carrousel du Louvre, a labyrinth of gift shops on the lower level, includes traditional museum store art books, high-end clothing boutiques, a post office, a rental car desk, and shops that sell souvenir items. There are also a number of excellent dining choices. In addition to the usual museum hours, the Louvre is open until 10:00 PM on Wednesdays and Fridays.

MUSEE JACQUEMART-ANDRE ♥

158 Boulevard Haussmann
Phone: 01-45-62-11-59
Website: www.musee-jacquemart-andre.com
8th *arrondissement*
Métro: St.-Philippe-du-Roule and Miromesnil
Cards: Accepted

Musée Jacquemart-André is a hidden treasure and offers a much more rewarding experience than many of the bigger, better-known museums. Edouard André built this mansion in 1875. He and his wife, artist Nelie Jacquemart, traveled throughout Europe collecting the masterpieces that now reside in the collection. In addition to works by major Italian and French painters, you are treated to a look at the living quarters of the former owners. The entrance is through a lovely courtyard, and Café Jacquemart-André is an excellent choice for an elegant lunch or afternoon tea in the former *salon*. Check the website for upcoming exhibitions and events. This museum is open 365 days a year.

MUSEE MARMOTTAN MONET ♥

2 Rue Louis-Boilly
Phone: 01-44-96-50-33
Website: www.marmottan.com
16th *arrondissement*
Métro: La-Muette
Cards: Accepted

One of my favorites! Tucked away in a nineteenth-century townhouse adjacent to a park in the sixteenth *arrondissement*, Musée Marmottan houses the largest single collection of Claude Monet's work. Over sixty-five original paintings, pastels, and drawings are displayed alongside a sampling of Monet's notebooks and palettes. One of Monet's signature works, *Impression, Soleil Levant* (*Impression, Sunrise*)—from which the name "Impressionist" was derived—was stolen in broad daylight by masked robbers during visiting hours several years ago. Thankfully, it was recovered by French police and is back on display. Marmottan is well worth the trip off the beaten path.

MUSEE PICASSO

5 Rue de Thorigny
Phone: 01-42-71-25-21
Website: www.musee-picasso.fr
3rd *arrondissement*
Métro: St.-Paul and Chemin-Vert
Cards: Accepted

When Pablo Picasso died in 1973, leaving no last will and testament, his heirs donated part of his personal collection to France in lieu of the more than $50 million owed in inheritance taxes. Musée Picasso, the beneficiary of this donation, was opened in 1973 by President François Mitterand in an opulent seventeenth-century mansion in the Marais district. In addition to housing the largest single collection of Picasso's work, the museum displays paintings by Paul Cézanne and Henri Matisse.

MUSEE RODIN ♥

This is a must-see. Surrounded by one of the larger gardens in Paris, the museum provides an idyllic setting for many of Auguste Rodin's beautiful sculptures. The building itself was once home and studio to many artists, including Henri Matisse, Isadora Duncan, and of course, Rodin. The room containing Rodin's *The Sculptor With His Muse* also displays several works by Camille Claudel, the talented sculptress who at seventeen became Rodin's muse, model, and lover. *Le Baiser* (*The Kiss*) is also on exhibit here.

Rodin said, "Intelligence designs, but the heart does the modeling." *Le Penseur* (*The Thinker*), his best-known work, stands in the garden.

77 Rue de Varenne
Phone: 01-44-18-61-10
Website:
   http://www.musee-rodin.fr/welcome.htm
7th *arrondissement*
Métro: Varenne and Invalides
Cards: Accepted

BOOKSTORES AND LIBRARIES

A wonderful way to experience the culture of Paris is to browse in one of its renowned bookstores, which have an ambience and history all their own. Ernest Hemingway, Gertrude Stein, F. Scott Fitzgerald, and other American writers congregated in Paris in the 1920s and contributed to the artistic renaissance of that era. In *A Moveable Feast,* Hemingway wrote fondly about his time spent at Shakespeare and Company, a popular bookstore still in existence, "On a cold windswept street, this was a warm, cheerful place with a big stove in winter, tables and shelves of books, new books in the window, and photographs on the wall of famous writers dead and living."

The two stores that are listed on the right offer good selections of books in English as well as one-of-a-kind small souvenirs and gift items. They also host free author events in the evenings. (Check their websites for calendars of upcoming talks.) The American Library in Paris, located near the Eiffel Tower, is another great venue for author events and a good place to meet interesting American expatriates.

AMERICAN LIBRARY IN PARIS
10 Rue du Général Camou
Phone: 01-53-59-12-60
Website: www.americanlibraryinparis.org
7th *arrondissement*
Métro: Ecole-Militaire and Alma-Marceau

SHAKESPEARE AND COMPANY
37 Rue de la Bûcherie
(across the river from Notre Dame)
Phone: 01-43-25-40-93
Website:
   www.shakespeareandcompany.com
5th *arrondissement*
Métro: St.-Michel
Cards: Accepted

WH SMITH
248 Rue de Rivoli
Phone: 01-44-77-88-99
Website: www.whsmith.fr
1st *arrondissement*
Métro: Concorde
Cards: Accepted

OPERA, BALLET, AND CONCERT HALLS

One of the best ways to gain a greater appreciation of French culture is to attend a concert, ballet, or opera in one of the city's grand venues. A less expensive option is to enjoy an intimate concert in one of the centuries-old churches, which are very romantic and likely to be a highlight of your trip.

Many hotels and Paris' Visitors Bureau (see page 39) post fliers that advertise concerts in nearby churches. For the opera or ballet, you're going to want to book ahead, either through the concierge at your hotel or through another service, like American Express. (Evening "spectacle" venues, like the Lido cabaret, are listed on pages 161 to 162.) While you're in Paris, both the hotel personnel and local event-oriented magazines will clue you into what's happening around town. Parisians swear by *Pariscope*, a weekly publication that covers all the attractions for the upcoming week, including *théâtre, concerts classiques, danse, opéras, discothèques,* jazz, pop-rock, sporting events, museum expositions, and more. *Pariscope* comes out each Wednesday, is available at most *tabacs* (newsstands), and is a reasonable .40 euros (about 60 cents) a copy. It's in French but fairly easy to figure out. If you prefer a publication that's written in English, look for the Paris version of *Where,* a monthly magazine that is available at the Welcome Desks of major department stores and the front desks of many deluxe hotels.

The following concert and performance sites stand out for their beauty and character.

OPERA DE PARIS BASTILLE

Until 1989, the Opéra National de Paris was housed in what is now the Palais Garnier (see the entry below.) Its new home—L'Opéra de Paris Bastille—was one of President François Mitterand's *grand travaux* (grand projects) and, as usual, the architecture sparked some controversy. Now its popularity has contributed to a revival of the surrounding Bastille *quartier.*

2 Place de la Bastille
Phone: 01-40-01-19-70
 (dial 0 for operator)
Website: http://visites.
 opera-de-paris.com/
 ?theatre=bastille
4th *arrondissement*
Métro: Bastille
Cards: Accepted

OPERA PALAIS GARNIER ♥

This former opera house now hosts world-class ballet performances. The renovated interior provides an amazing look into the elegance of times past, complete with an elaborate staircase, plush velvet decor, and a room of mirrored walls facing an exterior terrace that overlooks Avenue de l'Opéra. In 1964, the ceiling of the main performance hall was painted by Marc Chagall to depict scenes from famous musical works. To see the theater, you have to step into one of the theater boxes and view it from the balcony. The boxes themselves are also fascinating.

8 Rue Scribe
Phone: 01-71-25-24-23
Website:
 www.operadeparis.fr/
9th *arrondissement*
Métro: Opéra
Cards: Accepted

On the second floor, you'll find a small museum devoted to theater, with a beautiful library of bound plays and fascinating small architectural models of stage sets. Tours are conducted periodically, or you can explore on your own.

Concerts in Churches

Sainte-Chapelle (page 89) is one of my top recommendations for concert venues, but there are many other historic Paris churches that hold concerts, allowing you to enjoy superb music in lovely, inspirational settings. Tickets are available at FNAC (www.fnac.com), at reservation counters at the major department stores, and in the churches themselves.

CATHEDRALE AMERICAINE
A center of worship for English speakers living abroad, the Cathédrale Americaine, or American Church, often hosts free Sunday concerts.

23 Avenue George V
Phone: 01-53-23-84-09
Website: www.american
   cathedral.org
8th *arrondissement*
Métro: George-V
Cards: Accepted

EGLISE DE LA MADELEINE
Built in the nineteenth century as a monument to the glory of Napoleon Bonaparte, this large, elegant church was inspired by a Roman temple. Some of Paris' most fashionable weddings are celebrated here. The Madeleine features instrumental performances of works by classical composers like Mozart and Debussy as well as large choral groups.

Place de la Madeleine
Phone: 01-44-51-69-00
Website: http://www.
   eglise-lamadeleine.com
8th *arrondissement*
Métro: Madeleine
Cards: Accepted

EGLISE SAINT-GERMAIN-DES-PRES
Eglise Saint-Germain-des-Prés is all that remains of the larger Abbey of Saint-Germain, which played an important role in establishing the intellectual life of the Left Bank. A fine example of Romanesque architecture, the church stages religious and classical music concerts.

Place Saint-Germain
Phone: 01-55-42-81-33
6th *arrondissement*
Métro: St.-Germain-des-
   Prés
Cards: Not Accepted

EGLISE SAINT-JULIEN-LE-PAUVRE
Built in the Gothic style during the twelfth century, this is one of the oldest and most atmospheric churches in Paris. It is frequently used for chamber and religious music concerts.

1 Rue Saint-Julien-le-Pauvre
Phone: 01-43-54-52-16
5th *arrondissement*
Métro: St.-Michel
Cards: Not Accepted

EGLISE SAINT-SEVERIN
Built from the eleventh to the fifteenth centuries, Saint-Séverin has an exterior in the late Gothic style, and it is one of the prettiest churches in Paris. Its organ concerts are famous.

1 Rue des Prêtres
Phone: 01-42-34-93-50
Website: www.saint-
   severin.com
5th *arrondissement*
Métro: St.-Michel
Cards: Not Accepted

SAINTE-CHAPELLE ♥

Boasting immense stained-glass windows that are considered the finest in Paris, Sainte-Chapelle (Holy Chapel) is a Gothic jewel on the Ile de la Cité, near Notre Dame. Concerts are held in this romantic and historic locale from March through early November, so if you stay in Paris at that time of the year, I highly recommend attending. Tickets are a bit more expensive than those for other church venues, but the setting is well worth the money.

4 Boulevard du Palais
Phone: 01-42-50-96-18
Websites: http://sainte-chapelle.monuments-nationaux.fr/ (general information)
http://www.classictic.com/en/Concerts-at-La-Sainte-Chapelle/10055/115286 (tickets)
4th *arrondissement*
Métro: Cité and St.-Michel
Cards: Accepted

The Joys of French Culture

Even if you're normally not a museum buff or opera lover, the sights and sounds of Paris are bound to entrance you. The French culture is palpable throughout the city—in numerous statues, fountains, ancient buildings, and on every street—and is evolving all the time. The thrill of seeing the Eiffel Tower, Place de la Concorde, and other awe-inspiring monuments will last a lifetime, and Paris will draw you back time and time again.

5. La Cuisine

Delight in French Taste Treats

What better way to revel in the romance of Paris than to while away the hours in a cozy wine bar or linger over a candlelit dinner? For those who cherish a good meal in lovely surroundings, Paris is the quintessential dining capital *du monde* (of the world). There are an abundance of excellent restaurants, and many are within walking distance of the hotels listed in Chapter 1.

At the very top restaurants, gastronomy is king, Michelin's highest three-star rating is awarded, and prices are astronomical. We're talking easily $300 per person— and that's before wine! Fortunately, that's not the whole story; there are many up-and-coming neighborhood restaurants that serve gourmet cuisine at reasonable prices. Parisian restaurants and cafés offer a delicious glimpse into the French way of life. Dining is an integral part of each day, and meals can last for hours.

If you want to grab a snack or prepare a picnic, there is a new emphasis on healthy (organic) sandwich and salad eateries, particularly in the main tourist areas. For those who prefer traditional French cuisine, you can still find a *croque-monsieur*—a toasted ham and cheese sandwich—or simply buttery brie cheese on a fresh baguette. In Paris, the variety and abundance of mouthwatering food shops are very temping—the *pâtisserie* and *boulangerie* for fresh-baked pastries and flaky croissants; the fresh produce *marché* (market); the *fromagerie,* with hundreds of varieties of cheese; the *boucherie* for meat; and the *charcuterie* for beautifully prepared pâtés, salads, meats, and quiches, all ready to eat.

Many Paris restaurants are closed on Sundays, and a number are closed in August, the month that Parisians typically go on vacation. For that reason, if you have your heart set on dining at a certain establishment, you should be sure to make a reservation via the website or call ahead. If you choose to dine at one of Paris' most famous restaurants, such as Le Grand Véfour or Le Jules Verne, you *must* call as far in advance as possible to make a reservation.

This chapter highlights some of the most popular and traditional French dining spots, as well as more moderately priced neighborhood restaurants, cafés, bistros, wine bars, gourmet specialty stores, and cooking classes. If you're interested in a light lunch or a picnic in the park, I've suggested a few bakeries (boulangeries) that serve sandwiches and snacks. If you're in the mood for afternoon tea, see page 74 of Chapter 3 for recommended tea salons. Throughout this chapter, my favorite choices are indicated with the heart rating ♥.

Bon appétit!

Cafés

Cafés began to crop up at the end of the seventeenth century as all-male establishments. Eventually, women were allowed in specially designated rooms, but they were still prohibited from sitting alone on the terraces until well into the twentieth century. In the 1920s, American writers were drawn to Paris, and they frequented many now-famous cafés on the Left Bank.

Now, cafés offer a perfect setting to spend an hour or two sipping a *café au lait* or *coupe de champagne*. In *The Food Lover's Guide to Paris*, Patricia Wells writes, "As diverse as Parisians themselves, the cafés serve as an extension of the French living room, a place to start and end the day, to gossip and debate, a place for seeing and being seen."

This is one pastime that you will warm to quickly, and your tired feet will appreciate the break. Luckily, there are cafés on almost every block of this beautiful city, so you can grab a pick-me-up while pulling out a map or guidebook, catching up on your postcard writing, or deciding which romantic restaurant you want to check out that evening.

Café Terms

If you're like most travelers, one of the first places you'll visit after arriving in Paris is a lively neighborhood café—to relax, to soak up the atmosphere, and to tune into Paris' special rhythms. One hurdle to your adjustment will be the difference in language. Here are translations of basic café terms. Other food terms are listed on page 98.

Café noir (or *espresso*)	Plain, very strong black coffee
Café crème	Espresso in a large cup with hot cream or whole milk
Café au lait	Espresso with steamed milk
Noisette	Espresso with a dash of cream
Décafeiné or *déca*	Decaffeinated espresso
Café filter	What we call regular coffee; uses drip method
Infusion	Herb tea
Thé au citron	Tea with lemon
Thé au lait	Tea with milk
Thé nature	Plain tea
Chocolat chaud	Hot chocolate

Starbucks in Paris

If you're craving a comfortable setting with familiar coffee drinks, or you want to grab a large coffee to go (called *à emporter*), you may be happy to learn that Starbucks has a number of locations in Paris. The experience is practically identical to that in the US stores except that the drink menu on the wall is in French. The baristas speak some English, though. Here are two Starbucks in prime areas; you can find others by visiting the website www.starbucks.fr. (Click on *Où Nous Trouver* and then *Nos Addresses*.)

STARBUCKS ODEON
91 Boulevard St.-Germain
6th arrondissement
Métro: Odéon
Cards: Accepted

STARBUCKS OPERA
26 Avenue de l'Opéra
2nd arrondissement
Métro: Pyramides and Opéra
Cards: Accepted

FAMOUS CAFES

The following cafés are the most well known (*bien connu*), and are Paris institutions. They all serve meals and are open late. I don't recommend dining at these places, because they're very expensive, and some would say they take advantage of their fame. But it is worth the extra euros to enjoy the ambience while splurging on a *café au lait,* which is easily $8 (about 6 euros) and upwards. The list below includes my recommendations for well-known cafés. Following that, you'll find a list of less expensive, charming neighborhood cafés. (Café terms are listed in the inset on page 92.)

CAFE DE FLORE

Jean-Paul Sartre, Simone de Beauvoir, and Albert Camus used to gather here to discuss the ideas that led to the existentialist movement. The neighborhood's literati still frequent Flore in the late afternoon.

172 Boulevard St.-Germain
Phone: 01-45-48-55-26
Website: www.cafedeflore.fr
6th arrondissement
Métro: St.-Germain-des-Prés
Cards: Accepted

CAFE DE LA PAIX

Café de la Paix opened in 1862 and was declared a historic site in 1975. It is centrally located, near the Galeries Lafayette and across from the Opéra Garnier, and has lovely décor and ambience. The people-watching on the sidewalk terrace is a show in itself. I highly recommend that you step across the street and walk through the Opéra Garnier (see page 87 for details).

5 Place de l'Opéra
Phone: 01-40-07-36-36
Website: www.cafedelapaix.fr
9th arrondissement
Métro: Opéra
Cards: Accepted

LA CLOSERIE DES LILAS

Once a lilac-shaded country tavern, Closerie des Lilas was Hemingway's "watering hole" and his favorite place to converse with fellow writers. This is a bit off the beaten track, but if you happen to be in the neighborhood, it's definitely worth a visit.

171 Boulevard du Montparnasse
Phone: 01-40-51-34-50
Website: www.closeriedeslilas.fr
6th *arrondissement*
Métro: Vavin and Port-Royal
Cards: Accepted

LES DEUX MAGOTS ♥

Facing one of the oldest churches in Paris—sixth-century Eglise Saint-Germain-des-Prés—Deux Magots is a relative newcomer, having been built in 1875. It is one of the most inviting and popular cafés on the Left Bank and is open year-round except for the last few days in January. On many evenings, street performers add to the lively atmosphere in this central location.

6 Place St.-Germain-des-Prés
Phone: 01-45-48-55-25
Website: www.lesdeuxmagots.fr
6th *arrondissement*
Métro: St.-Germain-des-Prés
Cards: Accepted

LE FOUQUET'S

Smack in the middle of the Champs-Elysées, Fouquet's still manages to lure the *crème de Paris*. It is well known as *the* meeting spot for both politicians and the journalists who cover them.

99 Avenue des Champs-Elysées
Phone: 01-47-23-50-00
8th *arrondissement*
Métro: George-V
Cards: Accepted

BEST NEIGHBORHOOD CAFÉS

The cafés that have been included in this category are in prime locations, and on a lovely day, they offer plenty of outside tables that will allow you to soak up the sunshine and revel in the picturesque surroundings. All of the following establishments are worth a detour—for the ambience, for the wonderful fare, and for the neighborhood sights and shops.

CAFE LE NEMOURS

Located a block from the Louvre, adjoining Palais Royal and facing the Comédie Française theater, Café Le Nemours is a popular haunt for Parisians because most of its tables are placed outside on the large plaza. Drinks are somewhat pricey—5 euros for a *limonade pression,* or fresh lemonade—but my favorite meal, quiche and salad, is 11 euros and nicely done. The café's newest claim to fame is that it is featured in the long opening sequence of *The Tourist* starring Angelina Jolie.

2 Place Colette
Phone: 01-42-61-34-14
1st *arrondissement*
Métro: Palais-Royal-Musée-du-Louvre and Pyramides
Cards: Accepted

LE FLORE EN L'ILE ♥

Like the other two listings in this section, the location could not be more ideal. In this case, it's a few feet from Notre Dame on the adjoining small island of Ile Saint-Louis. The outdoor tables, which face Notre Dame, are in big demand. Happily, the quality of the service and cuisine are as superb as the setting. For an afternoon break, "Café Gourmand" is a great menu choice; it includes a cup of espresso and four small, tempting desserts for 9 euros.

42 Quai d'Orléans
Phone: 01-43-29-88-27
4th *arrondissement*
Métro: Hôtel-de–Ville,
   Pont-Marie, and Cité
Cards: Accepted

LA PALETTE ♥

Frequented by students from the nearby Ecole des Beaux-Arts (a prestigious school for artists and architects), this is my favorite "watering hole" in the Saint-Germain-des-Prés area. Located a few blocks from busy Boulevard St.-Germain, it is surrounded by elegant shops and art galleries.

43 Rue de Seine
Phone: 01-43-26-68-15
6th *arrondissement`
Métro: St.-Germain-des-
   Prés
Cards: Accepted

Restaurants

Many consider Paris to be the gastronomic capital of the world, and the French certainly share this belief. French chefs are viewed as national treasures and achieve the celebrity status reserved in most countries for actors and sports figures.

This section is divided into two categories—world-famous restaurants and my top picks for less pricey but still excellent restaurants. In addition, special insets explore restaurant customs (page 96), provide menu translations (page 98), and list acclaimed bistros (see page 108). Restaurants that are a good value for the price and/or imbued with a special romantic ambience are indicated with a heart rating ♥.

WORLD-FAMOUS RESTAURANTS BY NEIGHBORHOOD

A handful of the most famous restaurants—Alain Ducasse au Plaza Athénée and Alain Passard's L'Arpege, for instance—are an experience unto themselves. The setting is formal, elegant, and ornate; each individual plate takes hours to prepare and is presented as a work of art; and, as you would expect, the prices are astronomical. For that steep price, they offer an experience you're likely to never forget.

The following are my picks for the finest restaurants in Paris. Organized by *arrondissement,* they include the highest-rated Michelin three-star establishments as well as other restaurants that are recognized as being at "the top of their game." In most cases, you can make a selection from a multi-course menu that has a fixed price (*prix fixe*), or you can choose the more expensive *à la carte* option. A slightly more affordable way to enjoy these top chefs is to go at lunchtime, when the prices are a little lower, meaning that, before wine, a meal will cost you around 75 euros per person instead of 150 to 200 euros. You will need to make your reservation at least two to three months in advance; you should reconfirm a week before your trip; and you will have to provide your contact phone number in Paris. All of these establishments accept major credit cards.

Restaurant Tips and Customs

Navigating French restaurant customs is an ongoing adventure. You never know what to expect next. When in doubt, smile and preface your request with *"S'il vous plaît,"* which means "If you please." Then forge ahead. Here are a few guidelines.

- It is always wise to phone ahead for reservations or to reserve via the restaurant website, if that's an option. The top restaurants book a month or more in advance. To call from the United States, dial 011-33-1 and then the eight-digit Paris number.

- In old-fashioned formal restaurants, the prices are listed only on the menus handed to men or the host. Women can order to their hearts' content, oblivious of the cost.

- Not all restaurants carry menus in English. For those times when an English menu is not provided, a glossary of French food terms can be found on page 98.

- A *prix fixe* menu (also called a *formule*) offers a number of courses (usually, with a couple of choices in each course) for a set price. It is less costly than ordering the same number of courses *à la carte* (off the menu).

- A tasting or *dégustation* menu is a multi-course meal a chef prepares to show off his skills and use the best fresh ingredients available that day. It would probably be your most expensive but also most memorable option.

- Generally, a tip is included in the restaurant bill. This is often indicated by the term *service compris* (service included), printed at the bottom of the menu, but even if these words don't appear, you can assume that a gratuity has been added. If you are happy with the service, you are welcome to leave an additional tip, although it's certainly not required. Any amount from a single euro to 5 percent of the bill would be appreciated by the wait staff.

- If there is a hostess in the bathroom, you should leave a 1- or 2-euro tip. In some cases, the light in the toilet *cabine* (stall) doesn't go on until you lock the door.

The Premier (First) *Arrondissement*

LE CARRE DES FEUILLANTS

Chef Alain Dutournier specializes in delicious dishes that highlight his native southwestern French cuisine. This beautiful restaurant is in the high-rent district just off Place Vendôme. The prices are fairly reasonable compared with other restaurants of this caliber—and by "reasonable," I still mean expensive. For example, one fish dish—complete with caviar, broccoli semolina, and squid ink rice—will set you back 88 euros. A "Seasonal Menu" of five courses costs 150 euros per person when ordered for all diners at the table.

14 Rue de Castiglione
Phone: 01-42-86-82-82
1st *arrondissement*
Website: www.carredes feuillants.fr
Métro: Tuileries and Concorde
Cards: Accepted

LE GRAND VEFOUR

In the 1960s and '70s, Le Grand Véfour was *the* place to see and be seen in Paris, and celebrities flocked to this elegant establishment facing the beautiful Palais Royal garden. Its fortunes declined for a while, but since master chef Guy Martin came on board fifteen years ago, Véfour has been on the rise and is now a Michelin three-star restaurant—a tribute to its gourmet cuisine and luxurious ambience. At lunch, a three-course *prix fixe* costs 88 euros.

17 Rue de Beaujolais
Phone: 01-42-96-56-27
Website: www.grand-vefour.com
1st *arrondissement*
Métro: Palais-Royal-Musée-du-Louvre and Pyramides
Cards: Accepted

RESTAURANT LE MEURICE ♥

Hôtel Meurice is one of the most luxurious in Paris, and its flagship restaurant recreates the regal atmosphere of the Palace of Versailles, complete with antique mirrors, Louis XVI crystal chandeliers, and special Limoges china. In addition to receiving the coveted Michelin three-star rating, Le Meurice was called "one of the greatest establishments in Paris today" by French critic Gilles Pudlowski. The chef's "tasting menu" is 220 euros per person for a six-course meal.

228 Rue de Rivoli
Phone: 01-44-58-10-55
Website: www.meuricehotel.com
1st *arrondissement*
Métro: Concorde and Tuileries
Cards: Accepted

The *Quatrième* (Fourth) *Arrondissement*

L'AMBROISIE

This three-star restaurant is located in a charming eighteenth-century structure facing Place des Vosges, one of the city's prettiest squares. All the tables are in one intimate room, accented by wall tapestries, parquet flooring, and velvet chairs. Happily, the tables are spaced far enough apart for a romantic *tête-à-tête*. Chef Bernard Pacaud's creations are of such high quality that the French president has been known to entertain heads of state here. Prices are also in the stratosphere, running close to 300 euros per person.

9 Place des Vosges
Phone: 01-42-78-51-45
Website: www.ambroisie-placedesvosges.com
4th *arrondissement*
Métro: Bastille and St.-Paul
Cards: Accepted

The *Sixième* (Sixth) *Arrondissement*

HELENE DARROZE

Hélène Darroze trained under Alain Ducasse at his first restaurant in Monaco, and has now become a star in her own right. The restaurant—which is upstairs from a more casual ground-floor tapas eatery—is contemporary in décor. The cuisine receives critical raves for the inventiveness and quality of the dishes and has been awarded a Michelin one-star rating. But you can't order à la carte—only from the expensive many-course menus. For a less pricey, informal meal, the tapas bar is a good bet.

4 Rue d'Assas
Phone: 01-42-22-00-11
Website: www.helenedarroze.com
4th *arrondissement*
Métro: Sèvres-Babylone and St.-Sulpice
Cards: Accepted

Deciphering a French Menu

Now the fun begins. Deciphering a French menu (that doesn't have the English translations) is a herculean task. Some waiters speak a smattering of English, but you are likely to find yourself on your own. Since I suggest dining in neighborhood restaurants, off the beaten tourist track, you will definitely need some help in understanding what dishes are offered. The following two lists give the French/English and English/French translations for many of the basic terms. *Bonne chance!*

Je voudrais voir la carte. I would like to see the menu.

Avez-vous choisi? Have you decided?

L'addition, s'il vous plaît. The check, please.

Service compris. Service included (15 percent).

French/English

Addition. Bill.

Ananas. Pineapple.

Artichaut. Artichoke.

Asperge. Asparagus.

Assiette. Plate.

Avocat. Avocado.

Beurre. Butter.

Bifteck. Steak.
  Saignant. Rare.
  A point. Medium.
  Bien cuit. Well done.

Boissons. Drinks.

Brioche. Buttery roll.

Café. Coffee.*

Canard. Duck.

Carte. Menu.

Champignon. Mushroom.

Citron. Lemon.

Coquillages. Shellfish.

Côte d'agneau. Lamb chop.

Crème fraîche. Thick, sour, heavy cream.

Crudités. Raw vegetables.

Dégustation menu. Tasting menu.

Déjeuner. Lunch.

Dîner. Dinner; to dine.

Entrecôte. Beef rib steak.

Entrée. Appetizer course (first course).

Formule. Two- or three-course meal at set price.

Fromage. Cheese.

Gâteau. Cake.

Glace. Ice cream.

Haricot vert. Green bean.

Jambon. Ham.

Jus. Juice.

Lait. Milk.

Légume. Vegetable.

Oeuf. Egg.

Pain. Bread.

Pamplemousse. Grapefruit.

Pêche. Peach.

Petit déjeuner. Breakfast.

Plat. A dish; a main course.

Poisson. Fish.

Poivre. Pepper.

Pomme. Apple.

Pomme de terre. Potato.

Potage. Soup.

Poulet. Chicken.

Prix fixe. Two- or three-course meal at set price.

Raisin. Grape.

Reçu. Receipt.

Saumon. Salmon.

Sel. Salt.

Serviette. Napkin.

Thé. Tea.*

Thon. Tuna fish.

Veau. Veal.

Viande. Meat.

English/French

Appetizer (first) course. *Entrée.*

Apple. *Pomme.*

Artichoke. *Artichaut.*

Asparagus. *Asperge.*

Avocado. *Avocat.*

Beef rib steak. *Entrecôte.*

Bill, check. *Addition.*

Bread. *Pain.*

Breakfast. *Petit déjeuner.*

Butter. *Beurre.*

Buttery roll. *Brioche.*

Cake. *Gâteau.*

Cheese. *Fromage.*

Chicken. *Poulet.*

Coffee. *Café.**

Cold Cuts. *Charcuteries.*

Dinner, to dine. *Dîner.*

Dish. *Plat.*

Drinks. *Boissons.*

Duck. *Canard.*

Egg. *Oeuf.*

First (appetizer) course. *Entrée.*

Fish. *Poisson.*

Grape. *Raisin.*

Grapefruit. *Pamplemousse.*

Green bean. *Haricot vert.*

Ham. *Jambon.*

Ice cream. *Glace.*

Juice. *Jus.*

Lamb chop. *Côte d'agneau.*

Lemon. *Citron.*

Lunch. *Déjeuner.*

Main course. *Plat.*

Meat. *Viande.*

Menu. *Carte.*

Milk. *Lait.*

Mushroom. *Champignon.*

Napkin. *Serviette.*

Peach. *Pêche.*

Pepper. *Poivre.*

Pineapple. *Ananas.*

Plate. *Assiette.*

Potato. *Pomme de terre.*

Salmon. *Saumon.*

Salt. *Sel.*

Shellfish. *Coquillages.*

Soup. *Potage.*

Steak. *Bifteck.*
  Rare. *Saignant.*
  Medium. *A point.*
  Well done. *Bien cuit.*

Tea. *Thé.**

Tuna fish. *Thon.*

Veal. *Veau.*

* A complete listing and explanation of coffee and tea terms is found on page 92.

$ $ $ SAVE SOME MONEY $ $ $

Although dining in great restaurants and charming cafés is an important part of the Paris experience, sometimes you simply want a fast, inexpensive meal or snack to go. Fortunately, neighborhood supermarkets like Marché Franprix offer plenty of options, including salads, sandwiches, desserts, and bottled drinks. These stores are like US markets—with aisles of dry goods, refrigerated drinks, and sections of prepared food—but most of the choices have a decidedly French flair. According to your mood and your budget, you can buy a container of *mousse au chocolat* or a bag of cookies to munch on, or you can put together a more traditional meal. Other good sources of low-cost fare are the discount store chains Monoprix and Prisunic, both of which include food departments and can be found throughout the city. (For more information on these chains, see page 125.)

The Septième (Seventh) *Arrondissement*

L'ARPEGE ♥

84 Rue de Varenne
Phone: 01-45-51-47-33
Website: www.alain-passard.com
7th *arrondissement*
Métro: Varenne
Cards: Accepted

Under the guidance of one of my favorite chefs, Alain Passard, L'Arpège has held the coveted Michelin three-star rating for many years. The atmosphere is light and modern, as is the delicious cuisine. Passard is a wizard with vegetables and light fish dishes, and L'Arpège boasts unforgettable desserts as well, making this restaurant a favorite Paris *rendez-vous*. Plus, this wonderful restaurant is a block from the Rodin Museum, so you can walk off your long lunch in a beautiful art-filled garden. Prices here are high—135 euros for the multi-course lunch "tasting menu."

L'ATELIER DE JOEL ROBUCHON

Hôtel Pont Royal
7 Rue Montalembert
Phone: 01-42-22-56-56
Website: www.joel-robuchon.net (click on Paris)
7th *arrondissement*
Métro: Rue-du-Bac
Cards: Accepted

Arguably the best French chef of our era, Joël Robuchon retired for a few years and then came back with a vengeance. This time, Robuchon kept the atmosphere simple and brought the prices down. Other chefs carry out the preparations, but Robuchon's influence is seen in every dish, making this a popular destination for self-described "foodies." L'Atelier takes reservations only for the early seating of each meal. Alternatively, you can "queue up" to join other guests at the restaurant's unique counter service, which allows you to watch your food being prepared. Main courses run from 27 to 68 euros and small "tasting" plates range from 14 to 35 euros.

LE JULES VERNE ♥

Eiffel Tower, South Pillar
Champ-de-Mars
Phone: 01-45-55-61-44
Website: www.lejulesverne-paris.com
7th *arrondissement*
Métro: Bir-Hakeim and Trocadéro
Cards: Accepted

You can't get much more romantic than a world-class restaurant located on the second level of the Eiffel Tower. Add Alain Ducasse as head chef, and you have all the ingredients for a very special occasion. With stunning views of the city below, this is the most popular restaurant in Paris for visitors celebrating their anniversary or engagement. It is also quite pricey, but the lunch *prix fixe* menu available on weekdays is reasonable at 88 euros per person. Le Jules Verne has its own private elevator access with confirmed reservations, thank goodness; the lines for the other Eiffel Tower elevators are very long.

The Huitième (Eighth) *Arrondissement*

ALAIN DUCASSE AU PLAZA ATHENEE ♥

Set in one of the most luxurious hotels in Paris, this is gourmet cuisine on a grand scale in an elegant, refined setting. Prepare to be pampered. Alain Ducasse has received the highest Michelin three-star rating, and the prices are steep. The average price for an *à la carte* meal is 220 euros before drinks are added.

Hôtel Plaza Athénée
25 Avenue Montaigne
Phone: 01-53-67-65-00
Website: www.alain-
   ducasse.com
8th *arrondissement*
Métro: Alma-Marceau
   and Franklin-D.-
   Roosevelt
Cards: Accepted

APICIUS

Chef Jean-Pierre Vigato gears his menu to the seasons and is renowned for his flavorful seafood dishes. Located in a converted eighteenth-century mansion that looks out onto a private garden, Apicius draws a chic Parisian clientele along with visitors who appreciate Vigato's inventive cuisine. The meal will set you back approximately 200 euros per person before wine.

20 Rue d'Artois
Phone: 01-43-80-19-66
Website: www.restaurant-
   apicius.com
8th *arrondissement*
Métro: St.-Philippe-du-
   Roule, Franklin-
   D.–Roosevelt, and
   George-V
Cards: Accepted

SENDERENS ♥

This was formerly the Michelin three-star Lucas-Carton, but chef-owner Alain Senderens renounced his Michelin stars to focus on a more casual atmosphere and reasonably priced dining. This began a trend that several other top chefs have continued—cutting the exorbitant expense of maintaining a three-star Michelin rating. A "tasting" menu at Senderens costs 116 euros without wine or 160 euros for five courses, with wines served to complement each course. It's a very good deal.

9 Place de la Madeleine
Phone: 01-42-65-22-90
Website:
   www.senderens.fr
8th *arrondissement*
Métro: Madeleine
Cards: Accepted

TAILLEVANT

Long-time owner Jean-Claude Vrinat, a well-respected restaurateur who oversaw this luxurious dining destination for decades, passed away not long ago, but the same *équipe* (team) is maintaining his high standards. The contemporary décor in the Second Empire townhouse is described as "an escape towards nature," and both the cuisine and the wine list are first-class. A three-course *prix fixe* lunch costs 82 euros, and dining *à la carte* is approximately 140 euros before wine.

15 Rue Lamennais
Phone: 01-44-95-15-01
Website:
   www.taillevent.com
8th *arrondissement*
Métro: George-V
Cards: Accepted

The Dix-Septième (Seventeenth) *Arrondissement*

GUY SAVOY ♥

Guy Savoy is a star in the Parisian haute-cuisine firmament, and his restaurant is a temple to fine dining and attentive service. This flagship restaurant—Savoy also has several bistros—offers a special price to "web surfers": 110 euros buys a *prix fixe* lunch that includes an appetizer, main dish, and dessert on Tuesdays through Fridays. Plus you can order wines by the glass starting at 10 euros. You need to make your reservation on the website and request the "web surfer" price under comments. Only one table per day is reserved for this special deal.

18 Rue Troyon
Phone: 01-43-80-40-61
Website:
    www.guysavoy.com
17th *arrondissement*
Métro: Charles-de-
    Gaulle-Etoile
Cards: Accepted

RESTAURANTS AND CASUAL SPOTS BY NEIGHBORHOOD

The following is a select group of restaurants and casual dining spots listed by *arrondissement* so you can find good choices near your hotel or while you're out sightseeing. They are all *très populaire* with Parisians. The prices vary from very affordable to *très cher* (costly). A *prix fixe* menu is mentioned whenever it is applicable. At the casual, inexpensive spots, be prepared to pay for your meal in euros instead of using a credit card.

The Premier (First) *Arrondissement*

L'ABSINTHE

L'Absinthe, part of grand chef Michel Rostang's group of bistros, is ably run by his daughter, Caroline Rostang. It offers hearty, reasonably priced dishes (a *prix fixe* three-course meal runs about 32 euros) in a casual, comfortable setting. In warm weather, choose an outside table and watch the chic passersby.

24 Place du Marché St.-
    Honoré
Phone: 01-49-26-90-04
Website: www.michel
    rostang.com
1st *arrondissement*
Métro: Tuileries and
    Pyramides
Cards: Accepted

AUBERGE SAINT ROCH ♥

Tucked away on a small side street adjacent to the lovely Eglise Saint-Roch, this cozy restaurant is a find. It offers a charming, intimate setting, nice service, and good food for reasonable prices. A two-course meal is available for 19 euros at lunch and 23 euros at dinner.

33 Rue St.-Roch
Phone: 01-42-61-40-83
Website: www.auberge-
    saint-roch.com
1st *arrondissement*
Métro: Tuileries and
    Pyramides
Cards: Accepted

AUX DELICES DE MANON

This is a great inexpensive option for a casual lunch near Place de la Madeleine, a very pricey neighborhood. In addition to a nice choice of salads, sandwiches, and quiches for under 8 euros, there is a great selection of mouthwatering pastries you can enjoy along with a strong espresso.

400 Rue St.-Honoré
Phone: 01-42-60-83-03
1st *arrondissement*
Métro: Madeleine
Cards: Accepted

L'ECUME SAINT-HONORE

Fresh oysters are the specialty of this small *bar à huitrès* (oyster bar). There is limited seating at a few high tables with chairs. The display is mouthwatering, wines are offered by the glass, and for 12 euros, you can enjoy a plate of six oysters, a glass of Muscadet, and bread and butter. Plus the neighborhood boutiques are great for window-shopping.

6 Rue du Marché St.-Honoré
Phone: 01-42-61-93-87
1st *arrondissement*
Métro: Tuileries
Cards: Not Accepted

MACEO ♥

There are a number of reasons why Macéo deserves a heart rating. The décor is elegant yet comfortable, the cuisine is *bien fait* (well executed), you can enjoy a drink at the intimate bar, and there is a great selection of wines. (The proprietor, Mark Williamson, also owns Willi's Wine Bar, which is down the street.). A three-course *prix fixe* menu is available for 38 euros at lunch and dinner, and it's a great deal!

15 Rue des Petits Champs
Phone: 01-42-97-53-85
Website: www.maceo restaurant.com
1st *arrondissement*
Métro: Palais-Royal-Musée-du-Louvre and Pyramides
Cards: Accepted

PLAISIRS ET PAINS

This is one of numerous sandwich shops in the busy shopping area on Rue St.-Honoré, near Eglise Saint-Roch. Plaisirs et Pains has a bigger selection than the surrounding shops, and also has more tables. For 10 euros, you can get a *formule* (price-fixed meal) of a sandwich of your choice, a dessert, and a bottle of Evian water. This restaurant is open only for lunch.

215 Rue St.-Honoré
Phone: 01-42-61-18-04
1st *arrondissement*
Métro: Tuileries
Cards: Not Accepted

The Deuxième (Second) *Arrondissement*

DROUANT ♥

One of two good restaurants on charming Place Gaillon (the second is listed on page 104), Drouant is less formal than it was in years past, but still offers excellent cuisine in a beautiful setting for a good price. A three-course lunch costs 44 euros, and you can choose among suggested glasses of wine for 7 to 10 euros each. If you prefer small plates, you can order a choice of four hors d'oeuvres for 26 euros.

16-18 Place Gaillon
Phone: 01-42-65-15-16
Website: www.drouant.com
Métro: Opéra
Cards: Accepted

LA FONTAINE GAILLON

French actors Gerard Depardieu and Carole Bouquet are the owners of this beautiful restaurant on Place Gaillon. The enclosed patio is one of the most charming outdoor dining spots in Paris when the weather is accommodating. Be prepared to spend upwards of 40 euros for food (before wine) for reliably good cuisine and a wonderful atmosphere.

Place Gaillon
Phone: 01-47-42-63-22
Website: www.la-fontaine-gaillon.com
2nd *arrondissement*
Métro: Opéra
Cards: Accepted

LE GRAND COLBERT

This authentic-looking nineteenth-century brasserie was the setting for the last scene in *Something's Gotta Give,* which featured Diane Keaton as a writer torn between Keanu Reeves and Jack Nicholson. We should all have such luck! Seriously, the ambience is right out of a movie, and the cuisine is good (not great). The seafood platter is very popular, and main courses cost around 25 euros each.

2 Rue Vivienne
Phone: 01-42-86-87-88
Website: www.legrandcolbert.fr
2nd *arrondissement*
Métro: Bourse and Pyramides
Cards: Accepted

LE PASTEL

Located between Avenue de l'Opéra and Place Gaillon, Le Pastel is a very small, casual restaurant that looks like it is right out of an old Paris movie. A reasonably priced menu is posted on a chalkboard; there are paper placemats on wooden tables; and the bar counter is usually packed with neighborhood regulars. The three-course *prix fixe* menu is only 16 euros and includes an *entrée* (appetizer), *plat* (main course), and dessert. There is no phone or website; just drop by when you're in the neighborhood.

41 Rue St.-Augustin
2nd *arrondissement*
Métro: Opéra
Cards: Not Accepted

How Does a Café Differ From a Brasserie?

Just as we have diners, coffee shops, and restaurants, the French have several different kinds of places to eat. Here is a brief description of each. Since this is Paris, they all have romantic qualities and possibilities.

Bistro. This is usually a casual neighborhood place run by a husband-and-wife team—although some upscale eateries have taken the "bistro" moniker. The small menu is written on a blackboard to feature the daily specials.

Brasserie. Brasserie means brewery, and as you might expect, brasseries boast good selections of beer and wine. The menu tends to specialize in *charcuteries* (pork and other types of meat), and the atmosphere is lively and boisterous.

Café. Cafés vary in formality. Generally, they offer drinks and light meals. If there are two floors, the second level is usually more formal, with tablecloths and a bigger menu selection.

Restaurant. The word restaurant originated from a thick soup that "restored" the appetite. Now an elegant restaurant does much more than restore—it is a perfect setting for the celebration and enjoyment of life's finer pleasures on a grand scale.

The Troisième (Third) *and* Quatrième (Fourth) *Arrondissements*

BOFINGER ♥
Founded in 1864, Bofinger is reputed to be the oldest brasserie in Paris, although you wouldn't know it from the shiningly clean brass and stained glass. Visitors flock here for the authentic brasserie ambience and its selection of fresh seafood, among other dishes. It's also conveniently adjacent to the Bastille. Prices start at *prix fixe* menus of 29 euros for two plates (choose between appetizer, main course, and dessert) or 34 euros for three plates. This applies to both lunch and dinner.

5-7 Rue de la Bastille
Phone: 01-42-72-87-82
Website:
   www.bofingerparis.com
4th *arrondissement*
Métro: Bastille
Cards: Accepted

CAFÉ DES MUSEES
Just north of Place des Vosges, near the Carnavalet and Picasso museums, this "café of the museums" is an excellent place to stop for lunch when you're in the neighborhood. It is especially attractive when you consider that the *prix fixe* lunch costs 15 euros—half of what you'd pay at the cafés bordering Place des Vosges. Dinner prices are also quite reasonable.

49 Rue de Turenne
Phone: 01-42-72-96-17
3rd *arrondissement*
Métro: Chemin-Vert and
   St.-Paul
Cards: Accepted

CAMILLE
Amidst the trendy stores near Place des Vosges, this charming bistro offers a good selection of salads and light dishes. The bar area is lovely, and outside seating is available in nice weather. A two-course *prix fixe* lunch costs 24 euros.

24 Rue des Francs-
   Bourgeois
Phone: 01-42-72-20-50
3rd *arrondissement*
Métro: St.-Paul
Cards: Accepted

MA BOURGOGNE
Perfectly located in the arcade facing Place des Vosges, Ma Bourgogne is a popular bistro with hearty dishes and a good selection of wines, especially Beaujolais. Open *tous les jours* (everyday, including Sunday), it offers a 38-euro *prix fixe* menu that includes an appetizer, main course, and cheese or dessert. A simple *salade niçoise* costs 16 euros. This restaurant does not accept credit cards, so be sure you've got an ample supply of euros.

19 Place des Vosges
Phone: 01-42-78-44-64
Website: www.ma-
   bourgogne.fr
4th *arrondissement*
Métro: St.-Paul and
   Bastille
Cards: Not Accepted

AU LYS D'ARGENT ♥
A very good inexpensive option on Ile Saint-Louis, a charming island in the Seine River, this cozy restaurant specializes in crepes with various fillings that run 6 to 8 euros. Add a *café crème* for a reasonable 3.8 euros.

90 Rue St.-Louis-en-l'Ile
Phone: 01-46-33-56-13
4th *arrondissement*
Métro: Pont-Marie and
   Hôtel-de-Ville
Cards: Not Accepted

The Sixième (Sixth) *Arrondissement*

LA BOUSSOLE ♥

Situated on a small, picturesque street near Place Saint-Sulpice and surrounded by chic stores, La Boussole is a great choice for a romantic dinner. The intimate ambience is enhanced by exposed stone walls, wood-beam ceilings, warm colors, and soft lighting. The *prix fixe* menus for lunch and dinner offer excellent cuisine, like roasted salmon and grilled steak, at very good prices—24 euros at lunch and 29 euros at dinner. And the restaurant is *"ouvert tous les jours"*—open every day of the year.

12 Rue Guisarde
Phone: 01-56-24-82-20
Website: www.la-boussole.com
6th *arrondissement*
Métro: St.-Germain-des-Prés and Mabillon
Cards: Accepted

LA CHARRETTE

A few feet from Ecole des Beaux-Arts, the French art school, is La Charrette, a small, very authentic bistro with only a few tables. The daily menu, written on a chalkboard, features good, simple food for great prices. I loved this place! My two-course lunch of chicken with mushrooms, potatoes au gratin, and a salad came to 15 euros. Wines by the glass start at 3 euros, and a *café crème* is 3 euros—half the cost of La Palette, which is just around the corner. The portions at La Charrette are generous, and best of all, the habitués are local artsy types.

17 Rue des Beaux-Arts
Phone: 01-43-25-60-55
6th *arrondissement*
Métro: St.-Germain-des-Prés
Cards: Not Accepted

DEL PAPA

If you want to take a break from French cuisine, visit Del Papa, where you'll find mouthwatering Italian dishes, including tasty pastas. Just off Boulevard St.-Germain, in the heart of the action on the Left Bank, this charming "ristorante" features linen tablecloths, soft lighting, and the wonderful scent of pizza baking (the oven is near the door). A two-course *prix fixe* lunch with a drink is offered during the week for 17 euros.

38 Rue de Buci
Phone: 01-46-33-91-15
6th *arrondissement*
Métro: St.-Germain-des-Prés
Cards: Accepted

LES EDITEURS ♥

Only a short walk from the many movie theaters located on Boulevard St.-Germain, Les Editeurs is a great place to take a coffee break or enjoy an excellent dinner at reasonable prices. Very popular with Parisians, this restaurant has an atmosphere that's clubby and warm, with elegant wood bookshelves lining the walls. And it's open seven days a week until 2:00 AM.

4 Carrefour de l'Odéon
Phone: 01-43-26-67-76
Website: www.lesediteurs.fr
6th *arrondissement*
Métro: Odéon
Cards: Accepted

LA FERRANDAISE

Located a short distance from the Luxembourg Gardens, La Ferrandaise offers excellent food at very good prices. Beef is the specialty (Ferrandaise is a type of beef from the Auvergne region of France), although other dishes, like chicken, are also well prepared. A *prix fixe* dinner of three courses is a reasonable 34 euros, and a lunch special of three courses is only 16 euros.

8 Rue de Vaugirard
Phone: 01-43-26-36-36
Website:
   www.laferrandaise.com
6th *arrondissement*
Métro: Odéon and
   Cluny-La-Sorbonne
Cards: Accepted

FISH LA BOISSONNERIE ♥

This former fish shop is getting rave reviews for its inventive cuisine, featuring exotic fish dishes and other options at good prices. The *prix-fixe* dinner menus run 30 to 40 euros. There is also an excellent selection of wines, many by the glass. Word has gotten out, so you definitely need to book ahead for a table in this small dining room.

69 Rue de Seine
Phone: 01-43-54-34-69
6th *arrondissement*
Métro: Mabillon and St.-
   Germain-des-Prés
Cards: Accepted

LA MAIN A LA PATE

I normally don't recommend "pizza joints," but this casual Italian restaurant has good food for unbelievable prices. Their three-course *prix fixe* dinner is 15 euros. I chose the caprese salad (mozzarella and tomato), a pizza (ham and mushroom), and dessert (chocolate mousse), and everything was delicious.

35 Rue Dauphine
Phone: 01-46-33-58-97
6th *arrondissement*
Métro: Odéon
Cards: Accepted

LA PETITE COUR

La Petite Cour is earning raves for its gourmet French cuisine. The dining room colors are a bit bold (yellow walls and red chairs), but the terrace offers a lovely option, weather permitting. Dinner here is pricier than it is at some nearby restaurants—37 euros for a *prix fixe* dinner and around 60 euros *à la carte*—but customers aren't complaining.

8 Rue Mabillon
Phone: 01-43-26-52-26
Website:
   www.lapetitecour.fr/
6th *arrondissement*
Métro: Mabillon
Cards: Accepted

The Huitième (Eighth) *Arrondissement*

BAR DES THEATRES

Located amid haute couture stores, Bar des Théâtres is a reasonably priced option in this high-rent district. Tables are packed closely in this neighborhood hangout, so you'll be rubbing shoulders with Parisians. The menu highlights traditional French dishes like steak tartare, the house specialty, but I was able to order a chicken salad for 14 euros. Main dishes like grilled salmon run around 22 euros.

6 Avenue Montaigne
Phone: 01-47-23-34-63
8th *arrondissement*
Métro: Alma-Marceau
Cards: Accepted

Great Chefs' Bistros

A handful of the top chefs in Paris offer customers a chance to enjoy their first-class cuisine in bistro versions of their very expensive flagship restaurants. The atmosphere is more bustling and less formal, and the menu is not as extensive, but the reduced prices are a bargain for the quality of the dining experience.

Frankly, this list is the first place I'd look for a memorable meal in a charming setting at reasonable prices. I strongly recommend that you try one of these during your trip. Since these are popular spots, you should make a reservation at least a month or two before you depart. When you're planning your trip, check out the websites to see the menus and photos, and make your reservation online. In most cases, the site homepage lists many of the chefs' restaurants, so you will need to click on the specific bistro name.

For every bistro listed below, I have indicated the executive chef. Each of these finds has a *prix fixe* lunch menu for around 35 to 45 euros; dinner is more expensive.

L'ANGLE DU FAUBOURG
Restaurateur: Jean-Claude Vrinat's family
195 Rue du Faubourg St.-Honoré
Phone: 01-40-74-20-20
Website: www.taillevent.com
8th *arrondissement*
Métro: Charles-de-Gaulle-Etoile and George-V
Cards: Accepted

L'ATELIER MAITRE ALBERT
Executive Chef: Guy Savoy
1 Rue Maître Albert
Phone: 01-56-81-30-01
Website: www.ateliermaitrealbert.com
5th *arrondissement*
Métro: Maubert-Mutualité
Cards: Accepted

LE BISTRO D'A COTE FLAUBERT ♥
Executive Chef: Michel Rostang
10 Rue Gustave Flaubert
Phone: 01-42-67-05-81
Website: http://www.bistrotflaubert.com/
17th *arrondissement*
Métro: Ternes and Courcelles
Cards: Accepted

LES BOUQUINISTES
Executive Chef: Guy Savoy
53 Quai des Grands Augustins
Phone: 01-43-25-45-94
Website: www.lesbouquinistes.com
6th *arrondissement*
Métro: St.-Michel
Cards: Accepted

PINXO
Executive Chef: Alain Dutournier
Plaza Vendôme Hotel
9 Rue d'Alger
Phone: 01-40-20-72-00
Website: www.pinxo.fr
1st *arrondissement*
Métro: Tuileries
Cards: Accepted

LA ROTISSERIE D'EN FACE ♥
Executive Chef: Jacques Cagna
2 Rue Christine
Phone: 01-43-26-40-98
Website: www.jacques-cagna.com
6th *arrondissement*
Métro: Odéon
Cards: Accepted

LE CHIBERTA ♥

Top chef Guy Savoy has opened a beautiful new restaurant near the Arc de Triomphe. This is a great way to experience Savoy's gourmet cuisine in a luxurious setting at about half the price of his self-titled main restaurant (see page 102). A special tasting menu is either 100 euros or 155 euros with wine per person.

3 Rue Arsène Houssaye
Phone: 01-53-53-42-00
Website:
  www.lechiberta.com
8th *arrondissement*
Métro: Charles-de-
  Gaulle-Etoile
Cards: Accepted

MINIPALAIS ♥

MiniPalais is a wonderful new addition to the Champs-Elysées area. Chef Eric Frechon, who runs a three-star restaurant at the Bristol Hotel, also oversees this kitchen. The 25-euro price for a main plate is very reasonable for the quality, and the setting is right out of a palace—really. You'll find the entrance at one end of the Grand Palais, adjacent to the Seine and the lovely Pont Alexandre bridge.

Avenue Winston Churchill
  at Cours Albert Premier
Phone: 01-42-56-42-42
Website:
  www.minipalais.com
8th *arrondissement*
Métro: Champs-Elysées-
  Clemenceau
Cards: Accepted

LE RELAIS PLAZA ♥

A "chic bistro" in Hôtel Plaza Athénée, Le Relais Plaza is an upscale brasserie in a historic setting and a great place to see the *crème de la crème* of Paris. The menu is overseen by super-chef Alain Ducasse, whose flagship formal restaurant is in the same hotel, but charges much higher prices. A meal here is not inexpensive, but fortunately, "Le Menu Relais Plaza" includes a starter, main dish, and cheese or dessert for 48 euros. This menu is available for both lunch and dinner.

Hôtel Plaza Athénée
21 Avenue Montaigne
Phone: 01-53-67-64-00
Website: www.plaza-
  athenee-paris.com
  (click on restaurants)
8th *arrondissement*
Métro: Alma-Marceau
Cards: Accepted

SPOON

Spoon is Alain Ducasse's venture to offer "international" cuisine in a cool, modern setting. Innovative dishes are prepared with unusual ingredients, emphasizing light and flavorful combinations. Ducasse is one of the most acclaimed French chefs *du monde* (in the world). You can enjoy his traditional French cuisine at Le Jules Verne, in the Eiffel Tower (see page 100), or at his more formal and expensive restaurant, Alain Ducasse au Plaza Athénée (see page 101).

Hôtel Marignan
12 Rue de Marignan
Phone: 01-40-76-34-44
Website:
  www.spoon.tm.fr
8th *arrondissement*
Métro: Franklin-D.-
  Roosevelt
Cards: Accepted

TANTE LOUISE ♥

Highly recommended by friends who are connoisseurs, this is acclaimed chef Bernard Loiseau's Paris bistro. Located just off Place de la Madeleine, Tante Louise offers flawless cuisine, and the Art Deco ambience is a perfect setting for a romantic evening. The 26-euro *prix fixe* lunch menu for two courses is a great value.

41 Rue Boissy-d'Anglais
Phone: 01-42-65-06-85
Website: www.bernard-
  loiseau.com
8th *arrondissement*
Métro: Madeleine and
  Concorde
Cards: Accepted

The Arc de Triomphe at Night.

The Seizième (Sixteenth) *Arrondissement*

L'ARC ♥

L'Arc faces the Arc de Triomphe and provides an unob-
structed view of the monument, which is a breathtaking sight,
especially when it's lit up at night. Considering the quality of
the food and luxuriousness of the setting, prices are reasonable. A two-course *prix fixe* lunch with coffee is 38 euros. The
downstairs nightclub starts hopping around midnight, so if
you're having a late meal, you can inquire about going there
afterwards. There's no cover charge, but drinks are pricey.

12 Rue de Presbourg
Phone: 01-45-00-78-70
Website: www.larc-
   paris.com
16th *arrondissement*
Métro: Charles-de-
   Gaulle-Etoile
Cards: Accepted

AUX PAINS PERDUS

I came across this nice spot for a casual lunch when I stepped
off the yellow L'Open Tour bus to stroll along chic Avenue
Kléber. Just off the avenue, on equally chic Rue de
Longchamp, Aux Pains Perdus is a "sandwich shop" that also
offers great salads and gourmet coffee—as one would expect
in Paris. There are a few sidewalk tables where you can soak
up the Parisian atmosphere. The restaurant sells out most
items by mid-afternoon and closes at 4:00 PM.

40 Rue de Longchamp
Phone: 01-44-05-12-92
16th *arrondissement*
Métro: Trocadéro and
   Boissière
Cards: Not Accepted

The Dix-Septième (Seventeenth) *Arrondissement*

MICHEL ROSTANG ♥

Although it's in the seventeenth *arrondissement*, Michel Rostang is only one métro stop from the Arc de Triomphe. It is
worth the small detour to experience a two-star Michelin
restaurant that has been a Paris institution for decades. Michel
Rostang's French cuisine is *très populaire*, but the prices are
commensurately high. The most budget-friendly option is the
Déjeuner d'Affaires (business lunch) for 78 euros; you get
three courses, with five dishes to choose from in each course.

20 Rue Rennequin
Phone: 01-47-63-40-77
Website:
   www.michelrostang.com
17th *arrondissement*
Métro: Ternes
Cards: Accepted

Wine Bars

Paris wine bars allow you to sample delicious wines in an intimate setting while enjoying hearty French fare chosen to complement the wines. This is a great way to learn about new wines and have a reasonably priced meal. A few good choices are listed below. Because evening hours and availability of meals vary widely, this information has been provided for each bar.

LE GRIFFONIER

I discovered this hidden gem when walking to the nearby Astor Hôtel. It is a *bistrot à vins,* which means that it serves wines by the glass and offers a selection of steak, sausage, and the like. Prices are reasonable and the atmosphere can't be beat. This is a casual neighborhood hangout that will make you feel like a Parisian. But be forewarned—you will need your high school French. Le Griffonier serves lunch, and the bar stays open until 7:00 PM.

8 Rue des Saussaies
Phone: 01-42-65-17-17
8th *arrondissement*
Métro: Champs-Elysées-
   Clémenceau and
   Miromesnil
Cards: Not Accepted

LAVINIA ♥

Popular with chic Parisians who work near Place de la Madeleine and Rue St. Honoré, Lavinia is a renowned wine store that has a restaurant/wine bar one level up. From mid-afternoon on, the first floor is an elegant wine bar with an excellent selection of wine by the glass. If you stop by earlier in the day, you'll find a romantic setting for lunch. The ground-floor store sells a huge assortment of wines and accessories. Lavinia is pricier than the other wine bars as befits the formal setting and range of choices. It closes at 8:00 PM.

3 Boulevard de la
   Madeleine
Phone: 01-42-97-20-20
Website: www.lavinia.fr
1st *arrondissement*
Métro: Madeleine
Cards: Accepted

LEGRAND FILLES ET FILS ♥

Founded in 1880, Legrand is devoted to "the art of wine" and also sells glasses, decanters, and other accessories. The circular bar is an experience in itself and conjures up images of James Bond films. Legrand comes highly recommended by friends who work in the wine industry, and is a great option for a light lunch. It is open from 11:00 to 7:00 PM.

1 Rue de la Banque
Phone: 01-42-60-07-12
Website: www.caves-
   legrand.com
2nd *arrondissement*
Métro: Bourse and
   Pyramides
Cards: Accepted

LE RUBIS

This neighborhood hangout was packed every time I passed by, which was often, since I was staying in a hotel down the street. Many Beaujolais wines are featured, along with a good selection of other wines, to wash down the hearty fare. We're talking *big* servings. The retro 1950s décor will make you feel like you've stepped into a time capsule. Prices are reasonable and it's open until 9:30 PM, but full meals are served only at lunchtime.

10 Rue du Marché St.-
   Honoré
Phone: 01-42-61-03-34
1st *arrondissement*
Métro: Tuileries
Cards: Not Accepted

The Museum of Wine

Housed in what used to be limestone quarries that provided the stones to build Paris, the Musée du Vin, or Museum of Wine, displays more than 2,000 items and instruments related to winemaking. The museum also has a very atmospheric restaurant, set in a wine cellar, that serves traditional French cuisine. After learning about winemaking, you'll be tempted to try one of the hundreds of wines on the menu.

5 Square Charles Dickens on Rue des Eaux
Phone: 01-45-25-63-26
Website: www.musee duvinparis.com
16th *arrondissement*
Métro: Passy
Cards: Accepted

WILLI'S WINE BAR

Since 1980, Willi's Wine Bar, a few steps from Palais Royal, has been pleasing thirsty customers, who come for the great selection of wines by the glass and the excellent food. The bar is open from noon to midnight, lunch service runs from noon to 2:30 PM, and dinner is served from 7:00 to 11:00 PM.

13 Rue des Petits Champs
Phone: 01-42-61-05-09
Website: www.williswinebar.com
1st *arrondissement*
Métro: Bourse and Pyramides
Cards: Accepted

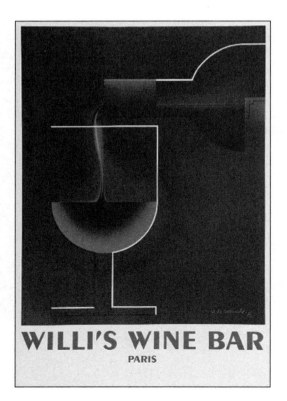

WILLI'S WINE BAR
PARIS

Willi's Wine Bar Poster.
For three decades, Willi's Wine Bar has produced posters that represent the spirit of the bar and its outstanding offerings. This, the first of Willi's poster series, was printed in 1984 using an original image created in 1935 by famed French artist Adolphe Mouron Cassandre.

Gourmet and Specialty Food Stores

Wandering through Paris' gourmet food stores is a delightful, entertaining, and delicious way to spend a few hours. These are good places to pick up gifts. Just steer clear of perishable items, like fruit, which aren't admitted through United States customs.

While you're shopping for ceramic jars of mustards, lovely bottles of spices, and beautifully wrapped boxes of chocolate, you'll definitely want to stop by Fauchon for its mouthwatering pastries and Berthillon for its famous ice cream. Every food connoisseur is able to satisfy his or her cravings in Paris. (If you're especially interested in purchasing teas, see the section on tea salons on page 74.)

BERTHILLON

Berthillon's ice cream is the most famous in Paris, and its ice cream parlor on the tiny island of Ile Saint-Louis is a popular destination for fanatics of this creamy dessert. The company's *glace* (ice cream) and sorbets come in dozens of unusual flavors, like pear caramel and mandarin chocolate. Just remember that the store is closed from mid-July through August.

31 Rue St.-Louis-en-l'Ile
Phone: 01-43-54-31-61
Website:
    www.berthillon.fr
4th *arrondissement*
Métro: Pont-Marie and
    Hôtel-de-Ville
Cards: Not Accepted

BON MARCHE'S LA GRANDE EPICERIE ♥

Bon Marché is the traditional French department store on the Left Bank, near Saint-Germain-des-Prés. Its Epicerie (from *épice,* meaning spice) is renowned among Parisians for the variety and quality of gourmet food items, arranged by country of origin. There is a beautiful display of fresh fruit, a selection of wines, shelves of chocolate and lovely gift items, and nearly anything else you could desire. In the back, you'll find a wonderful salad bar where you can grab a lunch or snack. Seating is at big communal tables, so you will be elbow-to-elbow with Parisians taking a break from their shopping.

38 Rue de Sèvres
Phone: 01-44-39-81-00
Website: www.lagrande
    epicerie.fr
7th *arrondissement*
Métro: Sèvres-Babylone
Cards: Accepted

Baguettes

Baguettes are a staple of the French diet. During the day, you will see many people on the street carrying their daily fresh-baked, crusty *baguettes* home for the evening meal. They are also eaten as a snack—a *tartine* is a baguette sliced in half lengthwise and spread with butter. *Baguettes* are also eaten at lunchtime (*déjeuner*) as a sandwich, often filled with ham and cheese.

FAUCHON ♥

Fauchon offers an unbelievable array of gourmet foodstuffs from around the world. You can order a delicious snack at the *traiteur* (deli/sandwich counter), or choose from wines, cheeses, pastries, and chocolates. The higher floors are devoted to packaged goods, including tea, coffee, condiments, and specialty food items. The Fauchon wrap lends an added flair if you're picking up gifts, and the store provides a shipping service, as well.

26 Place de la Madeleine
Phone: 01-70-39-38-00
Website:
   www.fauchon.com
8th *arrondissement*
Métro: Madeleine
Cards: Accepted

GALERIES LAFAYETTE ♥

Galeries Lafayette is best known for being a grand department store. It keeps expanding services and buildings, and now has a full floor devoted to gourmet food items and deli takeout. The spice table is something to see. Even if you're just craving a nice coffee and pastry, this is a great place to stop when you're in the Opéra Garnier area.

40 Boulevard
   Haussmann
Phone: 01-42-82-36-40
Website: www.galeries
   lafayette.com
9th *arrondissement*
Métro: Chaussée-d'Antin-
   La-Fayette and Opéra
Cards: Accepted

HEDIARD

Situated on Place de la Madeleine, just across from Fauchon, Hédiard also offers wonderful gourmet gift items in beautiful packaging. Each of its 6,000 products symbolizes "Quality, reliability, and tradition." There are other smaller Hédiard boutiques in other sections of the city, but this is the flagship store.

21 Place de la Madeleine
Phone: 01-43-12-88-88
Website: www.hediard.fr
8th *arrondissement*
Métro: Madeleine
Cards: Accepted

Boulangeries

Parisian *boulangeries,* or bakeries, sometimes serve sandwiches and coffee—just as they do in the United States. Here are two of my favorite *boulangeries* for snacks or a light lunch. They are both in lovely locales in major tourist areas. The first is on the Right Bank near Opéra Garnier, and the other is on the Left Bank near Boulevard St.-Germain.

BOULANGERIE DE LA FONTAINE GAILLON
15 Rue Gaillon
Phone: 01-47-42-22-49
2nd *arrondissement*
Métro: Opéra
Cards: Not Accepted

PAUL
77 Rue de Seine
Phone: 01-55-42-02-23
6th *arrondissement*
Métro: St.-Germain-des-Prés
Cards: Accepted

Cooking Classes

An afternoon or evening cooking class with *dégustation* (tasting) is a memorable way to learn about French cuisine firsthand and come away with a unique recipe that you can use at home. You need to reserve in advance and verify that the course you're interested in includes an English translation. The following schools offer a two-to-three-hour demonstration with tasting. Check their websites for information.

COOK'N WITH CLASS
A bit off the beaten track in the Montmartre area, near Sacré-Coeur, Cook'n With Class is very popular with Americans for its half-day morning and evening classes, which include a trip to the local market to purchase ingredients. A number of classes specialize in baking and desserts.

21 Rue Custine
Phone: 01-42-55-70-59
Website: www.cooknwith class.com
18th *arrondissement*
Métro: Château-Rouge
Cards: Accepted

LE CORDON BLEU PARIS ♥
Founded in 1895, this famous cooking school offers a variety of two-to-three-hour demonstrations, with tastings, that are translated into English. "Short Courses for Amateurs" include "Traditional Breadbaking" and "In Honor of Julia Child"—one of the school's most famous students. Check the website or call (they speak English) for the class calendar and for information on half- and full-day hands-on workshops. You must reserve in advance. For short courses, click on "Food Enthusiasts" and then "Culinary Discoveries."

8 Rue Léon Delhomme
Phone: 01-53-68-22-50
Website: www.lcbparis.com
15th *arrondissement*
Métro: Vaugirard
Cards: Accepted

ECOLE RITZ ESCOFFIER
Located in the basement of the Ritz Hôtel, the Ritz Escoffier School provides an elegant way to spend the afternoon. The demonstration lasts two and a half hours. Although it is usually easy to see the lesson, an overhead mirror is used to make sure that you don't miss anything. Conducted in French by a chef in whites, and translated into English, the lesson covers a three-course menu. You will be given printed recipes, and afterwards, you will taste the dishes.

38 Rue Cambon
Phone: 01-43-16-30-30
Website: www.ritzparis.com
1st *arrondissement*
Métro: Concorde and Madeleine
Cards: Accepted

Enjoying the Tastes of Paris

Dining in Paris is a wonderful way to partake of the French culture firsthand. If you're with your loved one, restaurants, cafés, and brasseries will allow you to enjoy each other's company and conversation in a special setting. If you're with friends, you will create lasting memories as you explore new dishes together. You may even bring home ideas for your own dinner parties. During one of my trips, I bought a French/English cookbook that contains some of my favorite recipes. And the gourmet and specialty stores described on pages 113 to 114 offer lovely items that you can bring home for your own cupboard or as gifts for friends, so that they, too, can enjoy a taste of Paris.

Galeries Lafayette.

6. Les Boutiques

Splurge in the Most Fashionable Shops in the World

The French fashion scene has been entertaining the rest of the world for decades. Each season, reporters arrive from distant lands to attend the *haute couture* designer shows and relay the latest styles to their readers back home. Will the hemlines be above the knee or below? What colors are *de rigeur*? Which designers are setting the trends?

Outside the showrooms, the streets of Paris are a show unto themselves. Frenchwomen place great value on pulling together an elegant yet individual look. This is an art form that has been passed from mother to daughter for generations. And men get into the act, too. In the French culture, fashion is as important and as much debated as politics and cuisine. Everyone has an opinion.

This chapter provides useful shopping tips, lists the top *couture* houses, includes the best department stores for women's *and* men's clothes, discusses French style and how you can make it your own, points the way to finding bargains, guides you in the art of choosing accessories, and explains tax-reimbursement and customs regulations. You'll also find a size conversion chart and a guide to the most fashionable streets to stroll. (If you're interested in home accessory boutiques, you'll find information in Chapter 7.)

Throughout the chapter, a heart rating ♥ is used to indicate my top choices or stores where you can find great bargains.

"Instinctive style is a particularly French quality, one that does not exist by accident or without historical references . . . important French ladies of the seventeenth and eighteenth centuries used their personal eccentricities to influence all the courts of Europe. An original, noticeable [fashion] mode was considered as essential as writing fascinating letters, commissioning masterpieces by the right composers and painters, or pushing for advantageous treaties, alliances, or boycotts. Powerful French females always had powerful styles."
—*Marian McEvoy*, European Travel & Life

Shopping Customs and Tips

Many Paris shopkeepers speak some English since it has become the predominant language spoken with tourists in Paris. I'm always amazed to hear French salespeople speaking English with customers from Japan, Italy, Germany, you name it. The accents are all over the map.

Still, some shopkeepers do not speak English. Also, as you may discover, French shopping customs are somewhat different from ours. The following guidelines and phrases should help you to better enjoy *les boutiques.*

• Shopping hours vary, depending on the season. Stores are usually closed Sundays and holidays, and many are closed on Mondays or just on Monday mornings. Most stores open by 10:00 AM and close around 7:00 PM, and many are closed during lunchtime. Since so many Parisians take their vacation in August, many stores close for a few weeks during that month.

• Paris shops usually accept major credit cards, but some smaller boutiques do not take the American Express card.

• If you notice a sign in the window saying *Soldes,* that does not mean that all the merchandise has already been purchased. On the contrary, it means that items are on sale and that you will save some euros. Normally, stores put their stock on sale twice a year, in January and in late June through July.

• The French government will reimburse the sales tax (about 12 percent) if you spend more than 175 euros in the same store on the same day. Remember to pick up the export sales invoice. (See page 131 for details.)

• Some bigger stores will ship your purchases to the United States for a small fee. Or you can go to the nearest post office and ship the goods yourself. (For more information on Paris post offices, see the inset on page 181.) Most post offices sell various size boxes for this purpose.

Common Shopping Phrases

How much does this cost?

Ça coute combien?

Do you accept credit cards?

Acceptez-vous les cartes de credit?

I would like the export sales form for sales tax reimbursement.

Je voudrais bordereau de détaxe.

I would like the package gift-wrapped.

Je voudrais un paquet cadeau.

TOP FASHION HOUSES

In *haute couture,* the epitome of French style, clothes are made *sur mesure* (by measure), meaning that each garment is custom-made. Top designers present their new creations twice a year at elaborate fashion shows attended by celebrities, journalists, and customers willing to pay tens of thousands of dollars for a unique, perfectly fitted gown. Guests are presented with a list of the garments to be modeled so that they can mark the items they may want to purchase. It is estimated that there are less than 2,500 serious *couture* customers in the world.

Prêt à porter, meaning ready-to-wear, is a wonderful development for those of us who don't want to spend our life's savings on one dress. The *prêt à porter* clothes are similar in design and style to *haute couture,* but are mass-produced and sold "off-the-rack" in boutiques at a fraction of the *couture* price. Most *couture* houses offer a *prêt à porter* line.

Here are some of the top showrooms in the Paris fashion world.

CHANEL
42 Avenue Montaigne
Phone: 01-47-23-74-12
Website: www.chanel.com
8th *arrondissement*
Métro: Franklin-D.-Roosevelt
Cards: Accepted
or
21 Rue du Faubourg St.-Honoré
Phone: 01-53-05-98-95
Website: www.chanel.com
8th *arrondissement*
Métro: Concorde and Madeleine
Cards: Accepted

CHLOE
44 Avenue Montaigne
Phone: 01-47-23-00-08
Website: www.chloe.com
8th *arrondissement*
Métro: Franklin-D.-Roosevelt
Cards: Accepted

CHRISTIAN DIOR
30 Avenue Montaigne
Phone: 01-40-73-73-73
Website: www.diorcouture.com
8th *arrondissement*
Métro: Franklin-D.-Roosevelt
Cards: Accepted

CHRISTIAN LACROIX
73 Rue du Faubourg St.-Honoré
Phone: 01-42-68-79-04
Website: www.christian-lacroix.com
8th *arrondissement*
Métro: Madeleine and Concorde
Cards: Accepted

EMANUEL UNGARO
2 Avenue Montaigne
Phone: 01-53-57-00-22
Website: www.ungaro.com
8th *arrondissement*
Métro: Alma-Marceau
Cards: Accepted

GIVENCHY
28 Rue du Faubourg St.-Honoré
Phone: 01-42-68-31-00
Website: www.givenchy.com
8th *arrondissement*
Métro: Madeleine and Concorde
Cards: Accepted

JEAN PAUL GAULTIER
44 Avenue George V
Phone: 01-44-43-00-44
Website: www.jeanpaulgaultier.com
8th *arrondissement*
Métro: George-V
Cards: Accepted

LANVIN
22 Rue du Fauboug St.-Honoré
Phone: 01-44-71-31-73
Website: www.lanvin.com
8th *arrondissement*
Métro: Madeleine and Concorde
Cards: Accepted

NINA RICCI
39 Avenue Montaigne
Phone: 01-40-88-65-36
Website: www.ninaricci.com
8th *arrondissement*
Métro: Franklin-D.-Roosevelt
Cards: Accepted

PIERRE CARDIN
59 Rue du Faubourg St.-Honoré
Phone: 01-42-66-68-98
Website: www.pierrecardin.com
8th *arrondissement*
Métro: Madeleine and Concorde
Cards: Accepted

SONIA RYKIEL
175 Boulevard St.-Germain
Phone: 01-49-54-60-60
Website: www.soniarykiel.com
6th *arrondissement*
Métro: Rue-du-Bac
Cards: Accepted

VALENTINO
17–19 Avenue Montaigne
Phone: 01-47-23-64-61
Website: www.valentino.com
8th *arrondissement*
Métro: Alma-Marceau
Cards: Accepted
or
27 Rue du Faubourg St.-Honoré
Phone: 01-42-66-95-94
Website: www.valentino.com
8th *arrondissement*
Métro: Madeleine and Concorde
Cards: Accepted

YVES SAINT LAURENT
38 Rue du Faubourg St.-Honoré
Phone: 01-42-65-74-59
Website: www.ysl.com
8th *arrondissement*
Métro: Concorde and Madeleine
Cards: Accepted
or
6 Place St.-Sulpice
Phone: 01-43-29-43-00
Website: www.ysl.com
6th *arrondissement*
Métro: St.-Sulpice
Cards: Accepted

DESIGNER OUTLETS AND VINTAGE STORES

While window-shopping on Avenue Montaigne and Rue du Faubourg St.-Honoré, you may succumb to "sticker shock" from the high price tags. Fear not. There are stores with designer labels at discount prices. The surroundings and service will not be as elegant as those of the *haute couture* houses, but you'll love the savings. Be forewarned, though—some shops do not accept credit cards, so bring your euros. In addition to fashionable clothes, many of these boutiques carry other items. Here are four good options. Miss Griffes sells new designer outfits, and the other stores carry designer vintage (used) clothes. Didier Ludot, found in the shopping arcade facing the Palais Royal garden, has Chanel jackets, shoes, and small leather clutches from big-name designers. Le Dépôt-Vente de Buci-Bourbon, situated in the Saint-Germain area, offers fur coats, designer clothes, and even vintage dishes.

LE DEPOT-VENTE
DE BUCI-BOURBON
6 Rue de Bourbon-le-Château
Phone: 01-46-34-45-05
6th *arrondissement*
Métro: St.-Germain-des-Prés
Cards: Accepted

DIDIER LUDOT
24 Galerie Montpensier
(in Jardin du Palais Royal)
Phone: 01-42-96-06-56
1st *arrondissement*
Métro: Palais-Royal or Pyramides
Cards: Accepted

MISS GRIFFES
19 Rue de Penthièvre
Phone: 01-42-65-10-00
8th *arrondissement*
Métro: Miromesnil
Cards: Acceptedd

RECIPROQUE
95 Rue de la Pompe
Phone: 01-47-04-30-28
Website: www.reciproque.fr
16th *arrondissement*
Métro: Rue-de-la-Pompe
Cards: Accepted

Fashion Through the Ages

The Musée de la Mode et du Costume displays one of the richest collections of fashion in the world. Over 5,000 complete costumes from the eighteenth century to the present day are housed in this Renaissance-style palace. The long history of French elegance is depicted through royal evening robes and many articles of clothing that were donated by *"les belles dames de la haute société"* (the beautiful women of high society). The museum also hosts revolving exhibitions.

MUSEE DE LA MODE ET DU COSTUME
Palais Galliera
10 Avenue Pierre Premier de Serbie
Phone: 01-47-20-85-23
Website: http://www.paris.org/Musees/Costume/info.html
16th *arrondissement*
Métro: Iéna and Alma-Marceau
Cards: Accepted

DEPARTMENT STORES

Parisian department stores (*grands magasins*) offer a great way to glimpse many of the top designer fashions in one place. Like US department stores, these establishments have separate sections for women's and men's clothes, shoes, accessories, children's clothes, and items for the home. By visiting any one of them, you will get a crash course in French style under one roof—or several roofs, since some stores take up more than one large building. Also, two of the stores—Galeries Lafayette and Printemps—offer a 10-percent discount to tourists. (See the individual discussions of the stores, below.) All of Paris' department stores have cafés where you can grab lunch, a snack, or a coffee, so you'll be able to maintain the energy to "shop 'til you drop."

LE BON MARCHE

Paris' oldest department store, Le Bon Marché opened in 1852, and is a bit off the beaten track on the Left Bank. It is the least "touristy" department store, and also the one most likely to surround you with stylish Parisians shopping for elegant goods. As described in Chapter 5 (page 113), Bon Marché also includes La Grande Epicerie, a large hall filled with gourmet food items, and a great salad bar with seating.

24 Rue de Sèvres
Phone: 01-44-39-80-00
Website:
   www.lebonmarche.fr
7th *arrondissement*
Métro: Sèvres-Babylone
Cards: Accepted

COLETTE

Colette's motto is "Style, Design, Art, Food," and this unique store lives up to its promise. Even though it's technically a department store, Colette is much smaller and more cutting-edge than the other establishments in this category. The ground floor is always mobbed with shoppers checking out music CDs, art books, perfumes, and candles. But the main event is on the second floor, where clothing created by trendy young French designers is displayed alongside purses and shoes. Many celebrities and models frequent this store. You might even catch some of them grabbing a healthy salad in the "Water Bar" café on the underground level.

213 Rue St.-Honoré
Phone: 01-55-35-33-90
Website: www.colette.fr
1st *arrondissement*
Métro: Tuileries and
   Pyramides
Cards: Accepted

GALERIES LAFAYETTE ♥

The Galeries Lafayette complex stretches over many buildings, giving you an opportunity to see a wide range of styles in clothing, accessories, and more. Galeries Lafayette is my top recommendation if you have time for only one department store. I found that the staff speaks more English than salespeople in other stores, and it's easy to get a 10-percent discount card. (For Printemps, you need to visit the store's website and print out the discount coupon before you go.) Start at the Welcome Desk to get the card, which is offered to all tourists who show a passport, and to pick up a floor plan to map out your visit. Even with the discount, these clothes are not a bargain, but if you spend over 175 euros in one day, you will quality for reimbursement of the French sales tax. (See page 131 for details.)

40 Boulevard
   Haussmann
Phone: 01-42-82-36-40
Email:
   welcome@galeriesla-
   fayette.com
Website: www.galeries
   lafayette.com
9th *arrondissement*
Métro: Chaussée-
   d'Antin-La-Fayette and
   Opéra
Cards: Accepted

The Galeries Lafayette Fashion Show

Every Friday at 3:00 PM, Galeries Lafayette department store hosts a live fashion show that is free to tourists. There are only 150 seats, so you have to make a reservation at least a few months ahead by calling 011-33-1-42-82-36-40 (from the US); ask for someone who speaks English. You can also book online (welcome@galeries-lafayette.com), in which case, you'll be able to print out your confirmation email and take it along with you to the show.

The Galeries Lafayette fashion show is held in the main Boulevard Haussmann store (see page 122) on the seventh-floor Salon Opéra. Be sure to get there by 2:00 PM for a good seat, or no later than 2:30, when they might give your seat to someone on standby.

I've attended the Galeries Lafayette show a few times, and it's always thrilling to see gorgeously dressed models strut down the catwalk to hip music. The fashions range from chic casual attire to elegant formal wear and include even wedding dresses. Each guest is given a booklet that lists the outfits and their location in the store. Of course, the prices are omitted. Remember that the store offers a 10-percent discount card to every shopper who presents a foreign passport.

To get the most out of your shopping trip, I suggest you reserve ahead for the Friday fashion show (see the inset above); browse for scarves, costume jewelry, and shoes; visit Lafayette Maison, the store's home furnishing building; and treat yourself to gourmet foodstuffs in Lafayette Gourmet, where you can also grab a coffee and dessert or sample delicacies at the tasting bar. If you have a few minutes to spare, take the elevator to the eighth floor, where the terrace offers a panoramic view of the city.

PRINTEMPS

A stunning example of nineteenth-century Art Nouveau architecture, Printemps is one block away from Galeries Lafayette on Boulevard Haussmann. My Parisian girlfriends prefer this store to Galeries Lafayette, saying that it's less "touristy," but I didn't find the layout as easy to navigate as that of the other store, and Printemps is also not quite as service oriented towards English-speaking visitors.

64 Boulevard
  Haussmann
Phone: 01-42-82-50-00
Website:
  www.printemps.com
9th *arrondissement*
Métro: Havre-Caumartin
  and Opéra
Cards: Accepted

Like Galeries Lafayette, Printemps offers a 10-percent discount to tourists, but it's complicated to obtain. You have to visit the store's website, click on services, and then click on 10-percent discount. Print out the coupon, which you can present at the store along with your passport. On the plus side, Printemps has an elaborate beauty salon for hair styling, facials, massages, manicures, you name it. The store also offers seven different restaurants, ranging from tea rooms to pub-style eateries.

Know Your Size

The following conversion charts will help you find clothes and shoes in your size. There is some variation, so you will still need to try things on for fit, but at least you'll be in the ballpark. The French translations for basic English clothing terms are in parentheses underneath each heading.

There are two words for size in French: *taille* is used for clothes, and *pointure* refers to shoes and gloves.

Women's Coats, Dresses, Blouses, Pants, and Skirts
(manteaux, robes, chemisiers, pantalons, et jupes)

American	4	6	8	10	12	14	16	18
French	34	36	38	40	42	44	46	48

Women's Shoes
(chaussures femmes)

American	5	6	7	8	9	10	11
French	35	36	37	38–39	40	41–42	43

Men's Suits
(complets)

American	34	36	38	40	42	44	46	48
French	44	46	48	50	52	54	56	58

Men's Shirts
(chemises)

American	14	$14^1/_2$	15	$15^1/_2$	16	$16^1/_2$	17	$17^1/_2$	18	$18^1/_2$
French	36	37	38	39	40	41	42	43	44	45

Men's Shoes
(chaussures hommes)

American	6	7	8	9	10	11	12
French	41	42	43	44	45	46	47

DISCOUNT STORES

When shopping for bargains, Parisians go to two discount store chains, Monoprix and Prisunic, which have locations throughout the city. (Check with the front desk of your hotel to find the one nearest you.) The quality of the women's clothes is not the best, but these are great places to shop for accessories like scarves and belts. You will also find a good selection of reasonably priced small gifts and everyday items, and, in some stores, an assortment of foods and wines (usually downstairs). On recent trips, I've picked up adorable children's clothes with attractive gift bags at a tenth the cost of similar boutique items. I've also bought small bottles of good champagne to enjoy before going out to dinner, and a stylish large black vinyl tote for bringing home extra purchases.

Accessories

Frenchwomen play at creating different moods by mixing and matching their belts, scarves, shoes, and purses, and by adding fun jewelry. The creative use of accessories (*accessoires*) has been developed into an art form and provides an inexpensive way to jazz up outfits and showcase each woman's originality and personality.

While you're strolling along the fashionable streets of Paris (see the inset on page 127), you'll have a great opportunity to view elegant Frenchwomen and take note of how they stylishly create an ensemble. Scarves are tied artfully, a beautiful watch adds an elegant touch, and that expensive leather handbag is a must.

If you're pressed for time, the top department stores (see page 122) are a good place to start because they offer a wide array of accessories under one roof. The following pages highlight a few of the top boutiques, many of which have smaller displays in the department stores.

PURSES AND SHOES

In *The Riches of Paris: A Shopping and Touring Guide,* French shopping expert Maribeth Clemente urges all her readers to "invest in a big, beautiful handbag that you love so much you'll never tire of it." According to Clemente, even budget-conscious Frenchwomen are willing to pay a hefty price for a handbag that makes a strong statement about who they are or who they're trying to be. Shopping in Paris will give you an opportunity to pick up a purse that will add style and polish to every outfit you wear long after you return home.

Shoes are another mainstay of a Frenchwoman's wardrobe, and shoe designers are as well known and coveted as their *couture* counterparts. The originality of these artists is astounding. Even if you're not interested in buying, you'll be inspired and entertained by their creations.

The following stores are top names in leather goods, including cutting-edge shoes and handbags.

"The French look consists of a variety of styles but a single spirit—self expression. And nowhere is it more evident than in a Frenchwoman's accessories, in the details that finish, but more often fashion, the entire outfit. Frenchwomen wear clever accessories, which they change at whim to instantly update any old thing and give it the stamp or originality. They seem to have an implicit understanding of the little touches needed to achieve just the effect they want."
—Susan Sommers, French Chic

BOTTEGA VENETA
14 Rue du Faubourg St.-Honoré
Phone: 01-42-65-59-70
Website: www.bottegaveneta.com
8th *arrondissement*
Métro: Concorde
Cards: Accepted

CAREL
4 Rue Tronchet
Phone: 01-42-66-21-58
Website: www.carel.fr
8th *arrondissement*
Métro: Madeleine
Cards: Accepted
or
171 Rue St.-Honoré
Phone: 01-42-96-29-29
Website: www.carel.fr
1st *arrondissement*
Métro: Palais-Royal-Musée-du-Louvre
Cards: Accepted

CHRISTIAN LOUBOUTIN
68 Rue du Faubourg St.-Honoré
Phone: 01-42-68-37-65
Website: www.christianlouboutin.com
8th *arrondissement*
Métro: Madeleine and Concorde
Cards: Accepted

ROBERT CLERGERIE
5 Rue du Cherche-Midi
Phone: 01-45-48-75-47
Website: www.robertclergerie.fr
6th *arrondissement*
Métro: St.-Sulpice
Cards: Accepted

ROGER VIVIER
29 Rue du Faubourg St.-Honoré
Phone: 01-53-43-00-85
Website: www.rogervivier.com
8th *arrondissement*
Métro: Madeleine
Cards: Accepted

SALVATORE FERRAGAMO
46 Rue du Faubourg St.-Honoré
Phone: 01-43-12-96-96
Website: www.ferragamo.com
8th *arrondissement*
Métro: Madeleine
Cards: Accepted
or
45 Avenue Montaigne
Phone: 01-47-23-36-37
8th *arrondissement*
Metro: Franklin-D.-Roosevelt
Cards: Accepted

STEPHANE KELIAN
19 Rue François Premier
Phone: 01-47-20-74-43
Website: www.stephane-kelian.com
8th *arrondissement*
Métro: Franklin-D.-Roosevelt
Cards: Accepted

Fashionable Streets to Stroll

Most of the top designers have a number of boutiques throughout Paris. However, the following four areas are especially wonderful for browsing, window-shopping, and mingling with the *crème* of Parisian society. Be sure to explore the side streets in these neighborhoods, as well.

Avenue Montaigne

Located in the eighth *arrondissement,* between the Champs-Elysées and the Seine River, Avenue Montaigne exemplifies elegance and plays host to Christian Dior, Nina Ricci, Valentino, and Chanel, among others.

Rue St.-Honoré ♥

The longest-running street of top stores in Paris, Rue St.-Honoré starts in the first *arrondissement,* near the Louvre, and continues into the eighth *arrondissement,* where it becomes Rue du Faubourg St.-Honoré.

Boulevard St.-Germain

Found in the sixth *arrondissement,* Boulevard St.-Germain boasts many designer stores. Be sure to check out the smaller streets on either side of the boulevard, around the St.-Germain-des-Prés métro stop. This area is highly recommended by my Parisian girlfriends, who love its small, trendy boutiques. While you're in the neighborhood, check out Place Saint-Sulpice.

Rue des Francs-Bourgeois

Situated in the fourth *arrondissement,* near Place des Vosges, this area is home to up-and-coming designers who offer avant-garde clothing and unique jewelry. As you stroll down this street, be sure to note the lovely Renaissance-era buildings.

SCARVES AND BELTS

Scarves are great accents to liven up and enhance your look and set off your face. Large scarves are also worn as shawls over the shoulder and held with a clasp or pin. Hermès scarves are a French institution. Whether worn with a suit or jeans, they are an integral part of the Frenchwoman's wardrobe.

The following stores have beautiful choices in classic styles and are among the top labels in Paris. Many also sell women's clothes and other accessories. As mentioned earlier, for a bigger selection of many designers' accessories—and to qualify for tax reimbursement—your best bet is one of the department stores listed on page 122. But for the experience of "stepping into another world," designer boutiques are in a class by themselves.

CHANEL
25 Rue Royale
Phone: 01-44-51-92-93
Website: www.chanel.com
8th *arrondissement*
Métro: Madeleine
Cards: Accepted
or
21 Rue du Faubourg
   St.-Honoré
Phone: 01-53-05-98-95
Website: www.chanel.com
8th *arrondissement*
Métro: Concorde and
   Madeleine
Cards: Accepted

CHRISTIAN DIOR ♥
30 Avenue Montaigne
Phone: 01-40-73-73-73
Website:
   www.diorcouture.com

8th *arrondissement*
Métro: Franklin-D.-
   Roosevelt
Cards: Accepted

HERMES ♥
24 Rue du Faubourg
   St.-Honoré
Phone: 01-40-17-47-17
Website:
   www.hermes.com
8th *arrondissement*
Métro: Concorde
Cards: Accepted

LOUIS VUITTON ♥
101 Avenue des Champs-
   Elysées
Phone: 01-53-57-52-00
Website:
   www.louisvuitton.com

8th *arrondissement*
Métro: George-V
Cards: Accepted

YVES SAINT LAURENT
38 Rue du Faubourg
   St.-Honoré
Phone: 01-42-65-74-59
Website: www.ysl.com
8th *arrondissement*
Métro: Madeleine and
   Concorde
Cards: Accepted
or
6 Place St.-Sulpice
Phone: 01-43-29-43-00
Website: www.ysl.com
6th *arrondissement*
Métro: St.-Sulpice
Cards: Accepted

$$$ SAVE SOME MONEY $$$

You'll notice that many Parisian women wear colorful scarves, tied in interesting ways, to add flair to their look. Believe me, not all these women are going to Hermès and Christian Dior and spending over $200. They know that deals can be found at the shops near tourist areas, particularly on Rue de Rivoli near the Louvre. These stores sell pashminettes in a wide variety of colors, usually for around 10 euros. These are narrow, long scarves, so they tie easily around the neck. The trick is to find ones of good-quality fabric; these are usually packaged in plastic rather than hanging on a rack.

JEWELRY

The French sense of whimsy was charmingly apparent when a recent ad campaign slogan was plastered across jewelry store windows—*"Bijoux mieux que bisous"* (Jewels are better than kisses). Hopefully, you can have both!

A stylish piece of jewelry is the finishing touch to add a note of glamour, formality, or just plain fun. It doesn't have to be expensive. I'm always picking up bargains at the department store counters, where you'll find great selections of costume jewelry (*faux bijoux*) for a wide range of prices.

The following four stores are *très cher* and great for window-shopping or serious jewelry purchases. Stores that carry less expensive jewelry—costume jewelry or pieces made with semiprecious stones and less costly metals—are listed on page 130. If you're looking for antique jewelry, your best bet may be the Paris flea markets, which are discussed in Chapter 7. Both Les Puces de Saint-Ouen (see page 139) and Porte de Vanves (see page 140) offer jewelry for many tastes and budgets.

Expensive Designer Jewelry

BOUCHERON
26 Place Vendôme
Phone: 01-42-61-58-16
Website: www.boucheron.com
1st *arrondissement*
Métro: Tuileries
Cards: Accepted

BULGARI
25 Place Vendôme
Phone: 01-55-35-00-50
Website: www.bulgari.com
1st *arrondissement*
Métro: Tuileries and Opéra
Cards: Accepted

CARTIER
13 Rue de la Paix
Phone: 01-58-18-23-00
Website: www.cartier.fr
2nd *arrondissement*
Métro: Opéra
Cards: Accepted

or

23 Place Vendôme
Phone: 01-44-55-32-20
Website: www.cartier.fr
1st *arrondissement*
Métro: Tuileries and Opéra
Cards: Accepted

VAN CLEEF & ARPELS
22 Place Vendôme
Phone: 01-53-45-35-50
Website: www.vancleef-arpels.com
1st *arrondissement*
Métro: Opéra
Cards: Accepted

or

3 Rue de la Paix
Phone: 01-53-45-35-60
Website: www.vancleef-arpels.com
2nd *arrondissement*
Métro: Opéra
Cards: Accepted

Lower-Priced and Costume Jewelry

ADELLINE ♥

In the midst of shopping heaven on the Left Bank, this store stands out for its one-of-a-kind jewelry pieces made from unpolished gold and set with smoky topaz, opaque ruby, and other colorful stones. The collection includes necklaces, bracelets, watches, rings, charms, and more.

54 Rue Jacob
Phone: 01-47-03-07-18
Website:
    www.adelline.com
6th *arrondissement*
Métro: St.-Germain-des-
    Prés and Mabillon
Cards: Accepted

AGATHA PARIS

Agatha is a major brand of *faux bijoux* (costume jewelry). Besides being offered in the following boutiques, Agatha jewelry is sold in major department stores.

45 Rue Bonaparte
Phone: 01-46-33-20-00
Website: www.agatha.fr
6th *arrondissement*
Métro: St.-Germain-des-
    Prés and Mabillon
Cards: Accepted

5 Place des Victoires
Phone: 01-40-39-08-25
Website: www.agatha.fr
1st *arrondissement*
Métro: Bourse
Cards: Accepted

FABRICE ♥

At Fabrice, necklaces, earrings, bracelets, brooches, and other pieces are created with flair, using unusual colorful stones and materials.

33 & 54 Rue Bonaparte
Phone: 01-43-26-57-95
Website:
    www.bijouxfabrice.com
6th *arrondissement*
Métro: St.-Germain-des-Prés
Cards: Accepted

LE GRAIN DE SABLE

This store carries inexpensive, artistic costume jewelry. It also stocks wonderful hats and other accessories—*and* it's on a street of charming shops on the island of Ile Saint-Louis.

79 Rue St.-Louis-en-l'Ile
Phone: 01-46-33-67-27
Website:
    www.legraindesable.fr
4th *arrondissement*
Métro: Pont-Marie and
    Hôtel-de-Ville
Cards: Accepted

Fabrice Jewelry.

Tax Refund and Customs Information

Paris is a shopper's dream, but you'll want to get your head out of the clouds long enough to take advantage of potential savings. For example, if you're tempted to buy items that total over 175 euros (about $245), you can save money by doing all your shopping in the same store so that you qualify for the sales tax reimbursement. Below are the details on this friendly French tax law for tourists, as well as regulations on entering the United States with purchases from abroad.

Applying for Sales Tax Reimbursement

To encourage tourists to shop, the French government has declared that if you spend more than 175 euros *in the same store on the same day,* you qualify for a refund of the sales tax. Because the tax is around 12 percent, this can amount to sizeable savings. To collect your money, you must do the following:

1. When making purchases that total 175 euros or more at the same store, request an export sales invoice, or *détaxe,* from the store, along with a stamped, addressed envelope. Make sure that you have three copies of the invoice.

2. When filling in the forms, be sure to choose the right refund option. Unless you have paid cash, the easiest option is to have the refund directly applied to your credit card. If you do not apply the refund to your credit card, a Global Refund Cheque will be mailed to you after the store receives the authorized form. (This can take months.)

3. When you go to the airport to take the flight home, after you get your boarding pass but before you go through security, find the "Détaxe" (French Customs) desk, which is normally near the airline check-in counters. (If you're leaving the country by train, contact the conductor.) You will need to present both the purchased items and the filled-in forms, so be sure to take the purchases with you in your carry-on bag. After the clerk has processed the forms, he will give you a receipt for your records and a completed form. Place the form in the stamped, addressed envelope, seal the envelope, and put it in a nearby yellow Paris mailbox.

If you will be visiting other countries in the European Union before your trip back home, wait until you leave the final country to process the tax-reimbursement forms.

Clearing United States Customs

When you return to the United States, you will be asked to fill out a Customs Declaration Form on which you list the items that you purchased in Paris to take back home. The United States does not charge tax on purchases that total less than $800 per person, but for the next $1,000 you spent, you will be taxed around 3 percent. This tax will have to be paid at the airport. Above that amount, the tax will vary, depending on the goods. For more details on US customs, visit the government's Customs and Border Protection (CBP) website.

UNITED STATES CUSTOMS INFORMATION
Website: http://www.cbp.gov/xp/cgov/travel/vacation/kbyg/

Keep in mind that this process was designed to impose a tax on people who are importing goods to resell, not to charge tourists who are bringing back souvenirs. Due to fear of contamination, US customs agents will not allow you to bring most fruits, vegetables, and meat products into the country.

Develop Your Own Take on Chic French Style

Paris is a wonderland for shopaholics, and even casual shoppers get caught up in the beauty of the displays and elegance of the fashions. You are bound to return with an urge to accessorize a casual jeans outfit, adopt the latest shoe style, sport a stunning handbag, or flash a fabulous piece of new jewelry.

7. Pour la Maison

Develop Your Decorating Style

A guide to Paris wouldn't be complete without a mention of the many beautiful shops devoted to *la maison*, the house. The quality and selection of household items in Paris are superb—from antique furniture, to luxurious sheets, to crystal and china, to original art pieces. This chapter will touch on museums that trace the history and evolution of home furnishings, antique stores, specialty boutiques, auction houses, and flea markets. Yes, there are still finds to be had. The following listings will give you many ideas for enhancing your environment and adding a new dimension to your decorating style.

"The French mix what they like with what they need with what the family has handed down. The look is eclectic and yet cohesive. The best of French country style is comfortable, graceful, and gracious—a mixture of color, texture, substance, and light that welcomes and charms in a way that is refreshingly open."

—Pierre Moulin, Pierre Le Vec, and Linda Dannenberg, Pierre Deux's French Country

MUSEUMS FOR HOME FURNISHINGS

While several Paris museums include some rooms that display antiques from specific time periods (see Musée Jacquemart-André on page 85), the city also has museums that are devoted solely to home furnishings. Musée des Arts Décoratifs—which is adjacent to the Louvre—is by far the largest of its kind. Collections that are still remarkable but smaller in scope include Musée Baccarat and Musée Nissim de Camondo. These museums provide a unique way of learning about French history as well as an eye-opening look into the lavish lifestyle of French aristocracy in times past. If this aspect of culture is of particular interest to you, consider saving some money by buying a combined entrance ticket for the Musée des Arts Decoratifs and the Musée Nissim de Camondo.

MUSEE DES ARTS DECORATIFS

Established in 1905, Musée des Arts Décoratifs is the largest home-furnishings museum in Europe, with four floors filled with furniture, tapestries, wallpaper, ceramics, glassware, and other interior design elements, most of which are French. A number of rooms recreate French interiors from the Middle Ages through the present day, and changing exhibitions highlight different aspects of design. A gift shop offers toys, books, jewelry, tableware, and other objects inspired by the museum's collection.

107 Rue de Rivoli
Phone: 01-44-55-57-50
Website:
  http://www.lesartsdeco
  ratifs.fr/english-439
1st *arrondissement*
Métro: Palais-Royal-
  Musée-du-Louvre
Cards: Accepted

MUSEE BACCARAT

Since the late 1700s, Baccarat's full-lead crystal has been sought by kings, presidents, and all those who can afford the high price tags. This museum traces the history of crystal and displays the company's most historic pieces, including sparkling stemware, perfume bottles, chandeliers, and award-winning crystal sculptures. A Baccarat store is adjacent to the museum. (For information on the Baccarat flagship store, see page 137.)

11 Place des Etats-Unis
Phone: 01-40-22-11-00
Website:
  http://www.baccarat.fr
  /fr/univers-baccarat/
  musees/museum-
  opening-hours.htm
16th *arrondissement*
Métro: Boissière and Iéna
Cards: Accepted

MUSEE NISSIM DE CAMONDO

Overlooking the beautiful Parc Monceau, this mansion—built in 1911 for Comte Moïse de Camondo—devotes three floors to the original owner's collection of eighteenth-century furnishings. Maintained as if it were still a private home, it offers lavish displays of furniture, tapestries, silver, porcelain, sculptures, and paintings.

63 Rue de Monceau
Phone: 01-45-63-26-32
Website: http://www.
  paris.org/Musees/
  Nissim.Camondo/
  info.html
8th *arrondissement*
Métro: Villiers
Cards: Accepted

ANTIQUE STORES

Paris has thousands of antique and secondhand stores. You'll pass many while you're walking around, especially on the smaller streets of the Left Bank between the Seine River and Boulevard St.-Germain. You will have better assurance of authenticity at established stores, and you should expect all stores to provide a certification document that includes the store's address and phone number, a description of the antique, and its age and provenance (history). If the item is over 100 years old, you will not have to pay tax in France or on your return to the United States.

In addition to the many stores you'll find on the Left Bank, there are two major centers that house a number of antique dealers under one roof.

LE LOUVRE DES ANTIQUAIRES ♥

Across from the Musée du Louvre, Le Louvre des Antiquaires houses 250 stores on three levels offering works of art starting from classical antiquity. The range is enormous; you'll find paintings and sculpture, furniture and specialty clocks, tableware and wine-related objects, antique jewelry, and more. The quality of items on display gives you the impression that you're in a museum tracing the lives of others, but in this case, you can actually buy what you like—assuming that your pocketbook can handle the hit.

2 Place du Palais Royal
Phone: 01-42-97-27-27
Website: www.louvre-
  antiquaires.com
1st *arrondissement*
Métro: Palais-Royal-
  Musée-du-Louvre
Cards: Accepted

LE VILLAGE SUISSE

Located near the Eiffel Tower, on the grounds of the 1900 World Fair, La Village Suisse—a recreated Swiss village—features over 150 antique dealers in two nearby buildings. Wares range from primitive to contemporary art, from furniture to ceramics, glassware, and textiles.

78 Avenue de Suffren
or 54 Avenue de la
  Motte-Picquet
Phone: 01-40-51-37-52
Website: www.levillage
  suisseparis.com
15th *arrondissement*
Métro: La-Motte-
  Picquet-Grenelle
Cards: Accepted

SPECIALTY BOUTIQUES FOR HOUSEHOLD ITEMS

The French have elevated dining and entertaining to a fine art. Dinner parties last for hours, and presentation is an important ingredient in the evening. The next few pages list the top stores for china, crystal, cutlery, linens, table accessories, silver, and the cookware needed to present a gourmet dinner at one of your future *soirées*. As you will see, some stores carry items from several different categories and some offer jewelry, as well.

China and Pottery

DINERS EN VILLE
As the name of this store implies, it carries many beautiful things for your dinner parties, including new and antique china place settings, luxury tablecloths and napkins, and delicate stemware and glasses.

27 Rue de Varenne
Phone: 01-42-22-78-33
7th *arrondissement*
Métro: Rue-du-Bac and
   Sèvres-Babylone
Cards: Accepted

HAVILAND
The Haviland family has been making Limoges china for over a hundred years. Their Paris boutique offers china, crystal, silverware, and giftware.

25 Rue Royale
Phone: 01-42-66-36-36
Website: www.haviland.fr
8th *arrondissement*
Métro: Madeleine
Cards: Accepted

LA MAISON IVRE
Specializing in French country style, La Maison Ivre sells not only pottery but also linens and other kitchen and dining room accessories.

38 Rue Jacob
Phone: 01-42-60-01-85
Website: www.maison-
   ivre.com
6th *arrondissement*
Métro: St.-Germain-des-
   Prés
Cards: Accepted

SEVRES CITE DE LA CERAMIQUE
After a large factory was established in 1740 to create special dishware for King Louis XV, Sèvres porcelain became a French institution in the decorative arts. Today, you can purchase elaborately decorated tea services, one-of-a-kind serving bowls and plates, vases, and decorative objects. This store specializes in unique porcelain dishes rather than place settings. Prices start at 150 euros for a Sèvres plate and go way up from there.

4 Place André-Malraux
Phone: 01-47-03-40-20
Website: www.sevrescite
   ceramique.fr
1st *arrondissement*
Métro: Palais-Royal-
   Musée-du-Louvre
Cards: Accepted

Lafayette Maison

Like their US counterparts, all French department stores have sections devoted to home furnishings. Galeries Lafayette deserves to be singled out in this respect because it has dedicated a whole building—Lafayette Maison—to the home. Under one roof, you will get a quick lesson in the art of French furnishing and decoration, be able to choose from a number of brands, and enjoy daily events such as short cooking demonstrations. You can combine purchases to reach the 175-euro requirement for sales tax reimbursement (see page 131 of Chapter 6 for details), and if you present your passport at the store's Welcome Desk, you will receive a 10-percent discount on your purchases.

35 Boulevard Haussman
Phone: 01-42-82-36-40
Website: www.galeries
lafayette.com
9th *arrondissement*
Métro: Opéra
Cards: Accepted

Crystal

BACCARAT

This is the most prestigious store that sells Baccarat crystal—even though the boutique adjacent to Musée Baccarat (see page 134) is actually larger. The prices are identical at both locations. My favorite item is the smoky-hued "heart of crystal" for 150 euros. It's stunning, and part of the proceeds go to a children's charity.

11 Place de la Madeleine
Phone: 01-42-65-36-26
Website: www.baccarat.fr
8th *arrondissement*
Métro: Madeleine
Cards: Accepted

CHRISTOFLE

From its founding in 1830, Christofle has remained "a symbol of luxury and elegance" and has always been associated with renowned artists and silversmiths. Branching out from flatware and fine porcelain table settings and accessories, Christofle now sells silver jewelry and a variety of specialty gifts, like money clips.

9 Rue Royale
Phone: 01-55-27-99-13
Website:
www.christofle.com
8th *arrondissement*
Métro: Concorde
Cards: Accepted

LALIQUE

One of the world's foremost crystal designers, Lalique offers glassware, decanters, candleholders, bowls, vases, and other high-quality crystal items.

11 Rue Royale
Phone: 01-53-05-12-81
Website:
www.cristallalique.fr *or*
www.lalique.com
8th *arrondissement*
Métro: Madeleine
Cards: Accepted

Cookware and Cutlery

E. DEHILLERIN
Serving both professional and "hobby" cooks, E. Dehillerin sells copper pots and pans, carbon and stainless steel knives, pastry utensils, and tableware.

18 Rue Coquillière
Phone: 01-42-36-53-13
Website: www.e-dehillerin.fr
1st *arrondissement*
Métro: Les-Halles
Cards: Accepted

LAGUIOLE ILE SAINT-LOUIS
Laguiole specializes in high-quality, sometimes exotic cutlery, as well as corkscrews and other wine-opening implements.

35 Rue des Deux-Ponts
Phone: 01-43-29-10-57
Website: www.laguiole.com
4th *arrondissement*
Métro: Pont-Marie
Cards: Accepted

Table Linens and Other Textiles

D. PORTHAULT
This store carries luxurious table linens, bed linens, quilts and coverlets, towels, and unique accessories, many in vibrant prints.

50 Avenue Montaigne
Phone: 01-47-20-75-25
Website: www.dporthault.com
8th *arrondissement*
Métro: Alma-Marceau
Cards: Accepted

PIERRE FREY
In addition to table linen, bedspreads, bedding, and fabrics, Pierre Frey offers furniture and extensive home accessories.

2 bis Rue de Furstenberg
Phone: 01-46-33-73-00
Website: www.pierrefrey.com
6th *arrondissement*
Métro: St.-Germain-des-Prés
Cards: Accepted

$$$ SAVE SOME MONEY $$$

During the weekends, as you stroll along the streets of Paris, be sure to keep your eye out for handmade signs saying "Brocante." These are spur-of-the moment flea markets that crop up in town squares. On recent trips, I've seen them next to Hôtel de Ville (Hôtel-de-Ville métro) and in Place du Marché St.-Honoré (Tuileries métro). There were many things I was tempted to purchase, including china, silverware, antique jewelry, interesting French bric-a-brac, oil paintings, children's toys, you name it. The prices are very good at these flea markets because the sellers are not professional antique dealers—they're just Parisians selling items that they no longer need. You will have to pay for your finds in euros.

Auction Houses

Many beautiful items for the home—from furniture and tapestries to ceramics and paintings—can be found at Paris auctions. Since the mid-1800s, Drouot has been the major Paris auction house, with several events being held every day. In their words, "Drouot is a magic museum open to all." But the auctions are conducted in French. You can view items the day before or at 11:00 AM on the day of the auction. Check Drouot's website to see if any upcoming sales are of interest to you. I'm told some paintings can be "won" for as little as 100 euros if there's no serious bidding competition, but in general, you won't find many deals here, although it's interesting to see this slice of Parisian life up close. The company's two main locations are listed below.

**HOTEL DES VENTES DROUOT—
RICHELIEU**
9 Rue Drouot
Phone: 01-48-00-20-20
Website: www.drouot.com
9th *arrondissement*
Métro: Richelieu-Drouot
Cards: Accepted

**HOTEL DES VENTES DROUOT—
MONTMARTRE**
64 Rue Doudeauville
Phone: 01-48-00-20-99
Website: www.drouot.com
18th *arrondissement*
Métro: Marcadet-Poissonniers
Cards: Accepted

FLEA MARKETS

Known as *marchés aux puces,* flea markets first appeared in Paris in 1890 as a means of selling used clothing and bedding. The selection and quality of the goods has vastly improved since then. My Parisian friends have made valuable finds, including paintings, old watches, and antique furniture.

Flea markets are generally open Saturday through Monday, but it's best to go early on Saturday before the good items are snatched up by professional antique hunters. Some vendors do not accept credit cards, so be sure to carry euros for your purchases. And don't forget to bargain on the price.

LES PUCES DE SAINT-OUEN
Known to regulars as Les Puces (The Fleas)—and sometimes called Clignancourt because of its location—Les Puces de Saint-Ouen features over 3,500 dealers, making it the biggest flea market in the world. The 2,000 antique dealers have permanent stands, while another 1,500 dealers display their goods on tables or from the backs of cars and trucks. Prices range from a few euros to astronomical figures for authenticated antiques. As you enter from the direction of the Porte-de-Clignancourt métro stop, you will have to walk past a few blocks of street vendors before you get to the real market. It opens on Saturday at 9:00 AM, on Sunday at 10:00 AM, and on Monday at 11:00 AM.

140 Rue des Rosiers
Phone: 01-40-12-32-58
Website:
www.parispuces.com
18th *arrondissement*
Métro: Porte-de-
Clignancourt
Cards: Accepted

French Posters and Prints

Among the many inexpensive decorative items that Paris has to offer, my favorites include the posters available at art galleries and the old prints sold by *bouquinistes* (bookstalls) along the Seine. These finds can be framed and used to add a distinctive French touch to your home.

As you walk past Paris shop windows, you'll see posters advertising current art gallery exhibits. When you spot one you like, make note of where the exhibit is being held. Art galleries are sprinkled throughout the city but are concentrated near Avenue des Champs-Elysées, on Rue St.-Honoré, and on the Left Bank near the Seine River. Their exhibition posters generally sell for 10 to 20 euros each.

Bouquinistes are the green stalls that run along both sides of the Seine River, near the Louvre and Notre Dame. They specialize in secondhand books but also sell attractive antique prints, old postcards, and other items that make lovely souvenirs, gifts, and decorations.

PORTE DE VANVES

Avenue Georges-Lafenestre
14th *arrondissement*
Métro: Porte-de-Vanves
Cards: Not Accepted

A much smaller flea market than Les Puces, Porte de Vanves runs only a few blocks and consists mainly of temporary tables that display silver, paintings, ceramics, art, jewelry, and small furniture. The advantage is that the métro stop is only a couple of blocks away, and the market is not overwhelming. A French artist friend comes here to pick up pieces for his home; he found an old map he sold to Sotheby's for ten times what he paid for it. This market is open Saturday and Sunday at 10:00 AM.

Enhance Your Home With French Style

On every trip to Paris, I bring back souvenirs that stir warm memories and reflect newly acquired tastes. And I've found that it's not necessary to spend a lot of money to add color, romance, and French flair to my home. Creating an inviting environment can be as simple as splurging on a beautiful vase and filling it with fresh flowers, buying a set of linen napkins to use when entertaining, or indulging in a scented candle for the bedroom or bath.

Good hunting!

8. Les Sports et Les Excursions

Enjoy the Great Outdoors

Paris is known far and wide as being one of the most attractive cities in the world, and the French spend a good deal of resources keeping it beautifully maintained. Skillfully designed gardens and parks create the perfect setting for a leisurely stroll, a brisk run, or a gourmet picnic. Add to that the city's many sporting events and it's clear that Paris is a place where natives and tourists alike can revel in the great outdoors.

This chapter begins by looking at the glorious parks and gardens that you'll find in and around Paris. It then fills you in on spectator sports such as the French Open and the Tour de France. Finally, you'll learn about outdoor activities in which you can participate during your stay. Whether you want to relax with a book under a chestnut tree, challenge a friend to a game of tennis, or stroll down a garden path with that special someone, the time you spend in Paris' great outdoors is sure to be a memorable part of your trip.

Jardin des Tuileries.

GARDENS

Paris has three beautifully landscaped and well-tended gardens in the *centre de la ville* (center of the city). The large Jardin des Tuileries (Tuileries Garden) is on the Right Bank, next to the Louvre; the more intimate Jardin du Palais Royal (Palais Royal Garden) is a few blocks away, sheltered from the noise of street traffic; and the Jardin du Luxembourg (Luxembourg Garden) is on the Left Bank, in Saint-Germain-des-Prés. These *jardins* are smaller than the parks discussed on page 144, and because they are located in the heart of the city, it's easy to visit them after touring a museum, before a shopping trip, or whenever the spirit moves you. They each have received my heart rating ♥, indicating they are all great choices for a romantic interlude.

In addition to the three gardens highlighted in this chapter, there are many small neighborhood squares with shade trees, benches, and well-tended flower beds that you will pass during your sightseeing. By design, Paris has more green space than any other major city in the world. Two of these tiny parks are located on the Ile de la Cité island in the Seine River—Square du Vert-Galant is at the western tip, and there is a lovely small park right behind Notre Dame. You are sure to see and enjoy many other lovely grounds, as well.

JARDIN DES TUILERIES ♥

The Tuileries Garden, built for "Sun King" Louis XIV in the 1600s, is adjacent to the Louvre, which was the king's residence. The garden's landscape artist, André Le Nôtre, also designed the beautiful grounds of Versailles. This is the most central garden in Paris, stretching along the River Seine from the Louvre to Place de la Concorde, where you'll find Musée de l'Orangerie (details on page 84). Because of its location, this is also the most visited of Paris' gardens.

1st *arrondissement*
Métro: Tuileries and Concorde

The Tuileries covers about sixty-three acres and includes several fountains, two large basins, and many sculptures, including some new pieces that were added in the 1990s. A few steps from Musée de l'Orangerie, just on the other side of the garden's entrance from Place de la Concorde, is a nicely stocked small boutique of museum gifts and cards. There is also a reasonably priced outdoor café in the middle of the Tuileries Garden that offers light meals and drinks at casual tree-shaded tables. Conveniently, there is a new footbridge over the River Seine, linking the Tuileries to Musée d'Orsay on the other side.

JARDIN DU LUXEMBOURG ♥

Located in the heart of Saint-Germain-des-Prés, this sixty-acre oasis is a wonderful option for a few hours' respite from the bustle of the city. At the center of the park is an octagonal pond known as the *Grand Bassin*. It is framed by rows of well-manicured trees and plenty of lovely walking paths, some showcasing interesting statues in tribute to historical French luminaries. In warm weather, there are puppet shows, pony rides, and a small café that serves drinks and light snacks on a terrace overlooking the pond.

PALAIS DU LUXEMBOURG
15 Rue de Vaugirard
Phone: 01-44-54-19-49
(to reserve a tour)
Website: http://www.senat.fr/visite
6th *arrondissement*
Métro: Luxembourg
Cards: Accepted

The *Palais du Luxembourg*, located on the north end of the garden, was built in the seventeenth century for Queen Marie de Medici, and it is now occupied by the French Senate. The palace is open the first Saturday of each month, and can be toured only by reservation. (See the phone number on page 142.) Next to the palace is the Musée du Luxembourg, which features revolving exhibitions.

MUSEE DU LUXEMBOURG
19 Rue de Vaugirard
Phone: 01-40-13-62-00
Website: www.musee duluxembourg.fr.
6th *arrondissement*
Métro: Luxembourg
Cards: Accepted

JARDIN DU PALAIS ROYAL ♥

1st *arrondissement*
Métro: Palais-Royal-Musée-du-Louvre and Pyramides

Commissioned by Cardinal Richelieu in the seventeenth century, Palais Royal is steeped in history and intrigue. Originally, the elegant apartments facing the garden housed members of the royal court. Legend has it that the French Revolution began on the steps of Rue Montpensier, which is at one end of the garden. In the 1800s, the area fell into disrepute when it became overrun with gambling halls. Today, both the garden and the surrounding arcade have been restored to their former grace.

Since Jardin du Palais Royal is not visible from the nearby streets, but is entered on foot by passageways, this gem is not well known by tourists, but is a favorite haunt of Parisians. Visitors are struck by the large central fountain surrounded by rows of lime trees. Beautiful statues are found throughout the grounds. The arcade includes interesting curio shops, trendy designer boutiques, and a café with outdoor tables facing the garden. Le Grand Véfour (page 97), a formal restaurant that has been a Paris landmark for decades, is located at the far end of the garden, on Rue de Beaujolais.

Paris Beaches

If you're traveling to Paris in the summer, you may think that you'll miss out on beach-going during your stay. Not true! Since 2002, every summer, the City of Paris has trucked in tons of sand and built artificial beaches along the River Seine. Known as *Paris Plage* (Paris Beach), this project has grown to involve the construction of three beaches that include umbrellas, deck chairs, drink stands, misting fountains, mini-pools, and even palm trees. At night, there are free outdoor concerts. The most central *plage* is on the Right Bank, starting at the Louvre and running east to the Pont de Sully bridge. The other two beaches are farther from the center of the city. One of them (La Villette) is dedicated to water sports and provides kayaks, pedal boats, and sailboats.

Unlike the beaches in the south of France where "anything goes," these Seine-side beaches are subject to the Paris dress code, which requires women to wear tops in public. So if you're thinking about eliminating that tan line, you'll have to do that somewhere else.

Paris beaches are open from the last week in July through most of August, from 8:00 AM to midnight.

PARKS

Two large parks, Bois de Boulogne and Bois de Vincennes, frame Paris at opposite ends—Bois de Boulogne to the west, and Bois de Vincennes to the east. Napoleon III commissioned their development in the mid-nineteenth century. *Bois* means "woods," and both of these parks have miles of forest with paths for strolling and bicycling, châteaux from former royal hunting days, flower gardens, and tables for picnics. This is a wonderful way to spend a a few hours surrounded by nature in a setting very similar to what French royalty and their guests enjoyed centuries ago.

BOIS DE BOULOGNE ♥

Running along the western edge of the sixteenth *arrondisse-ment,* Bois de Boulogne is considered the more fashionable park of the two. Covering more than 2,000 acres, it is also enormous—more than twice the size of New York's Central Park. In addition to the forests and lakes, there are two courses for horse races, and Roland Garros tennis center is on the edge of the park. On weekends, the park hums with activity, from jogging to biking, boat rowing, and picnicking. (To learn more about biking in the park, see page 147.) One of the loveliest areas in the Bois is Parc de Bagatelle, which has formal rose gardens, manicured lawns, and a restaurant surrounded by oak trees. (For information on the restaurant, see the inset "Les Jardins de Bagatelle" below.)

16th *arrondissement*
Métro: Porte-Maillot and Porte-Dauphine

Les Jardins de Bagatelle

One of the most wonderful features of Paris is that no matter where you go, you are likely to find superb food in an enchanting setting. Located in the midst of the Parc de Bagatelle—a large Anglo-Chinese-style garden in Paris' sprawling Bois de Boulogne—is a gourmet restaurant housed in former horse stables (you wouldn't know that now). Les Jardins de Bagatelle is a lovely place to stop for lunch or afternoon tea after enjoying a romantic stroll in the park.

42 Route de Sèvres à Neuilly
Phone: 01-40-67-98-29
Website:
   www.lesjardinsdebagatelle.fr
16th *arrondissement*
Métro: Pont-de–Neuilly (then take Bus 43)
Cards: Accepted

BOIS DE VINCENNES

Located on the eastern edge of Paris, Bois de Vincennes covers nearly 2,500 acres, making it larger than the Bois de Boulogne. Vincennes has miles of walking paths, a large manmade lake that is popular for boating, a beautiful flower garden (Parc Floral, which charges a small admission fee), and a zoo. On the north end of the woods, you'll find a fourteenth-century medieval fortress, Château de Vincennes, which is considered one of the best-preserved castles in Europe.

12th *arrondissement*
Métro: Château-de-Vincennes and Porte-Dorée

ATTENDING A SPORTING EVENT

If you love sports—or if you are traveling with a sports enthusiast—Paris has more than its share of exciting spectator events, including some that are world-class. Attending a horse race or a tennis match is a great way to experience the French culture firsthand while making memories that will last a lifetime. In most cases, you'll need to buy tickets before your departure for Paris, either on the Internet or with the help of your hotel concierge.

Horse Races

Paris has two racecourses, or *hippodromes,* Auteuil and Longchamp. Both tracks are located in Bois de Boulogne, and each has a restaurant. Hippodrome de l'Auteuil is designed exclusively for steeplechasing and is renowned for the diversity of its jumps. Hippodrome de Longchamp is used for flat-racing and is best known for the elegant Prix de l'Arc de Triomphe race, which takes place in early October. This is such a celebrated course that its races were a favorite subject of Impressionists Edouard Manet and Edgar Degas. The French still love horse racing and dress well for the occasion.

HIPPODROME DE L'AUTEUIL
Bois de Boulogne
Route des Lacs
Phone: 01-40-71-47-47
16th *arrondissement*
Métro: Porte-d'Auteuil
Cards: Accepted

HIPPODROME DE LONGCHAMP ♥
Bois de Boulogne
Route des Tribunes
Phone: 01-44-30-75-00
16th *arrondissement*
Métro: Suresnes-Longchamps
Cards: Accepted

Team Sports

Within Paris, there are two large venues for team sports. The Palais Omnisports de Paris-Bercy, located in the twelfth *arrondissement,* is a large indoor stadium that hosts a number of competitions, including hockey, basketball, boxing, gymnastics, and show jumping. Parc des Princes, found in Paris' sixteenth *arrondissement,* is the home of the French soccer team Paris Saint-Germain. It also features rugby matches and is the venue for many big-name concerts.

**PALAIS OMNISPORTS DE
  PARIS-BERCY**
8 Boulevard de Bercy
Phone: 01-44-68-44-68
Website: www.bercy.fr
12th *arrondissement*
Métro: Bercy
Cards: Accepted

PARC DES PRINCES
24 Rue du Commandant Guilbaud
Phone: 01-47-43-72-54
Website: www.leparcdesprinces.fr
16th *arrondissement*
Métro: Porte-de-St.-Cloud and
  Porte-d'Auteuil
Cards: Accepted

Tennis Matches

Located adjacent to the Bois de Boulogne on the western periphery of Paris, the Roland Garros Stadium (Stade Roland Garros) plays host to the French Open, which starts in late May and runs for two weeks. The twenty-one-acre complex includes twenty courts and three large stadiums. Seats sell out well in advance, so you'll need to book ahead. If you're a true tennis fan, you may want to stop at the stadium's Musée de la FFT (Museum of the French Federation of Tennis), a multimedia tennis museum that's open daily, except on Mondays.

ROLAND GARROS
2 Avenue Gordon Bennett
Phone: 01-47-43-48-00
Website: www.rolandgarros.com (tickets)
www.fft.fr/site-tenniseum (museum)
16th *arrondissement*
Métro: Porte-d'Auteuil (then take tournament bus)
Cards: Accepted

The Tour de France

The first Tour de France was held in 1903. More than a century later, it is the most famous bicycle race in the world. The course of the three-week over-2,000-mile race changes every year, but the contest always ends in Paris, along the Champs-Elysées. There, it creates quite a spectacle with its world-class contestants and cavalcade of colorful floats and vehicles. The race is run every July and you can view it anywhere along its route. Check the official website (www.letour.fr) for dates and other details.

A Fat Tire Bike Tour.

ENGAGING IN YOUR FAVORITE SPORT

With so much beautiful outdoor space, Paris is a wonderful place for visitors to walk, run, cycle, play a game of tennis, or go ice skating in winter. Here are some great options. And if you prefer to get your exercise indoors, especially during colder weather, two gyms/sports clubs are suggested.

Bicycling

Bicycles, known as *vélos,* are a wonderful way to get some exercise while touring a park or exploring new surroundings, and Paris is an exceptionally bike-friendly city. Some lanes have been set aside for bicycles alone. But keep in mind that you must follow the traffic rules, and you could get ticketed if you violate them.

Chapter 2 explored Vélib, Paris's system of self-service bicycle rentals. (See page 56.) This is the most convenient way to rent (*louer*) bicycles in Paris, because you can turn them in at any Vélib station along your route.

Bois de Boulogne, discussed on page 144, has over twenty miles of bicycle routes and is a favorite destination of Paris cyclists. You can rent bicycles at two locations in the park—on Avenue du Mahatma Gandhi (the Les-Sablons métro), across from the Porte Sablons entrance to the Jardin d'Acclimatation amusement park, and at the northern end of Lac Inférieur, near the Pavillon Royal (the Avenue-Foch métro).

If you want to combine cycling with sightseeing, consider taking a bike tour of the city. Here are my two favorites.

BIKE ABOUT TOURS

This three-and-a-half-hour bicycle tour starts at Notre Dame and is one of the most popular activities with American tourists. It runs ten months a year, from mid-February through mid-December, "rain or shine." You will pass secret gardens and passageways, learn about French history, and see major sights, all at a "leisurely" pace that is advertised as easy for every level of bike rider. The cost is 30 euros, and the groups are small (no more than twelve people), so you should reserve ahead. This is a fun activity for families.

4 Rue Lobau
Phone: 06-18-80-84-92
Website: www.bikeabout
tours.com
4th *arrondissement*
Métro: Hôtel-de-Ville
Cards: Accepted

FAT TIRE BIKE TOURS ♥

The Day Bike Tour—which is only one of several options offered—starts at the Eiffel Tower and includes commentary on Napoleon's Tomb, Musée Rodin, Musée d'Orsay, the Tuleries Garden, the Louvre, and Place de la Concorde, as well as other sights. It lasts four hours and costs 28 euros. When the company's bicycles are not out on tour, they are available for rental.

Phone: 1-866-614-6218
(in the U.S.)
01-56-58-10-54 (in Paris)
Website: www.fattirebike
tours.com/paris
15th *arrondissement*
Métro: Bir-Hakeim
Cards: Accepted

Exercise Clubs and Swimming

There are numerous gyms in Paris, but their day passes can be costly. If exercise is an important part of your life, your best bet may be to stay at a large hotel that offers some exercise equipment and steam and sauna rooms at no extra cost. But if your hotel doesn't have those amenities and you're aching for a workout, here are two good choices: Aquaboulevard and Club Med Gym. I particularly recommend Aquaboulevard, a sports complex with a wide variety of activities. True to its name, it has an impressive aquatic indoor park with large swimming pools featuring exotic trees, slides, and waves, but it also offers tennis, squash, and other options. This is the largest complex of its kind in the city.

AQUABOULEVARD
4 Rue Louis-Armand
Phone: 01-40-60-10-00
Website: www.aquaboulevard.com
15th *arrondissement*
Métro: Balard and Porte-de-Versailles
Cards: Accepted
Cost: 20–25 euros for a day pass
  (depending on the season); certain
  activities may involve additional fees.

**CLUB MED GYM—CHAMPS
  ELYSEES**
26 Rue de Berri
Phone: 01-43-59-04-58
Website: http://www.clubmedgym.com
  /club/champs-elysees
8th *arrondissement*
Métro: George-V
Cards: Accepted
Cost: 10 euros per hour.

Ice Skating

In the wintertime, the city of Paris welcomes the holidays and the blast of cold weather by setting up ice skating rinks for the public. Free ice skating is offered in front of the Hôtel de Ville, which is Paris' City Hall, and at the railroad station at Montparnasse. In both locations, you can rent skates for about 5 euros. After a round of skating, you can catch your breath and enjoy a hot drink at one of the many nearby cafés.

HOTEL DE VILLE
Place de l'Hôtel-de-Ville
4th *arrondissement*
Métro: Hôtel-de-Ville

MONTPARNASSE
Place Raoul-Dautry
15th *arrondissement*
Métro: Montparnasse-Bienvenüe

Tennis

Your best bet for a fun tennis outing is Aquaboulevard, which is mentioned above. This sports complex offers indoor and outdoor courts, so you won't be hampered by the weather, and also provides racquets and balls. Be sure to call ahead for court time.

$$$ SAVE SOME MONEY $$$

A good way to enjoy the parks and the great outdoors is to take a walking tour. Amazingly, Sandmans New Paris Tours offers daily free walking tours that last three and a half hours and cover many of the major sights. The only payment is a tip of your choosing at the end. Tours run twice a day, starting at 11:00 AM and 1:00 PM at Place Saint-Michel—just across the Seine from Notre Dame. Be prepared for a lot of walking, since the tour travels from Notre Dame, past the Louvre and Place de la Concorde, up to the Arc de Triomphe, and over to the Eiffel Tower. Check the website at right to make a reservation.

**SANDMANS
NEW PARIS TOURS**
http://www.newparistours.com

Romantic Horse Carriage Ride

It may sound a bit touristy, but a horse-and-carriage ride through Paris is a charming way to revel in the romance of the city while touring some of its top sights. Starting at 1:00 PM and departing four times each afternoon from the Eiffel Tower, the comfortable carriage can accommodate up to four people. If you and your companion want to enjoy the carriage alone, it will cost 170 euros for a one-hour ride. If you include another couple, the price will be split among four people. The horse is normally off on Mondays and Tuesdays.

The tour companies listed below—both of which can arrange your carriage ride—suggest that you make your booking at least forty-eight hours ahead of time, so this can't be a spontaneously romantic choice unless you want to take your chances and try at the last minute. You can book a Viator tour through the website or by phone from the States before your trip. If you choose Experience Paris, you can call from your hotel, but be aware that this company's website is a little bit tricky to navigate.

EXPERIENCE PARIS
Phone: 01-45-51-53-80
Website: http://manstouch.com/travel/
   horse-and-carriage.html
15th *arrondissement*
Métro: Bir-Hakeim
Cards: Accepted

VIATOR
Phone: 888-651-9785 (in the US)
Website: http://www.viator.com/tours/
   Paris/Romantic-Horse-and-Carriage-Ride-
   through-Paris/d479-3061HORSE
15th *arrondissement*
Métro: Bir-Hakeim
Cards: Accepted

Walking and Jogging

You will probably be doing a lot of walking during your visit, because it's the easiest and most enjoyable way to see Paris. Virtually any route you take will be charming. The most picturesque gardens and parks are listed at the beginning of this chapter on pages 142 to 144. If you would like to learn about Paris history and culture while you stroll, check out Context travel's scholar-led walking tours. (See the inset on page 79.) There are even photo tours so you can hone your camera skills as you enjoy the beauty of the city. (See page 178 of Chapter 11.)

Jogging is popular in Paris, although it is limited to certain parks and to paths along the Seine River. You won't have the spectacle we have in the States of joggers running down busy boulevards at the height of rush-hour traffic inhaling fumes. The French tend to be more "correct" about such things. If you are in Paris on a Sunday, you will be able to enjoy a peaceful run along the riverbanks, which are closed to vehicles from 9:00 AM to 5:00 AM. Enter on the Left Bank at Quai Branly or Quai Anatole France, or on the Right Bank at Quai des Tuileries and Pont Charles de Gaulle.

Join Parisians Outdoors

Paris boasts some of the most beautiful gardens and parks in the world, as well as world-famous sporting events and well-equipped health clubs—countless opportunities to unwind and relax. Whether you spend an afternoon in one of the city's breathtaking gardens, observe a tennis match at Roland Garros Stadium, or bicycle past centuries-old monuments, this is bound to be an exhilarating change of pace from shopping and museum hopping.

9. La Nuit

Romantic Paris by Night

Once the sun goes down, a different Paris comes alive. Cleverly designed floodlights provide dramatic illumination of historic monuments, and the Eiffel Tower sparkles with 20,000 lights. Even ordinary buildings seem to glow after a Paris dusk. The result is magical and *very* romantic.

If you are traveling with a loved one, you'll find that Paris at night offers endless ways to keep the flames burning brightly. If you simply want to have a good time with friends, you'll discover that this cosmopolitan city offers a wide array of choices for spending an entertaining evening out.

This chapter includes intimate bars where you can cozy up with your sweetheart; jazz clubs where you can groove to the beat or kick up your heels on the dance floor; nighttime tours—by boat, bus, bicycle, or foot; elegant nightclubs, many of which serve a late supper; sexy spectacles such as the Moulin Rouge's quintessentially Parisian cancan dancers; and movie theaters, many of which feature American blockbusters (with French subtitles) along with French films.

Throughout the chapter, a heart rating ♥ indicates my top recommendations. If you are interested in evening cultural performances, such as the ballet, see page 87 of Chapter 4. Listings of restaurants and wine bars begin on page 95 of Chapter 5. Wherever you choose to spend your evening, Paris is guaranteed to keep you up past your bedtime.

Paris' Night Lights

The beautiful lighting of Paris did not occur by chance. In 1981, the city created a special department to focus on improving the view at night. At that time, buildings were lit by large spotlights, which did not enhance the architecture or add theatrical ambience. Today, the department includes a staff of thirty specialists who are responsible for the artistic illumination of hundreds of monuments, centuries-old government buildings, and numerous bridges over the Seine.

There are a few theories about how Paris came to be known as the City of Light. One is that the name was derived from the spectacular electrical light displays at Paris' World's Fair of 1900. Another traces its origin to the city's early adoption of street lighting. Whatever the reason, Paris truly is the City of Light and—day or night—is one of the most beautiful places in the world.

INTIMATE BARS

If you want to enjoy a good drink and quiet conversation in an elegant atmosphere, visit one of Paris' intimate bars. Most of the establishments listed below are found in luxurious hotels that cater to pampered clientele. These are some of the most stylishly appointed spaces in Paris, and the service is first-class. You will pay dearly for the drinks—about 25 euros each—but in this case, it's worth the splurge to enjoy good company in an unforgettable setting.

You'll need to dress appropriately; jeans are frowned upon and jackets for men are preferred, and in some cases required. Most hotel bars serve a good selection of appetizers and light dishes, so you can grab a late-night bite as you savor your wine or cocktail.

LE BAR DU PLAZA ATHENEE

Voted "Best Bar" at the Virtuoso Awards, this one is so hot that it's cold—the illuminated bar is sculpted entirely of sandblasted glass to resemble an iceberg. There is also a separate area with large leather chairs. This bar gets busy, so if you want a seat, look the part and get there early. On Thursdays through Saturdays, a DJ spins electro-rock music after 11:00 PM, so if you're looking for intimacy, arrive earlier.

25 Avenue Montaigne
Phone: 01-53-67-66-55
Website: www.plaza-athenee-paris.com
8th *arrondissement*
Métro: Franklin-D.-Roosevelt and Alma-Marceau
Cards: Accepted

THE BAR HEMINGWAY

Located in the Hôtel Ritz, the Bar Hemingway, as its name implies, was one of the author's favorite "watering holes" in Paris and keeps his memory alive by displaying twenty-five of his photographs on the walls. The elegant décor has been restored to resemble the original wood paneling, and leather armchairs provide comfortable seating. Service is impeccable and drinks are delicious. (For information on another Hôtel Ritz bar, see page 154.)

15 Place Vendôme
Phone: 01-43-16-33-65 *or* 01-43-16-30-30
Website: www.ritzparis.com
1st *arrondissement*
Métro: Tuileries and Madeleine
Cards: Accepted

Harry's New York Bar

For Americans, Harry's Bar is one of Paris' most famous landmarks. Most notably, Ernest Hemingway and F. Scott Fitzgerald were regulars. Drinks are pricey, the quality of service is intermittent, and wine is not served. But the walls do evoke a sense of history, and the intimate downstairs cellar has live piano music Tuesday through Saturday from 10:00 PM to 2:00 AM. This establishment may not be on my "A" list, but if you're in the mood for an American-style bar with American-style cocktails, you may want to pay Harry's a call.

5 Rue Daunou
Phone: 01-42-61-71-14
Website: www.harrys-bar.fr
2nd *arrondissement*
Métro: Opéra
Cards: Accepted

LE BAR 228 DU MEURICE ♥
My favorite hotel bar is at the luxurious Meurice near Place de la Concorde. Le Bar 228, named for its street address, is all you could seek for a romantic *rendez-vous* or a memorable evening among friends. The setting is intimate and luxurious. Comfortable leather chairs are arranged in cozy groupings; beautiful paintings adorn the wood-paneled walls; and the service and elegant presentation are impeccable. Live jazz piano every evening after 7:00 PM completes the mood.

228 Rue de Rivoli
Phone: 01-44-58-10-66
Website: http://www.lemeurice.com/bar-228
1st *arrondissement*
Métro: Concorde and Tuileries
Cards: Accepted

L'HOTEL BAR ♥
This is the perfect place to take a break at the end of a day of sightseeing, or to grab an after-dinner drink if you're in this area of the Left Bank. L'Hôtel was renovated by famed designer Jacques Garcia, and it's yummy—the sumptuous fabrics in warm colors are seductive and inviting. The bar area is very small and intimate, with only a few tables, so you could have trouble getting a seat if it's a busy night.

13 Rue des Beaux-Arts
Phone: 01-44-41-99-00
Website: www.l-hotel.com
6th *arrondissement*
Métro: St.-Germain-des-Prés
Cards: Accepted

HOTEL RAPHAEL BAR
A few steps from the Arc de Triomphe, this luxury hotel has a lovely *Bar Anglais* (English Bar) decorated in warm wood paneling and red-velvet upholstered chairs reminiscent of a private British club. Besides aperitifs and nightcaps, the bar offers lunch and afternoon tea.

17 Avenue Kléber
Phone: 01-53-64-32-00
Website: www.raphael-hotel.com
16th *arrondissement*
Métro: Kléber and Charles-de-Gaulle-Etoile
Cards: Accepted

HOTEL REGINA ENGLISH BAR ♥
You won't find this establishment on any other list of top bars, and that's one of the reasons I like it. This well-kept secret is intimate (read "darkly lit with close seating"), attractive, and well-located. Adjacent to the Louvre Museum and Tuileries Garden, the English Bar is a good choice for a quiet drink and a cozy *tête-à-tête*. Coffered ceilings, a polished oak bar, well-stocked bookshelves, nicely upholstered couches and armchairs, and good service all add up to a heart rating.

2 Place des Pyramides
Phone: 01-42-60-31-10
Website: www.regina-hotel.com
1st *arrondissement*
Métro: Tuileries and Palais-Royal-Musée-du-Louvre
Cards: Accepted

PARK HYATT PARIS—VENDOME BAR
Adjacent to Place Vendôme, this is in an ideal spot for an afternoon cocktail and a favorite watering hole among hip Parisians, who are drawn to the contemporary décor and the wide variety of whiskies, champagnes, and cocktails. Twice a month, the head barman offers "Cocktail Courses." Eight participants learn to mix two cocktails and enjoy their final products with a tasting of tapas plates. The cost, a pricey 140 euros per person, includes a booklet of cocktail recipes.

5 Rue de la Paix
Phone: 01-58-71-12-34
Website: www.paris.vendome.hyatt.com
2nd *arrondissement*
Métro: Opéra and Madeleine
Cards: Accepted

LE RITZ BAR ♥

My top recommendation for the Hôtel Ritz—which also offers the stylish Bar Hemingway, described on page 152—is this elegant bar/nightclub, which has a separate entrance at the back of the hotel on Rue Cambon. It is very atmospheric with sumptuous red décor and flatteringly dim lighting. Le Ritz Bar is open Tuesday through Saturday, but the best night is Thursday, when the beautiful people come out and a DJ rocks the room with trendy music until 2:00 in the morning. This bar has no cover charge, but drinks are a pricey 30 euros.

38 Rue Cambon
Phone: 01-43-16-33-65
or 01-43-16-30-30
Website:
   www.ritzparis.com
1st *arrondissement*
Métro: Madeleine and
   Concorde
Cards: Accepted

JAZZ CLUBS

Jazz clubs are among the best places to spend a fun evening in Paris. Good jazz is revered in France; in times gone by, American jazz musicians found more success in France than they did in the United States. Today, there are still a number of American jazz groups performing in Paris, and if you're not familiar with French jazz performers, this will be a fine opportunity to hear a new group and perhaps pick up their CD as a souvenir.

Small atmospheric clubs are found in almost every neighborhood. Many serve meals, so you can enjoy a full evening in one spot. They usually have two seatings (starting around 10:00 PM) and a cover charge, which is sometimes included in the price of the first drink. If you dine at the club, the fee is normally waived.

If you are looking for a specific style of jazz or you want to learn who will be performing during your stay in Paris, visit the Paris Jazz Club website at www.parisjazzclub.net, which lists most of the Paris clubs. Click on "Calendar" to see the bands that are playing each night, or try "Sort by Style" to choose from among thirty options, ranging from Be Bop and Blues to New Orleans and Swing. The "Sort by Club" menu lists the venues in alphabetical order. The clubs that are listed below are conveniently located in the center of the city and are my top recommendations.

PARIS JAZZ CLUB
Website:
   www.parisjazzclub.net

CAFÉ LAURENT ♥

Located in the lovely Hotel d'Aubusson, Café Laurent comes alive on Thursday, Friday, and Saturday nights when a jazz trio performs. You don't have to reserve in advance, but it's best to get there by 9:00 PM so you're sure to get a seat. There is no cover charge, and drinks cost 14 euros. This is a very romantic venue with plush seating at small wooden tables where you can enjoy good drinks, great service, and lovely music—a hidden gem at a reasonable price.

33 Rue Dauphine
Phone: 01-43-29-03-33
Website: http://cafe-
   laurent.com/
6th *arrondissement*
Métro: Odéon and Pont-
   Neuf
Cards: Accepted

CAVEAU DE LA HUCHETTE ♥

Opened in the aftermath of World War II and reputed to be one of the first jazz clubs in Paris, the Caveau, with its atmospheric stone walls and vaulted ceilings, has been used as a set for several French films. Located near Notre Dame, this club is geared more to casual jazz enthusiasts than to aficionados; some nights feature swing dancing. The cover charge is 14 euros and drinks are a reasonable 6 to 8 euros each. Check the website to learn which acts will be playing during your stay.

5 Rue de la Huchette
Phone: 01-43-26-65-05
Website:
www.caveaudelahuchette.fr
5th *arrondissement*
Métro: St.-Michel and Cité
Cards: Accepted

DUC DES LOMBARDS ♥

One of the most famous jazz clubs in Paris because of its big-name acts and intimate surroundings, Duc des Lombards is on a "jazz street" that has two other clubs nearby. Check the website for a calendar of upcoming performances and Internet specials, which discount the usual 30-euro entrance fee. The dinner menu includes casual dishes at good prices, such as a salmon club sandwich for 11 euros.

42 Rue des Lombards
Phone: 01-42-33-22-88
Website:
www.ducdeslombards.fr
1st *arrondissement*
Métro: Châtelet
Cards: Accepted

JAZZ CLUB ETOILE

Located at the top of Le Meridien Etoile hotel, opposite the Palais des Congrès, Jazz Club Etoile is larger and more formal than the other clubs listed. Over the years, B.B. King, Cab Calloway, Fats Domino, Count Basie, Lionel Hampton, and many other jazz greats have performed here. Admission is 32 euros and includes the first drink, or, for about 60 euros, you can opt for a *prix fixe* dinner menu that includes wine and champagne.

81 Boulevard Gouvion Saint-Cyr
Phone: 01-40-68-30-42
Website: www.jazzclub-paris.com
17th *arrondissement*
Métro: Porte-Maillot
Cards: Accepted

LE PETIT JOURNAL SAINT MICHEL

Located across from the Luxembourg Garden, this jazz club and restaurant specializes in New Orleans jazz. It holds only eighty people, so it's best to reserve ahead. A three-course dinner is 50 euros per person and includes one drink and admittance to the performance. Admission for the jazz alone is 20 euros and includes the first drink.

71 Boulevard St.-Michel
Phone: 01-43-26-28-59
Website: www.petitjournal-saintmichel.com
5th *arrondissement*
Métro: Cluny-La-Sorbonne
Cards: Accepted

SUNSET-SUNSIDE ♥

A Parisian friend who loves jazz took me here, explaining that it's for serious jazz devotees. These are two adjoining jazz clubs, so you can "shop" for whatever group you're in the mood to hear that night. Seating is first come, first serve; the entrance fee is 25 euros and includes the first drink. The website lists 50-percent-off specials as well as free performances.

60 Rue des Lombards
Phone: 01-40-26-46-60
Website: www.sunset-sunside.com
1st *arrondissement*
Métro: Châtelet
Cards: Accepted

Paris Jazz Festivals

If you're a jazz fan, you may want to plan your Paris vacation around one of the city's jazz festivals. Each of the following events runs for a week or more and features a good selection of top musicians.

JAZZ A LA VILLETTE

Every September, the Cité de la Musique at Parc de la Villette hosts this popular festival. In addition to ticketed events for the big-name performers, there are open-air concerts in the park that are free of charge. Visit the festival website—which is updated a few months before the event—to make plans before your trip, or check out the schedule in *Pariscope* during your visit.

Parc de la Villette
Phone: 01-44-84-44-84
Website:
   www.jazzalavillette.com
19th *arrondissement*
Métro: Porte-de-la-Villette

JAZZ A SAINT-GERMAIN-DES-PRES

This free festival runs for two weeks in May at various locations, including cafés, boutiques, theaters, and churches. If you're in Paris during this time, pick up an issue of *Pariscope* to learn which musicians will be playing. The website offers a day-by-day schedule.

Website: www.festivaljazz
   saintgermainparis.com

PARIS JAZZ FESTIVAL ♥

During June and July, weekend afternoon jazz concerts are held in Parc Floral, a beautiful area in the Bois de Vincennes. There is a 5-euro admission fee to enter the park; the concert is free. Best of all, you can bring a picnic and sit on the grassy hill nearby. This festival has drawn big-name acts, including Wynton Marsalis, Joe Sample, and Randy Crawford.

Parc Floral
Phone: 01-48-76-83-01
Website:
   www.parisjazzfestival.fr
12th *arrondissement*
Métro: Château-de-
   Vincennes

Duc des Lombards Jazz Club.

MOVIE THEATERS

With over one hundred movie theaters and three hundred films playing on any given week, Paris is a great place to catch a movie after dark. Both American and French films are shown in many theaters, and old American movies are often presented in English. Here are a few good choices that are centrally located. Check the current issue of *Pariscope* to find what's playing in these and other venues throughout the city. (Note that the theater phone recordings are in French.) American movies marked "VO"—for *version originale*, or original language—are in English and have French subtitles, and French movies marked "VO" are in French. "VF" means *version française* and indicates that the movie is in French. If a French film is marked "VOST"—meaning that it's an original version with subtitles—you should be able to understand it by reading the English subtitles. Just make sure that you don't accidentally buy a ticket for an American movie that has been dubbed in French—unless you're fluent in French and figure that this would be a good way to polish up your language skills.

GAUMONT OPERA
2 Boulevard des Capucines
Phone: 08-92-69-66-96
9th *arrondissement*
Métro: Opéra
Cards: Accepted

MK2 ODEON ♥
113 Boulevard St.-Germain
Phone: 08-92-68-68-12
6th *arrondissement*
Métro: Odéon
Cards: Accepted

PUBLICIS CINEMAS
129 Avenue des Champs-Elysées
Phone: 08-92-68-90-75
8th *arrondissement*
Métro: Charles-de-Gaulle-Etoile
Cards: Accepted

UGC GEORGE V
146 Avenue des Champs-Elysées
Phone: 08-92-70-00-00
8th *arrondissement*
Métro: George-V and Charles-de-Gaulle-Etoile
Cards: Accepted

$ $ $ SAVE SOME MONEY $ $ $

If you're a movie lover and plan to visit Paris during the summer, check out the free outdoor movies shown at Parc de la Villette, in the northeast section of the city. This program runs from mid-July to late August. Movies are played in the original language—American movies are in English with French subtitles—and the show begins after dark at around 10:00 PM. You can't get much more romantic than an old-fashioned outdoor movie, so bring your own picnic, including a bottle of good French wine, and find plentiful seating on a grassy hill. Take a blanket with you, or indulge and rent chairs for about 6 euros each.

PARC DE LA VILLETTE
211 Avenue Jean Jaurès
Phone: 01-40-03-75-75
Website:
www.villette.com
19th *arrondissement*
Métro: Porte-de-la-Villette and Porte-de-Pantin

PARIS TOURS AT NIGHT

Much like the tours available by day, night tours offer a great way to see Paris' highlights. With so many different options available, you're sure to find an excursion that suits your interests and offers a fun evening. You can choose tours by boat, bus, or bicycle; tours that combine trips on a bus or bike with a cruise; or even a walking tour that provides in-depth information on the city's history and architecture (see the inset on page 160). Some bus tours will pick you up at your hotel and drop you off afterwards. Many tours are combined with dinner; for instance, you might end your outing by dining at Altitude 95, on the first level of the Eiffel Tower, or at a restaurant on the Champs-Elysées. Some of Cityrama's packages even include tickets to a cabaret performance at the Lido, the Moulin Rouge, or another venue.

My top recommendation is to take a boat cruise along the River Seine to see the beautifully illuminated monuments and historical buildings and to view the sparkling lights of the Eiffel Tower. Another great option is to take the Fat Tire Night Bike Tour, which combines a boat cruise with a bicycle trip around Paris. Should you choose a tour that includes dinner at a restaurant or seating at a show? You may prefer the ease of an arranged evening that provides transportation to all your activities. However, some people who select the combination tours feel as if they're being rushed from one activity to another, or that the meal and service are lacking because an entire group is being served en masse. Also, you can save money on cabaret tickets by buying them directly (see page 161). I suggest that you select one of the romantic restaurants listed in Chapter 5 and enjoy a boat cruise, bus tour, or cabaret show separately. This will allow you to handpick each component of your evening. Dinner cruises are another good option, even if they are a bit "touristy." Yes, there is a lot to choose from—that's the beauty of Paris!

Popular Music Concerts and Shows

Paris plays host to the world's top musical acts, including American groups that are as well-loved in France as they are in the United States. These shows are held in large stadiums and sell out quickly. While large-venue concerts aren't my top recommendations for a romantic evening, they will give you an opportunity to see favorite performers in a setting where you'll probably be the only tourist. Two major venues are Palais Omnisports de Paris-Bercy, which presents hugely popular artists like Madonna and Lady Gaga, and Le Palais des Congrès de Paris, which features French singers such as Sylvie Vartan and musicals like *Mamma Mia!*

PALAIS OMNISPORTS DE PARIS-BERCY
8 Boulevard de Bercy
Phone: 01-40-02-60-60
Website: www.bercy.fr
12th *arrondissement*
Métro: Bercy
Cards: Accepted

LE PALAIS DES CONGRES DE PARIS
2 Place de la Porte Maillot
Phone: 01-40-68-22-22
Website: www.palaisdescongres-paris.com
16th *arrondissement*
Métro: Porte-Maillot-Palais-des-Congrès
Cards: Accepted

Each of the following companies offers a range of options for touring Paris at night. (For information on bus tours by day, see the inset on page 43 of Chapter 2. For information on boat tours by day, see the inset on page 80 of Chapter 4.)

BATEAUX PARISIENS ♥
Bateaux Parisiens dinner cruises offer authentic French dishes prepared on-board by first-rate chefs. Prices start at 70 euros per person, excluding wine, for the "Paris Essential" tour. This is less expensive than Paris Connection (see below), but you will have to find your own transportation to the point of embarkation below the Eiffel Tower.

Phone: 01-76-64-14-66
Website: www.bateaux parisiens.com
15th *arrondissement*
Métro: Bir-Hakeim and Trocadéro
Cards: Accepted

CITYRAMA
Cityrama offers a myriad of night and day tours. If you don't mind riding in a big motorcoach with other tourists, the "Cruise + Illuminations"—a trip down the Seine River followed by a bus tour of illuminated monuments—is a good deal, with prices starting at 36 euros per person. Tours depart from the Cityrama office near the Louvre.

2 Rue des Pyramides
Phone: 01-44-55-61-00
Website: www.pariscityrama.com
1st *arrondissement*
Métro: Palais-Royal-Musée-du-Louvre and Pyramides
Cards: Accepted

FAT TIRE BIKE TOURS ♥
The nighttime Fat Tire bicycle tour lasts four hours and includes a one-hour boat cruise with a complimentary glass of wine, all for 28 euros. Among the tour highlights are Notre Dame, Sainte-Chapelle, the Louvre, the Champs-Elysées, and Hôtel de Ville. You meet at the south leg (*pilier sud*) of the Eiffel Tower.

Phone: 01-56-58-10-54
Website: www.FatTire BikeToursParis.com/paris
15th *arrondissement*
Métro: Bir-Hakeim and Trocadéro
Cards: Accepted

LA MARINA DE PARIS ♥
My top choice for a reasonably priced evening dinner cruise, La Marina departs from a convenient central location just below Musée d'Orsay (between the Pont Royal and Passerelle Solférino bridges). The first cruise of the evening costs 50 euros per person, and includes a glass of wine. The later cruise is 79 euros per person for the "Menu Prestige," which includes a half-bottle of wine. Plus the website is very easy to navigate.

Phone: 01-43-43-40-30
Website: www.marinade paris.com
7th *arrondissement*
Métro: Solférino
Cards: Accepted

PARIS CONNECTION TOURS
This company offers more personalized service with smaller groups. The excursions are pricier, but all evening tours include hotel pickup and return by minibus—which is the main advantage of choosing Paris Connection. The website lists many options, starting with the "Early Evening Dinner Cruise" at 105 euros per person. Jacket and tie are requested.

Phone: 01-60-70-81-12
Website: www.parisconnection.fr
Cards: Accepted

NIGHTCLUBS

Paris nightclubs are among the most exciting in the world; these people know how to party. Known as *boîtes de nuit* ("night boxes"), they are also a fun way to spend a romantic evening. If you turn to the back of the weekly *Pariscope* event guide, you'll find an up-do-date listing of many dance clubs and discos under "Paris la nuit." You'll want to get your hotel desk clerk to translate it if your French isn't up to the task. Nightlife starts late in Paris, so clubs open around midnight and don't get "hopping" until even later.

All of the clubs listed below are at the top of the scale for atmosphere and Paris glamour. Be sure to dress up to pass muster with the doorman, and to guarantee that you will be admitted, book dinner at the club beforehand. Prices run around 40 euros per person for two courses before wine, and the quality of the cuisine at all these places is extremely good. Drink prices at the clubs start at around 15 to 20 euros each. Although it's an expensive evening, clubs like these are rare, so it's worth the splurge.

L'ARC

Also mentioned in the restaurant section (see page 110), this classy restaurant/bar/club faces the Arc de Triomphe, which is striking when it's illuminated at night. The easiest way to gain admittance to the club is to reserve a table for dinner upstairs, and explain that you'd like to go to the club when your meal is over. There is no cover charge, but drinks are pricey—about 20 euros each. The DJ plays a mix of music, from disco to contemporary, and there is plenty of room on the dance floor.

12 Rue de Presbourg
Phone: 01-45-00-78-70
Website: www.larc-paris.com
16th *arrondissement*
Métro: Charles-de-Gaulle-Etoile
Cards: Accepted

A Unique Nighttime Walking Tour

If you're looking for an unusual and informative experience, consider Context travel's walking tours. Led by scholars and historians, the "Rive Gauche Evening Stroll" includes some of the most beautiful monuments while paying particular attention to small squares and quieter side streets, "where Paris' evening majesty is most discernible." Or you can take the two-hour "Le Jazz Hot" walk through the Latin Quarter to explore the "magic and history of jazz in Paris." Tours are limited to six people in each group, and the cost is 40 euros per person.

CONTEXT
14 Rue Charles V
Phone: 800-691-6036 (in US)
01-72-81-36-35 (in Paris)
Website: www.contexttravel.com/city/Paris
4th *arrondissement*
Métro: St.-Paul
Cards: Accepted

LE CABARET ♥

Le Cab, as it is known, has been a Paris late-night destination for many years. Conveniently located adjacent to the Louvre, it is still a draw for beautiful people who come to dine, dance, and mingle. Reserve dinner in the restaurant ahead of time to guarantee entrance to the club, and get ready for a night you'll never forget.

2 Place du Palais Royal
Phone: 01-58-62-56-25
Website: www.cabaret.fr
1st *arrondissement*
Métro: Palais-Royal-
   Musée-du-Louvre
Cards: Accepted

LE DANDY

Le Dandy is a "new address" on the Left Bank for those looking for a chic, fun evening. Located a few steps from the Panthéon, it attracts a young crowd of artsy types who are drawn to the inventive drinks, eighties revival décor, and good dancing music.

7 Rue Tournefort
Phone: 01-43-36-90-11
5th *arrondissement*
Métro: Place-Monge and
   Cardinal-Lemoine
Cards: Accepted

CABARETS

If you're looking for a lavish show with an unmistakably French flavor, consider the three cabarets listed below. Even though many critics claim that the shows are not as good as those in Las Vegas, the entertainment is well-staged and world-renowned. Prices are high, and this is not an intimate evening; these venues are usually crowded with other tourists.

I recommend that you bypass the dinner show and attend the later show so that you pay just for admittance and drinks. You can enjoy dinner at a nice restaurant beforehand, probably pay half the price that they charge at the cabarets, and avoid the likelihood of being seated with strangers. "Elegant attire" is requested, and you should plan to arrive thirty minutes before the show.

If you haven't purchased cabaret tickets in advance and would like to snag discount seats, check out Le Kiosque Théâtre. Similar to the TKTS booth in New York City, this stand-alone kiosk, located on the west side of the large Madeleine Church in Place de Madeleine, offers reduced-price tickets on the day of the performance. If you're lucky, you'll be able to catch a cabaret show at a bargain price. The kiosk is open Tuesday through Saturday, from 12:30 PM to 8:00 PM.

LE KIOSQUE
   THEATRE
15 Place de la Madeleine
Website: www.kiosque
   theatre.com
8th *arrondissement*
Métro: Madeleine
Cards: Accepted

CRAZY HORSE

With a smaller stage and fewer performers than the other cabarets, Crazy Horse is more intimate. The shows here are focused on the sexy dance routines of scantily clad girls rather than big production numbers. Occasionally there are guest stars such as Pamela Anderson of *Baywatch* fame. The price for the second performance (the after-dinner show) starts at 125 euros per person and includes admittance and champagne.

12 Avenue George V
Phone: 01-47-23-32-32
Website: www.lecrazy
   horseparis.com
8th *arrondissement*
Métro: Alma-Marceau
   and George-V
Cards: Accepted

LIDO

The Lido offers extravagant productions with dazzling costumes, special effects, and a water display. When dinner is included, prices start at 160 euros per person, depending on the menu you choose. If you skip dinner, the "Champagne Revue" price starts at 105 euros and includes entrance and a half-bottle of champagne per person.

116 bis Avenue des
   Champs-Elysées
Phone: 01-40-76-56-10
Website: www.lido.fr
8th *arrondissement*
Métro: George-V
Cards: Accepted

MOULIN ROUGE

Moulin Rouge's fame is partly due to the paintings of Henri de Toulouse-Lautrec, who was a regular customer during the late nineteenth century. It is regarded as the birthplace of the French cancan, which features a line of beautiful women kicking their legs in unison. You'll recognize the exterior of this nightspot, with its distinctive red windmill, from numerous French posters. (*Moulin* means "windmill.") You may have time to study the windmill at length, since guests have been known to wait in line for hours. Moulin Rouge is not in a good neighborhood; the other cabarets are more centrally located. Entrance and a half-bottle of champagne cost 105 euros for the first and second shows.

82 Boulevard de Clichy
Phone: 01-53-09-82-82
Website:
   www.moulinrouge.fr
18th *arrondissement*
Métro: Blanche
Cards: Accepted

Revel in Paris Nightlife

Paris after dark is seductive and conducive to romance. Be sure to bring at least one dressy outfit so that you will be ready for those special nights. I wouldn't plan any early morning sightseeing the next day; clubs stay open late and the party atmosphere is infectious, so you're likely to be out on the town way past midnight.

10. Les Promenades

Journey Into the Countryside

One of the wonderful things about Paris is that so many interesting and beautiful places can be found just a short drive from the city, allowing you to idle away a day or two in bucolic surroundings. During your travels, you will glimpse a very different side of France as lush green fields unfold before your eyes. You may even feel as if you were being transported back to a time when kings and queens ruled the land. A great many royal retreats remain intact and are open to visitors—a testament to an era of luxury, elegance, and privilege.

Your options are almost limitless. This chapter discusses touring wine cellars in the Champagne region, where you can dine on gourmet cuisine; exploring the royal château at Fontainebleau; strolling through the gardens of Giverny, the inspiration for some of Claude Monet's best-known paintings; visiting Honfleur, a fishing village made world-famous by the Impressionist painters who congregated there; and journeying to Versailles on the outskirts of Paris.

Cityrama and Paris Vision, the two bus tour companies discussed on page 43 of Chapter 2, are the easiest way to get to many of the sights discussed in the following pages, but you will be traveling in a crowd. For a more adventurous experience, you can take the train (see the inset on page 164 for details) and then catch a cab or bus to your final destination. Your most daring option is to rent a car as I did recently—although this is a costly choice, to be sure. In some cases, I've suggested restaurants and hotels in the vicinity of the listings. My favorite romantic choices have been given a heart rating ♥.

Using the French Railroad

The French railroad, or Société Nationale de Chemins de Fer Français (S.N.C.F.), is one of the best in Europe. The cars are neat, clean, and comfortable, and the trains run on time. To purchase tickets, you can go to any travel agency in Paris that has the S.N.C.F. sign posted outside; or you can buy the ticket at the station before your train departs–but you'll need to allow plenty of extra time.

If you're sure of your plans, it's best to buy the ticket a month or two in advance to get a better rate and guarantee your seat. This website, www.raileurope.com, is a handy way to view all the schedules and prices and buy your ticket online. (Note: In the "From" box, type the train station you plan to depart from, rather than "Paris.")

Paris has six main train stations serving various geographical regions:

East	Gare de l'Est
South and Southeast	Gare de Lyon
Southwest	Gare d'Austerlitz
West and Southwest	Gare Montparnasse
North	Gare du Nord
Northwest	Gare St. Lazare

An Important Regulation

Before boarding, you must validate your ticket by punching it in one of the orange machines placed before the *quais* (platforms) where the trains pull up. (Just follow all the other passengers.) If you don't do this, the conductor can charge you a fine.

French Terms

When using the French railroad, you may come across signs containing a number of unfamiliar terms. The following are those most commonly used in railway stations and on the trains themselves.

Première Classe	First Class
Deuxième Classe	Second Class
Banlieue	Suburbs (trains going near Paris)
Grandes Lignes	Big Lines (long-distance routes)
Quai	Platform
Fumeur	Smoking
Non-Fumeur	Nonsmoking
Voie	Track
Voiture	Car
Potable	Drinkable water
Non-potable	Nondrinkable water

Champagne Country

A day in the Champagne region of France is my idea of heaven on earth! The history and culture surrounding the creation and celebration of champagne are fascinating, and it's so much fun to sample the product—especially when it accompanies a gourmet meal.

There are two main cities in the Champagne region, Reims and Epernay. I've included some of the top champagne houses in each area; you can get more details about visits on their websites or at the tourist offices listed in the following pages. Most of the champagne houses are closed during lunchtime, and some require reservations. The average cost is around 15 euros for a tour and complimentary tasting of one of their champagne *cuvées* (blends).

If you have the time, I recommend that you take two days, rent a car, and immerse yourself in the experience. Area hotels are less expensive than those in Paris (I've suggested a few in the pages that follow), and a car will allow you to visit a number of the champagne houses while touring the countryside. I've also suggested a few good restaurants that you can enjoy during a day trip or longer stay. If you call the phone numbers in Champagne from the United States, you must dial 011-33-3-26 and then the last six digits. If you call from within France, you need to dial the 0 that has been added to the numbers provided in this chapter.

REIMS OFFICE DU TOURISME
2 Rue Guillaume de Machault
Phone: 03-26-77-45-19
Website: www.reims-tourism.com

The Cellars of Moët & Chandon.

Trains leave Gare de l'Est (East Station) frequently for Reims and Epernay. The high-speed TGV train (*Train à Grande Vitesse*) gets to Reims in forty-five minutes; tickets are cheaper if you book a few months ahead and grab one of the "leisure fare" tickets in first class, about 28 euros each way. Make sure you get off at the TGV stop in the center of Reims, rather than the one on the outskirts of the city. Normal trains to Epernay, which is a bit farther and is not a TGV stop, cost about 22 euros each way and take one hour and twenty minutes. (For more information on the French railroad system, see the inset on page 164.)

REIMS

Reims is the larger of the cities in the Champagne region, and is closer to Paris than Epernay. I recommend that you get an early start and catch a mid-morning train. This will give you time to visit the historic Gothic *cathédrale* in the center of town before you set off to wine and dine the rest of the day. Formerly known as Notre-Dame de Reims, and now known simply as Reims Cathedral, it was originally built in the thirteenth century and was rebuilt in the twentieth century after sustaining extensive damage during World War I. In addition to the grandeur of its size—the interior is 455 feet long and 125 feet high in the center—it features an abundance of statues and spires and a not-to-be-missed Marc Chagall stained glass window in the apse.

Conveniently located next to the *cathédrale* is Reims' tourist office, where you can pick up a city map, get advice on transportation, find information on the tour schedules of nearby champagne houses, and even make on-the-spot tour reservations. Check out Reims' office of tourism website for the history of champagne, contact information for the champagne houses, suggested hotels and restaurants, special exhibits, maps, and brochures that can be downloaded. The office is open from Monday through Saturday, from 9:00 AM to 6:00 PM. It opens Sundays at 10:00 AM.

The following list includes a few suggested restaurants and hotels that are well located near the *cathédrale* and train station. In addition to having a charming ambience, they are reasonably priced and offer good service. For a splurge, I recommend that you stay or dine at Les Crayères (see the inset below).

Château Les Crayères in Reims ♥

If Reims' proximity to wineries isn't reason enough to pay a visit to this centuries-old town, here's another incentive—the palatial Les Crayères hotel. Located on a gorgeous seventeen-acre park, Les Crayères offers luxury and pampering, and its restaurant is one of the top dining spots in France. Pommery Champagne's headquarters and cellar tour are across the street, and the sights of Reims are nearby. Prices are astronomical—rooms range from 380 to 700 euros in high season—but this is a top choice for a honeymoon stay or important anniversary. Visit the website and you'll find special offers that combine accommodations with extras such as meals in the restaurant, golf at a private golf course, and champagne.

64 Boulevard Henry Vasnier
Phone: 03-26-24-90-00
Website: www.lescrayeres.com
Cards: Accepted

If you want to experience Les Crayères without breaking the bank, another option is to stop there for lunch in the more casual glass-enclosed restaurant in the garden, for mid-afternoon tea and dessert on the outdoor terrace, or for a late-afternoon drink in the wood-paneled bar. Whether you decide to spend a night or just an hour or two, I urge you to stop and enjoy this beautiful property.

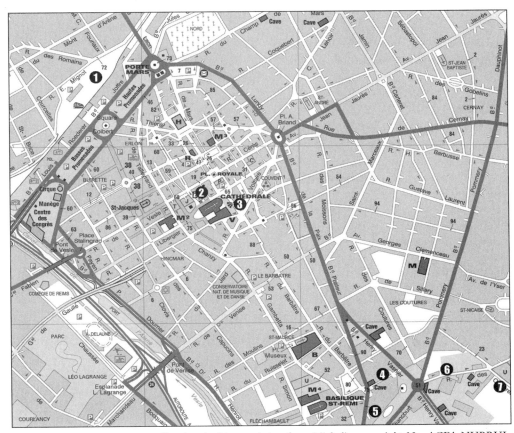

Reprinted with permission from Michelin, copyright No. AGFA-NUBRUL.

The City of Reims. If you take the train to Reims, as suggested, you'll find that the train station (1) is about one mile northwest of the tourist office (2), which is next to the Reims Cathedral (3). Many of the champagne houses—such as Taittinger (4), Veuve Clicquot (5), and Pommery (6)—and Les Crayères hotel (7) are about three miles to the southeast and easily reachable by taxi.

Reims Restaurants

CAFE DU PALAIS ♥

A couple of blocks from Reims' *cathédrale*, located on a main street with lots of stores, Café du Palais is a traditional restaurant, popular with the locals. It has a lovely Art Deco ambience and serves bistro fare and salads. A three-course *prix fixe* menu is 36 euros.

14 Place Myron Herrick
Phone: 03-26-47-52-54
Website:
  www.cafedupalais.fr
Cards: Accepted

LE GRAND CAFE

Le Grand Café is *très populaire* for its authentic French cuisine and its *specialité de la maison* (specialty of the house), a variety of mussel dishes. The approximate cost of a meal with a glass of wine is 25 euros per person.

92 Place Drouet d'Erlon
Phone: 03-26-47-61-50
Website: www.le-grandcafe.com
Cards: Accepted

Reims Hotels

GRAND HOTEL CONTINENTAL

Located near the train station at the center of the action, this is a very good choice for a comfortable stay in attractive surroundings. All sixty-one rooms and suites have air conditioning. The least expensive rooms, *Chambre Classique,* start at 100 euros, but they're very small. The next level up, *Chambre Supérieure,* starts at 159 euros.

93 Place Drouet d'Erlon
Phone: 03-26-40-39-35
Website: www.grandhotelcontinental.com
Cards: Accepted

HOTEL AZUR

Hôtel Azur is a small, charming hotel that is very reasonably priced for the central location. Be sure to ask for a renovated room and one with air conditioning during the summer months. A superior double with air conditioning costs 80 euros, and there is no elevator.

9 Rue des Ecrevées
Phone: 03-26-47-43-39
Website: www.hotel-azur-reims.com
Cards: Accepted

Reims Champagne Houses

CHARLES DE CAZANOVE
8 Place de la République
Phone: 03-26-88-53-86
Website:
    www.champagnedecazanove.com
Cards: Accepted

LOUIS ROEDERER
74 Rue Savoye
Phone: 03-26-07-61-40
Website: www.champagne-roederer.com
Cards: Accepted

MARTEL
17 Rue des Créneaux
Phone: 03-26-82-70-67
Website: www.champagnemartel.com
Cards: Accepted

MUMM
32 Rue du Champ de Mars
Phone: 03-26-49-59-70
Website: www.mumm.com
Cards: Accepted

POMMERY ♥
5 Place du Général Gouraud
Phone: 03-26-61-62-63
Website: www.pommery.fr
Cards: Accepted

RUINART ♥
4 Rue des Crayères
Phone: 03-26-77-51-51
Website: www.ruinart.com
Cards: Accepted

TAITTINGER
9 Place Saint-Nicaise
Phone: 03-26-85-45-35 and
03-26-85-84-33
Website: www.taittinger.fr
Cards: Accepted

VEUVE CLICQUOT ♥
1 Place des Droits de l'Homme
Phone: 03-26-89-53-90
Website: www.veuve-clicquot.com
Cards: Accepted

EPERNAY

Locals consider Epernay the "Capital of Champagne." Certainly, this small picturesque city is surrounded by vineyards. It is a short distance from Reims, so you can visit both cities in a few days. There are more champagne houses to visit in Reims, but Epernay is a smaller, more charming place for an overnight stay.

Epernay's tourist office is centrally located near the train station. Both the office and its website can provide up-to-date information on all the champagne houses' hours of operation. The office is open Monday through Saturday, but closes from 12:30 PM to 1:30 PM each day.

EPERNAY OFFICE DU TOURISME
7 Avenue de Champagne
Phone: 03-26-53-33-00
Website: www.ot-epernay.fr

Epernay Restaurants

LA CAVE A CHAMPAGNE
La Cave à Champagne serves traditional French cuisine and offers a wonderful selection of fish dishes that use champagne in their recipes. The *prix-fixe* menus are reasonable, especially the weekday lunch *formule*—18 euros for two plates (appetizer and main course or dessert), a glass of wine, and coffee.

16 Rue Léon Gambetta
Phone: 03-26-55-50-70
Website: www.la-cave-a-champagne.com
Cards: Accepted

A L'OEIL DE BOEUF
This is a small neighborhood restaurant with good service and very reasonable prices. The traditional French cuisine includes some excellent meat dishes and a good selection of wines by the glass. It's best to reserve a table ahead.

40 Rue de Sézanne
Phone: 03-26-54-81-90
Cards: Accepted

ROYAL CHAMPAGNE ♥
Located between Epernay and Reims and surrounded by vineyards, this restaurant is worth the picturesque drive. The dining room is luxurious, with great views of the vineyards, making this the perfect spot for a romantic occasion. The *prix fixe* menu prices are reasonable, starting at 40 euros for a three-plate weekday "Menu Bistronomique" for lunch. A Relais & Châteaux property, Royal Champagne has sumptuous rooms if you care to stay the night.

In Champillon
Phone: 03-26-52-87-11
Website: www.royalchampagne.com
Cards: Accepted

Epernay Hotels

LE CLOS RAYMI

A nineteenth-century mansion that used to be the home of Monsieur Chandon, Le Clos Raymi has only seven rooms (double rates start at 150 euros), and it is perfectly located a few blocks from the champagne houses on Avenue de Champagne.

3 Rue Joseph de Venoge
Phone: 03-26-51-00-58
Website: www.closraymi-hotel.com
Cards: Accepted

PARVA DOMUS

Parva Domus, a lovely bed and breakfast with a small garden, is very reasonably priced at 90 euros per night, and is in the heart of town. The champagne welcome is warm and hospitable, and there are only five rooms, so you need to book a few months ahead. Credit cards are not accepted here, so be prepared to pay in euros.

27 Avenue de Champagne
Phone: 03-26-32-40-74
Website: www.parva domusrimaire.com
Cards: Not Accepted

The Art of Making Champagne

The Benedictine monk Dom Perignon discovered and developed the secrets of making champagne at the end of the seventeenth century at the Abbey of Hautvillers near Epernay. For many years, champagne was so scarce and so costly that the sparkling wine was available only for royalty and the very rich. Today, we are all able to celebrate in style. Here is how champagne is made.

• Late in September, the grapes are harvested and taken in baskets to the presshouse, where they are emptied into large winepresses.

• After the pressing, the juice runs into vats for the *débourbage,* where extraneous substances and particles are removed. The juice is then transferred to giant vats, where it is fermented and becomes wine.

• When the first fermentation is over, the *chef de cave* prepares the *cuvée,* a blend of various wines, to give a balanced, consistent quality to the champagne.

• In the spring, the *cuvée* is bottled and taken below to the cellars for a second fermentation, during which the wine becomes effervescent.

• At the end of the second fermentation, the bottles are placed neck-down, and *remueurs* (riddlers) turn them slightly each day for three months to coax the sediment down to the cork. A *remueur's* special training takes years, and he turns 40,000 bottles a day—which is quite a feat.

• After three to seven years of aging, depending on the grapes and vintage, the bottles are uncorked to allow for the disposal of the remaining sediment, and a liqueur mixture is added. According to the amount of liqueur added, the champagne is half-dry, dry, extra-dry, or Brut.

LA VILLA EUGENE ♥
This beautiful hotel, set in a park, is a bit farther away from the center of Epernay. There is an outdoor heated swimming pool, and the hotel has an arrangement that allows you to have meals brought in from local restaurants. La Villa Eugène offers only fifteen rooms beautifully decorated in the Louis XVI style, so reserve ahead. Prices range from 130 to 300 euros.

82 Avenue de Champagne
Phone: 03-26-32-44-76
Website: www.villa-eugene.com
Cards: Accepted

Epernay Champagne Houses

The jewel of Epernay, Moët & Chandon is the largest champagne house in the world and is only a ten-minute walk from the train station. When you arrive, you'll be greeted at the reception desk and grouped with other visitors for an underground tour of the cellars, or *caves,* conducted by an English-speaking guide. During an intriguing hour, you'll observe firsthand the dimly lit, cool, cavernous rooms where experts oversee the three-to-seven year process of making champagne. Moët's cellars stretch for twenty miles below ground! The 17-euro admission fee includes a flute of Moët's Brut Impérial in the tasting room afterwards—a fitting finale, and you'll definitely be ready to savor the flavors after learning about its origins and complexity.

Tour times are posted on Moët & Chandon's website (click on "Guided Tours"), and it is wise to reserve ahead, especially during high season. Between mid-March and mid-November, tours are generally offered seven days a week. At other times of the year, the winery is open only on weekdays.

Although Moët is the largest champagne marker in the world, it is not the only one in the Epernay area. Four good choices—including Moët—are listed below. In all cases, it's best to call or email ahead to check when the winery is open. Most champagne houses are closed for a few months in winter and on certain holidays, as well. The Epernay office of tourism (see page 169) can help you plan your visit—*and* the staff speaks English.

CASTELLANE
63 Avenue de Champagne
Phone: 03-26-51-19-19
Website: www.castellane.com
Cards: Accepted

CHAMPAGNE ACHILLE PRINCIER
9 Rue Jean Chandon Moët
Phone: 03-26-32-06-22
Website: www.achilleprincier.com
Cards: Accepted

MERCIER
70 Avenue de Champagne
Phone: 03-26-51-22-22
Website: www.champagnemercier.fr
Cards: Accepted

MOET & CHANDON ♥
20 Avenue de Champagne
Phone: 03-26-51-20-20
Website: www.moet.com
Cards: Accepted

$$$ SAVE SOME MONEY $$$

Looking for an affordable but thoroughly rewarding day trip? Try the picturesque town of Saint-Germain-en-Laye. This lovely destination is only twenty minutes from Etoile/Arc de Triomphe on the RER (fast train), Line A. Not only is the price right—11 euros for an all-day pass on the RER—but once you arrive, you'll find that the sights, shops, and restaurants are also easy on the wallet.

Château de Saint-Germain is an impressive royal palace that dates back to the sixteenth century and played a big part in the history of France. Louis XIV was born there, and Napoleon added what is now called the Musée d'Archéologie Nationale, which houses artifacts from the Stone Age to the eighth century. The magnificent park and gardens of the château, which were designed by André le Nôtre of Versailles fame, provide a lovely place to stroll and enjoy a picnic lunch. Another great option is to check out one of the charming nearby cafés.

CHATEAU DE SAINT-GERMAIN-EN-LAYE
Phone: 01-39-10-13-00
Website:
   http://www.rmn.fr/
   francais/sortir/musees/
   en-ile-de-france
Cards: Accepted

Château de Fontainebleau

Starting in the twelfth century, French kings and their courts made Fontainebleau their country home. Although not as grand as Versailles, Fontainebleau is viewed by the French as being important historically. In fact, Napoleon abdicated his crown here.

Phone: 01-60-71-50-60
   or 01-60-74-99-99
Website:
   www.uk.fontainebleau-tourisme.com
Cards: Accepted

Named after the freshwater spring that gave rise to the town, Fontainebleau is surrounded by breathtaking gardens, statuary, and fountains, and the nearby forest, where kings used to hunt, is excellent for hiking and long romantic walks. Since it is "off the beaten track," Fontainebleau is much less crowded than Versailles. Follow a tour guide or rent an audio guide, and you will see how royalty lived in centuries past. Included in the tour are Fontainebleau's ornate private apartments (Napoleon held Pope Pius VII prisoner in one of them for two years), as well as its drawing rooms, bed chambers, throne room, chapel, theater, and ballroom.

Trains depart frequently from Gare de Lyon in Paris for the forty-five-minute ride to Avon, a nearby town. My favorite mode of transportation from the Avon station to Fontainebleau, two miles away, is a bicycle (*vélo*), which can be rented from many train stations. The bike paths through the adjacent forest are *très romantique*. Another option is to take the local bus marked "Château."

Admission to the château is 6.5 euros. To visit a small museum devoted to Napolean and to see his private apartments, you must pay an additional 3 euros for a special tour; it's best to reserve ahead. Fontainebleau is open year-round and closed on Tuesdays and major holidays. The helpful website provides historical information and offers a free audio guide download.

Enjoying the French Countryside by Bike

Fat Tire Bike Tours (discussed in Chapters 8 and 9) offers an intimate way to experience Monet's gardens and the grounds of Versailles.

For the "Monet's Gardens" tour, you travel by train to Vernon, then hop on a bicycle, pick up a picnic lunch at the local market, and pedal out to view the gardens and enjoy your meal. The cost is 75 euros per person.

The Versailles tour starts at the company's office near the Eiffel Tower. From there, you travel via bike to the nearby train station. When you arrive at Versailles, you ride your bikes to a market for picnic supplies. After touring Versailles' beautiful tree-lined paths and gardens, you eat lunch and then tour the palace itself. The cost is 85 euros per person and covers the bicycle, train trip, bicycle guide, entrance to Versailles, and audio guide—not the picnic lunch.

FAT TIRE BIKE TOURS
24 Rue Edgar Faure
Phone: 01-56-58-10-54
Website: www.fattirebike
    tours.com/paris
15th *arrondissement*
Métro: La-Motte-Piquet-
    Grenelle and Dupleix
Cards: Accepted

Giverny ♥

Through his paintings, Claude Monet portrayed the French gentry of his day as well as the scenic countryside. He is widely acclaimed for his masterful ability to create an "impression" of a scene through his use of colors and depiction of light. In 1883, Monet moved his family to Giverny, north of Paris. There he lived and worked for more than forty years, until his death. Monet went one step further than many of his colleagues by creating the setting that he painted. In *Monet's Years at Giverny*, Philippe de Montebello writes:

84 Rue Claude Monet
Phone: 02-32-51-28-21
Website: www.fondation-
    monet.com (in French)
www.giverny.org/gardens
    (in English)
Cards: Accepted

> The paintings immortalized the actual garden, which was the *tour de force* of the master gardener Monet, who planned every aspect of it. . . . There is no more happenstance in the arrangement of the flower beds, garden paths, lily pond and footbridge than there is in the many striking color juxtapositions and broad brushstrokes in the late canvases that depict them.

The gardens stretch over many acres and encompass the water lily pond and Japanese footbridge that were the focus of Monet's later paintings. (The largest of these paintings can be seen in the Musée de l'Orangerie, described on page 84.) The flower beds near the house are laid out in rows divided by walking paths, and small nameplates describe each variety.

Don't miss touring Monet's restored house—the colors are stunning. The dining room glows in shades of yellow; the kitchen sparkles in blue and white; and the salmon pink exterior is accented with green shutters. The gift shop carries an extensive selection of books, posters, notecards, desk items, children's puzzles, and more.

Giverny is open from April through October, and is closed on Mondays. Admission is 9 euros, and reservations are accepted for large groups only.

Trains depart from Gare St. Lazare station in Paris and take forty-five minutes to arrive in nearby Vernon. From the Vernon station, it's a fifteen-minute bus or taxi ride to Giverny.

Honfleur

A visit to the charming fishing village of Honfleur is best planned as an overnight trip from Paris. The picturesque harbor began luring visitors even before the Impressionist painters made the village more widely known. Now, reasonably priced accommodations can be found in the center of town, or you can opt for a luxurious splurge at Ferme Saint-Siméon, a first-class hotel and restaurant a few miles away.

The most celebrated of Honfleur's four harbors, Vieux Bassin, is flanked by seventeenth-century houses. Many of the quaint shops are found between Rue de la Ville and Rue de la Prison. Musée Municipal Eugène Boudin, built to honor Honfleur native Boudin, displays his works as well as many paintings of his fellow Impressionists.

The train ride from Gare St. Lazare to Deauville (or Lisieux nearby) takes two hours. You can then catch a bus or taxi to Honfleur on the *Côte de Grâce* (Coast of Grace). Honfleur's office of tourism is a good source of information on hotels, restaurants, festivals, and sights.

" 'The jewel of Normandy' I'd heard Honfleur called, and I'm finding it difficult to disagree. A fishing town since the Middle Ages—the local fleet still unloads its catch almost daily—it unfurls a parade of Norman architectural styles as I drive in."
—Alan Richman, National Geographic Traveler

HONFLEUR'S OFFICE DU TOURISME
Phone: 02-31-89-23-30
Website: www.ot-honfleur.fr

HOTEL FERME SAINT-SIMEON AND RESTAURANT ♥

Located off the coast highway, west of Honfleur, this hotel won my heart rating because it offers a warm welcome, charming rooms, a gourmet restaurant, beautiful grounds, and prices that are much lower than those you would pay in Paris. This is romantic! Double rooms start at 150 euros, and on the website, you'll find packages that include a room, a continental breakfast, dinner for two, and use of the spa and swimming pool.

Rue Adolphe-Marais
Phone: 02-31-81-78-00
Website: www.fermesaint simeon.fr
Cards: Accepted

LES MAISONS DE LEA

This charming hotel is moderately priced and in a great location at the center of town. The rooms are attractively furnished, although some are reached by steep stairs, so inquire ahead if that is an issue. Doubles start at 145 euros.

Place Sainte-Catherine
Phone: 02-31-14-49-49
Website: www.lesmaisons delea.com
Cards: Accepted

Versailles

A half-century in the making, Versailles became the center of French society when King Louis XIV established court there. In addition to the large Palace of Versailles, there are two smaller mansions—the Grand and Petit Trianons. The whole complex is set off by fountains, sculpture, and vast gardens that stretch as far as the eye can see. It is awesome.

Highlights of the palace include the *Galerie des Glaces,* or Hall of Mirrors, where the World War I peace treaty was signed; the *Chapelle Royale,* or Royal Chapel, where the king worshipped; the king's bedchamber; and galleries depicting the history of France in the last few centuries.

Because of the size of the grounds and palace, you'll definitely want to wear comfortable walking shoes, and you should be prepared for crowds. The best time to visit is during the week. The bus companies mentioned on page 163 offer various guided tours of Versailles, but it is much less expensive to catch the RER (fast train) Line C from various stops in Paris, including Gare d'Austerlitz, St-Michel, Musée d'Orsay, Pont de l'Alma, and Champ de Mars. There are two C trains going in that direction, so be sure to take the train that ends at the Versailles-Rive Gauche station. Then follow the signs to take the short walk to Versailles.

Versailles is open daily except Mondays and holidays. You can now purchase your tickets in advance on the website. (Click on "Purchase Tickets" on the right side of the home-page.) I strongly recommend this; you will avoid standing in line for an hour or more. In addition, the website presents a wealth of information not only on entrance fees, but also on Versailles history, Versailles sights, and special shows—like a fountain water display accompanied by recorded classical music and a fireworks show on summer evenings.

CHATEAU DE VERSAILLES
Website: www.chateau versailles.fr
Cards: Accepted

A Romantic Interlude in the Country

If you're in Paris for more than a few days, I strongly recommend taking a short excursion into the countryside. What can be more romantic than a bicycle ride through lush parkland, luscious meals served in attractive rustic settings, and small charming towns that have changed little in the last hundred years? This is guaranteed to be a memorable highlight of your trip!

11. Les Souvenirs

Preserve and Share Your Memories

As Ernest Hemingway so aptly stated, "Paris is a moveable feast." Once you've experienced Paris' charms, she will enhance and enlighten the rest of your life. You will return home with lasting memories and a new outlook that may change you in subtle but profound ways.

- You might seek out sidewalk cafés or afternoon tea salons for a *tête-à-tête* with your loved one or a close friend.

- When you go to the local French restaurant, you will understand some of the items on the menu and enjoy ordering your favorite dish.

- You may spend more time in the accessory section of the department store selecting scarves, belts, and fun jewelry to accentuate your new "signature look."

- When special exhibits come to a nearby museum, you will revisit paintings you saw first in their permanent collection in Paris, and fond memories of your trip will come flooding back.

This chapter discusses how you can capture your fabulous experiences and share them with friends and family. You'll learn about taking photographs and using them in creative ways, recording your experiences in a journal or scrapbook, posting your impressions on social networking and video-sharing websites like Facebook and YouTube, sending postcards (*cartes postales*) to the folks back home, collecting memorabilia to decorate your home or office, and buying gifts.

Taking Photographs

Taking photographs is a great way to preserve your memories for years to come. I prefer photographing the people and places that make Paris special for me—the view from my hotel window, the waiter at the nearby café who serves my morning croissant and *café au lait,* buckets of fresh-cut flowers on the sidewalk in front of the local florist's shop, and the window display of the lingerie store where I bought those sexy unmentionables. (Keep in mind that most stores do not allow photos to be taken *inside.*) I also snap photos of signs to help me remember where each grouping of photos was taken. My goal is to choose images that tell the story of my unique trip.

Photography Tours

If you're a shutterbug and want to improve your camera techniques while preserving your memories of Paris, photography tours are a great option. They're costly—well over 100 euros for a half-day—but the groups are very small and the tours include technical and creative instruction. In some cases, they will let you bring a "non-photographer" companion at no extra charge. Both companies below offer half-day tours as well as longer workshops, and you do need to bring your own equipment. No addresses have been listed because you will be advised of the meeting point after you make your reservation.

BETTER PARIS PHOTOS
Phone: 06-74-04-21-84
Website: www.betterparisphotos.com
Cards: Accepted

PHOTO TOURS IN PARIS
Phone: 06-40-14-84-49
Website: www.phototoursinparis.com
Cards: Accepted

I recommend taking an inexpensive lightweight camera to Paris. Theft is common, so it's best not to carry expensive equipment unless you plan on taking a photography tour (see the inset above). These days, high-pixel digital cameras with a good array of shooting options can be found at reasonable prices. Make sure you bring the correct adapter to use for charging your battery pack (details on page 34), or use a camera that runs on disposable batteries, and bring extras. (Remember that according to TSA rules, you have to pack any spare batteries in your carry-on bag—not in checked luggage.) Even if you're bringing your phone and can use it for taking photos, it's good to have the camera as a backup in case something goes wrong with the phone.

When you return home, there are a number of things you can do with the photos. You can opt for a traditional photo album, produce photo slide shows on websites such as Shutterfly and Snapfish, design personalized calendars or mugs, or incorporate your images in a scrapbook (see below). These websites will even allow you to create photo notecards and printed books. Or visit drugstore websites, most of which have special photo sections geared to making calendars, posters, and other photo gifts.

Creating a Journal or Scrapbook

Your trip to Paris will be a unique experience to savor for years to come, and a journal will help you remember all the events, large and small. My Paris journal provided the starting point for this book. Whenever I have a few minutes—while I'm sitting in a café or waiting to catch a bus—I jot down my impressions, feelings, encounters, and notes on favorite haunts. I also collect the *carte de la maison,* or business card, of each place I visit and want to share with others.

Scrapbooks are a fun, creative way to record the story of your trip and share the journey with others. Capture the sense of being there by including museum fliers, ticket stubs, travel brochures and postcards of places you visited, and even your airline luggage tags. If you draw, incorporate sketches of the places you visited. Add descriptive captions so that years from now, your photos, drawings, and other memorabilia will still have meaning for you, your friends, and your family. Scrapbooking has become very popular over the last few years, so you will be able to choose from a range of formats, including three-ring notebooks that allow you to easily add and move pages. Many of the photo websites, like Shutterfly, even enable you to have the finished product printed and bound as a book. Whatever method you choose, years later, you will be glad you took the time to record your trip's highlights when they were fresh in your mind.

Reaching Out Through Facebook, Twitter, and YouTube

Not everyone chooses to post their experiences on the rapidly evolving social network and video-sharing sites, but if this option appeals to you—and if you have the necessary resources at your disposal—you'll be able to keep friends and family up-to-date on your trip as it unfolds, or even post a video so that they can see the sights that Paris has to offer. But a word of caution is in order: You may not want hundreds of Internet users knowing that you're out of the country, especially if you're concerned about burglars finding out you're on vacation—a real problem these days. In that case, check your privacy settings to be sure your Facebook posts are visible only to friends. If you're at all worried about people knowing that you're away from home, it's best to post on Twitter and YouTube *after* you get back, as these sites are open to everyone.

If you are traveling with a laptop computer or a tablet such as an iPad, you can load your pictures, edit them, and then send them to a website for friends to view. Another option is to access the web at an Internet café (see page 59 for listings). Most hotels have a computer hooked up to the Internet for use by guests at a nominal fee. This will enable you to post on-the-scene "bulletins" about your adventures without being burdened with equipment.

Your options and flexibility will increase if you are traveling with a cell phone that has international roaming and web access. You can then hop onto Facebook and describe your gourmet lunch while you're still comfortably seated at that trendy chef's new bistro.

Since the microblogging service Twitter is limited to 140 characters per entry, Facebook is usually a better tool for describing your experiences. You might use Twitter for short trip highlights and refer readers to your Facebook page, where you can post a full description of your day's activities.

If you shoot videos of your trip, you will give your communications the added dimension of sound. You can speak into the microphone to narrate what you're seeing or capture the ambient sound—the resonant organ music at Notre Dame or the laughter of Parisian children at play in a park. You can also film a guided tour, like a boat cruise on the Seine River, and tape the guide's lively description of the monuments along the riverbank.

Depending on the sophistication of your equipment and software, you can edit a professional-looking travel documentary or go the simplest route with a cell phone that shoots video or with a Flip camcorder, which basically allows you to point and shoot. Transmitting video to the web can get pretty complicated unless you are traveling with equipment that has been set up for the task, so if you want to post a video on YouTube or a similar site, I recommend that you handle it after your return home.

$ $ $ SAVE SOME MONEY $ $ $

After your trip, when you want to share your Paris adventure with friends and family, nothing is easier than sending out a simple email. But if you wish to go further and treat them to a gorgeous-looking email newsletter (ezine) that chronicles your trip, pay a visit to the Constant Contact website. The company offers a *free trial* if you're sending your email out to less than one hundred addresses.

I'm a big fan of Constant Contact (www.constantcontact.com), which was one of the first sites to offer a template that you can use to send out a professional-looking email. Visually, a completed ezine looks nearly like the page of a magazine, with columns, separate "article" boxes, and, of course, photos. You write the contents, upload the photos, input the email addresses, and send it off. The recipients will be delighted, and you'll have preserved your memories in a unique and unforgettable way.

Sending Postcards

Granted, it's a bit old-fashioned to send postcards these days, and you will probably be back in the States before they reach their intended recipients. But postcards remain a gracious, personal way to send your thoughts to friends and loved ones. You can also stock up on beautiful postcards, as I do, and use them to enliven scrapbook pages or as gift and notecards later on.

Cartes postales, as they are called in French, are sold at newsstands, in souvenir stores, and in museum gift shops. Prices can vary widely, from a half-euro per card to ten cards for one euro. Incredibly, you are likely to find the best prices in major "tourist" areas adjacent to Notre Dame and the Louvre. If you prefer old postcards, visit the *bouquinistes*—the bookstalls found along the Seine River near Notre Dame. (For information on mailing postcards, see the inset on page 181.)

Collecting Memorabilia

Paris' treasures are boundless. My home and office are full of souvenirs from previous trips, so wonderful memories remain vivid. Lovely ceramic bowls with drawings of Paris scenes hold keys, and coasters depicting "touristy" sights like the Eiffel Tower are set out when guests come over. Numerous posters from art galleries adorn walls in my office.

Most of the souvenirs I collect are inexpensive, but to me they have a value far beyond their cost in euros. There are many quintessentially Parisian items sold on the streets—old books in stands along the Seine River, small antique household objects sold at flea markets (see page 139), and artists' watercolors displayed for sale near major tourist sights. The main areas frequented by sidewalk artists include Boulevard St.-Germain, near Eglise de Saint-Germain-des-Prés; the bridges leading to Ile Saint-Louis and Notre Dame; and Place du Tertre, near Sacré-Coeur. At many of these locations, you can have your portrait drawn on the spot. This may sound corny, but the sketch is sure to put a smile on your face every time you pass it in your home, and also makes a fun conversation piece with friends.

The Bureau de Poste

Neighborhood post offices are identified by the yellow PTT sign. They are normally open from 9:00 AM to 7:00 PM on weekdays and from 9:00 AM to noon on Saturdays. Although the city places PTT signs with arrows blocks away from post offices to help you locate them, it's easier to simply inquire about their location at your hotel. If you're a night owl, the Louvre post office is open twenty-four hours a day.

BUREAU DE POSTE AT THE LOUVRE
52 Rue du Louvre
1st *arrondissement*
Métro: Palais-Royal-
   Musée-du-Louvre

As of this writing, the cost of mailing a postcard from Paris to the United States is .85 euro—a little over a dollar. You may be able to buy stamps at your hotel or a nearby newsstand (*tabac*). If not, when you enter the post office, look for the window marked *timbres* (stamps), as not all windows sell stamps. Here are some other common terms that may be helpful:

Cartes postales	Postcards
Aux Etats Unis	To the United States
Par Avion	Airmail
Une lettre	A letter
A l'etranger	To foreign destinations

If you want to use one of the cute yellow mailboxes on the street to send off your postcards, select the slot marked *Autres Départements Etranger* (To Foreign Destinations).

Buying Souvenirs for Friends and Family

Small gifts—especially those that are distinctly French in flavor—make wonderful mementos to bring home to friends and family. I look for lightweight items like posters and original sketches, designer silk scarves, and gourmet food items such as French teas, coffees, and chocolate in distinctive wrapping.

Of course, many of the specialty food stores mentioned in Chapter 5, the clothing boutiques discussed in Chapter 6, and the household-item shops discussed in Chapter 7 offer a variety of beautiful gift items, but there are many more options available to you throughout the city. The

"There's nothing quite like the satisfaction of stumbling upon the perfect travel souvenir. . . . The idea of bringing objects back home from the places we have been is as old as travel itself. . . . What connects the things I collect is that they each contain a discovery, a cultural insight, that I can't wait to share, which is why I find my best mementos where local people work, live, and shop. Some of the coolest souvenirs are everyday objects that are culturally specific, like kitchen items and housewares found on supermarket shelves. . . ."

—*Daisann McLane*, National Geographic Traveler

inexpensive department stores such as Monoprix and Prisunic (see page 125) and neighborhood drugstores, called *pharmacies,* are great places to find lovely but inexpensive gifts. I found aromatic soaps from Provence at one of the Marionnaud beauty stores (see page 72), and the salesperson was kind enough to gift-wrap them in beautiful linen paper.

If you are looking for a small keepsake, consider the "touristy" souvenir and gift shops. Some seasoned travelers shun these shops, but I beg to differ. If you look carefully, you will find useful, charming, inexpensive items, including small ceramics, costume jewelry, coasters imprinted with well-known Paris scenes, t-shirts bearing French phrases, colorful low-priced shawls, and even key chains. And when most stores are closed on Sundays, the majority of tourist shops near major sights are still open. Travelers often don't realize that a tote bag with a sketch of Notre Dame is worth more than its dollar value to recipients, who are intrigued by the novelty of the object or have fond memories of their trip taken long ago. To them, these small gifts are priceless. Below, you'll find a few of the gift shops that I recommend for their nice selection of souvenirs, for their quintessentially Parisian knickknacks, and for their very reasonable prices. They are conveniently located in the heart of the city near main tourist attractions.

SOUVENIR AND GIFT SHOPS

LA BOUTIQUE

Adjacent to Musée d'Orsay, this store specializes in hand-painted porcelain from Limoges and also carries many other interesting souvenir items and inexpensive jewelry. It is closed on Mondays.

6 Rue de Bellechasse
Phone: 01-47-05-31-45
7th *arrondissement*
Métro: Solférino
Cards: Accepted

BUCI NEWS

Located in the midst of the Left Bank shopping area, Buci News is open seven days a week and sells small gifts, in addition to notecards, other paper items, and a big selection of magazines.

4 Rue Grégoire de Tours
Phone: 01-43-54-62-65
6th *arrondissement*
Métro: St-Germain-des-
   Prés
Cards: Accepted

LE JARDIN DE CHANTAL

I discovered this lovely shop one Sunday, when I was visiting the bird market near Notre Dame. There weren't as many cute birds in cages as I'd hoped to see, but there were interesting shops, some selling colorful fresh flowers. This boutique was especially nice and carried beautiful cards printed in France, baskets, wreaths, scented gifts, and signs you can post in your home.

25 Place Louis Lépine
   (in the flower market)
Phone: 01-43-26-67-41
4th *arrondissement*
Métro: Cité
Cards: Accepted

PALAIS ROYAL SOUVENIRS DE PARIS

As the name states, this store is crammed with traditional souvenirs, from coasters and ashtrays to t-shirts and shot glasses—just about anything that can be imprinted with the image of the Eiffel Tower. Located across from the Louvre, Palais Royal has especially good prices for postcards, offering around ten of them for one euro. It is open on Sundays.

182 Rue de Rivoli
Phone: 01-42-60-79-49
1st *arrondissement*
Métro: Palais-Royal-
   Musée-du-Louvre
Cards: Accepted

TUILERIES IMAGES

Facing the lovely Tuileries Garden, Tuileries Images has a great selection of posters and cards suitable for framing. It is in a blocks-long arcade with other tourist shops, most of which are open on Sundays.

210 Rue de Rivoli
Phone: 01-42-60-65-50
1st *arrondissement*
Métro: Tuileries and
   Concorde
Cards: Accepted

When you leave Paris, you will have a final chance to pick up souvenirs and gifts in the airport's duty-free shops before your flight back home. I urge you to leave enough time to take advantage of this opportunity. At Charles de Gaulle Airport, you'll find boutiques selling cosmetics; perfume; bath products; gourmet foodstuffs like tea, coffee, and chocolate; liquor; and high-end clothes and jewelry. My favorite stop for inexpensive gifts is a newsstand called Relais. In addition to newspapers and snacks, it offers a nice selection of Paris souvenirs, including scarves depicting Paris landmarks, small purses, and high-quality chocolate bars. Remember that you will be asked for your passport and boarding pass to show that you're visiting from another country and that your final destination is outside the European Union.

Your Paris Adventure Lives On

Your Paris photos and souvenirs will help keep your memories alive and allow you to share them with others. However you preserve your trip's highlights, you can be sure that friends will come to you for advice before taking their exciting trip to the City of Light . . . and romance.

Glossary

This glossary includes most of the French terms used throughout the guide, as well as some additional terms that may prove useful during your stay in Paris. The glossary has been organized into the following sections:

General Terms and Phrases

- Conversational Phrases
- Common Terms
- Days of the Week
- Months of the Year
- Numbers
- Building Terms
- Computer and Internet Terms

Food Terms

- General Food Terms
- Café Terms
- Restaurant Phrases
- Menu Terms

Post Office Terms and Phrases
Recreation Terms
Salon Terms

- General Salon Terms
- Beauty Salon Terms
- Hair Salon Terms

Shopping Phrases and Terms

- Shopping Phrases
- General Shopping Terms
- Clothing Terms

Transportation Terms

- Métro Terms
- Train Terms

Each section starts with an alphabetical listing of the English words, along with the French translations. In most cases this is followed by the French/English version. *Bonne chance!* Translation: Good luck!

GENERAL TERMS AND PHRASES
Conversational Phrases

English/French

Do you speak English? *Parlez-vous anglais?*

Excuse me. *Excusez-moi.*

Good-bye. *Au revoir.*

Hello. *Bonjour.*

How are you? *Comment allez-vous?*

How do you say _____ in French? *Comment dit-on _____ en français?*

Madame. *Madame.*

My name is _____. *Je m'appelle _____.*

No. *Non.*

Please. *S'il vous plaît.*

Sir. *Monsieur.*

Thank you. *Merci.*

Very well, thanks. And you? *Très bien, merci. Et vous?*

What's your name? *Comment-vous appelez-vous?*

Yes. *Oui.*

You're welcome. *Je vous en prie.*

French/English

Au revoir. Good-bye.

Bonjour. Hello.

Comment allez-vous? How are you?

Comment dit-on_____ en français? How do you say_____ in French?

Comment-vous appelez-vous? What's your name?

Excusez-moi. Excuse me.

Je m'appelle _____. My name is _____.

Je vous en prie. You're welcome.

Madame. Madame.

Merci. Thank you.

Monsieur. Sir.

Non. No.

Oui. Yes.

Parlez-vous anglais? Do you speak English?

S'il vous plaît. Please.

Très bien, merci. Et vous? Very well, thanks. And you?

Common Terms

English/French

A lot. *Beaucoup.*

Air conditioning. *Climatisé.*

Bookstall. *Bouquiniste.*

Bridges. *Ponts.*

Business card. *Carte de la maison.*

Courtesy. *Courtoisie.*

District. *Arrondissement.*

Dry cleaners. *Nettoyage à sec.*

Eighth. *Huitième.*

First. *Premier.*

Forbidden. *Interdit.*

Fourth. *Quatrième.*

Gifts. *Cadeaux.*

House. *Maison.*

Kindness. *Gentillesse.*

Left Bank. *Rive Gauche.*

Most popular. *Plus populaire.*

Museum. *Musée.*

Newsstands. *Kiosks* or *tabacs.*

Nightclub. *Boîte de nuit.*

Offices. *Bureaux.*

Right Bank. *Rive Droite.*

Sixteenth. *Seizième.*

Sixth. *Sixième.*

Songs. *Chansons.*

The good life. *La belle vie.*

Very chic. *Très mode.*

Very expensive. *Très cher.*

Well known. *Bien connu.*

French/English

Arrondissement. District.
Beaucoup. A lot.
Bien connu. Well known.
Boîte de nuit. Nightclub.
Bouquiniste. Bookstall.
Bureaux. Offices.
Cadeaux. Gifts.
Carte de la maison. Business card.
Chansons. Songs.
Climatisé. Air conditioning.
Courtoisie. Courtesy.
Gentillesse. Kindness.
Huitième. Eighth.
Interdit. Forbidden.
Kiosks. Newsstands.
La belle vie. The good life.
Maison. House.
Musée. Museum.
Nettoyage à sec. Dry cleaners.
Plus populaire. Most popular.
Ponts. Bridges.
Premier. First.
Quatrième. Fourth.
Rive Droite. Right Bank.
Rive Gauche. Left Bank.
Seizième. Sixteenth.
Sixième. Sixth.
Très cher. Very expensive.
Très mode. Very chic.

Days of the Week

English/French

Monday. *Lundi.*
Tuesday. *Mardi.*
Wednesday. *Mercredi.*
Thursday. *Jeudi.*
Friday. *Vendredi.*
Saturday. *Samedi.*
Sunday. *Dimanche.*

French/English

Lundi. Monday.
Mardi. Tuesday.
Mercredi. Wednesday.
Jeudi. Thursday.
Vendredi. Friday.
Samedi. Saturday.
Dimanche. Sunday.

Months of the Year

English/French

January. *Janvier.*
February. *Février.*
March. *Mars.*
April. *Avril.*
May. *Mai.*
June. *Juin.*
July. *Juillet.*
August. *Août.*
September. *Septembre.*
October. *Octobre.*
November. *Novembre.*
December. *Décembre.*

French/English

Janvier. January.
Février. February.
Mars. March.
Avril. April.
Mai. May.
Juin. June.
Juillet. July.
Août. August.
Septembre. September.
Octobre. October.
Novembre. November.
Décembre. December.

Numbers

English/French	French/English
One. *Un.*	*Un.* One.
Two. *Deux.*	*Deux.* Two.
Three. *Trois.*	*Trois.* Three.
Four. *Quatre.*	*Quatre.* Four.
Five. *Cinq.*	*Cinq.* Five.
Six. *Six.*	*Six.* Six.
Seven. *Sept.*	*Sept.* Seven.
Eight. *Huit.*	*Huit.* Eight.
Nine. *Neuf.*	*Neuf.* Nine.
Ten. *Dix.*	*Dix.* Ten.
Eleven. *Onze.*	*Onze.* Eleven.
Twelve. *Douze.*	*Douze.* Twelve.
Thirteen. *Treize.*	*Treize.* Thirteen.
Fourteen. *Quatorze.*	*Quatorze.* Fourteen.
Fifteen. *Quinze.*	*Quinze.* Fifteen.
Sixteen. *Seize.*	*Seize.* Sixteen.
Seventeen. *Dix-sept.*	*Dix-sept.* Seventeen.
Eighteen. *Dix-huit.*	*Dix-huit.* Eighteen.
Nineteen. *Dix-neuf.*	*Dix-neuf.* Nineteen.
Twenty. *Vingt.*	*Vingt.* Twenty.
Thirty. *Trente.*	*Trente.* Thirty.
Forty. *Quarante.*	*Quarante.* Forty.
Fifty. *Cinquante.*	*Cinquante.* Fifty.

Building Terms

English/French	French/English
Bath. *Bain.*	*Ascenseur.* Elevator.
Cashier. *Caisse.*	*Bain.* Bath.
Do not enter. *Interdit.*	*Caisse.* Cashier.
Elevator. *Ascenseur.*	*Dames.* Ladies (for restroom).
Emergency exit. *Sortie de secours.*	*Douche.* Shower.
Escalator. *Escalier roulant.*	*Escalier roulant.* Escalator.
Exit. *Sortie.*	*Escaliers.* Stairs.
Ladies (for restroom). *Dames.*	*Interdit.* Do not enter.
Men (for restroom). *Messieurs.*	*Messieurs.* Men (for restroom).
Pull. *Tirez.*	*Poussez.* Push.
Push. *Poussez.*	*Sortie.* Exit.
Shower. *Douche.*	*Sortie de secours.* Emergency exit.
Stairs. *Escaliers.*	*Tirez.* Pull.

Computer and Internet Terms

English/French
Connect. *Connexion.*
Delete. *Supprimer.*
Disconnect. *Deconnecter.*
Edit. *Fichier.*
Password. *Mot de passé.*
Print. *Imprimer.*
Start. *Demarrer.*
User name. *Nom d'utilisateur.*

French/English
Connexion. Connect.
Deconnecter. Disconnect.
Demarrer. Start.
Fichier. Edit.
Imprimer. Print.
Mot de passé. Password.
Nom d'utilisateur. User name.
Supprimer. Delete.

FOOD TERMS
Types of Food and Dining Establishments

English/French
Bakery. *Boulangerie.*
Cheese shop. *Fromagerie.*
Delicatessen with gourmet take-out foods. *Charcuterie.*
Market. *Marché.*
Meat shop. *Boucherie.*
Pastry shop. *Pâtisserie.*
Tea salon. *Salon de thé.*
Wine bars. *Bars à vins.*

French/English
Bars à vins. Wine bars.
Boucherie. Meat shop.
Boulangerie. Bakery.
Charcuterie. Gourmet take-out, like a delicatessen.
Fromagerie. Cheese shop.
Marché. Market.
Pâtisserie. Pastry shop.
Salon de thé. Tea salon.

Café Terms

English/French
Black coffee that's very strong (or espresso). *Café noir.*
Coffee with steamed milk. *Café au lait* (or *café crème*).
Decaffeinated coffee. *Décafeiné* or *déca.*
Drip coffee, which is less strong than other types. *Café filtre.*
Espresso with cream. *Noisette.*
Herb tea. *Infusion.*
Hot chocolate. *Chocolat chaud.*
Lemonade, fresh. *Limonade pression.*
Tea with lemon. *Thé au citron.*
Tea with milk. *Thé au lait.*
Tea without milk or lemon. *Thé nature.*

French/English
Café au lait (or *café crème*). Coffee with steamed milk.
Café filtre. Uses drip method, less strong.
Café noir. Plain, very strong black coffee (or espresso).
Chocolat chaud. Hot chocolate.
Décafeiné or *déca.* Decaffeinated coffee.
Infusion. Herb tea.
Lemonade pression. Fresh lemonade.
Noisette. Expresso with cream.
Thé au citron. Tea with lemon.
Thé au lait. Tea with milk.
Thé nature. Plain tea.

Restaurant Phrases

English/French
Have you decided? *Avez-vous choisi?*
I would like to see the menu. *Je voudrais voir la carte.*
Service included (15 percent). *Service compris.*
The check, please. *L'addition, s'il vous plaît.*

French/English
Avez-vous choisi? Have you decided?
Je voudrais voir la carte. I would like to see the menu.
L'addition, s'il vous plaît. The check, please.
Service compris. Service included (15 percent).

Menu Terms

English/French
Apple. *Pomme.*
Artichoke. *Artichaut.*
Asparagus. *Asperge.*
Avocado. *Avocat.*
Beef rib steak. *Entrecôte.*
Bill; check. *Addition.*
Bread. *Pain.*
Butter. *Beurre.*
Buttery roll. *Brioche.*
Cake. *Gâteau.*
Cheese. *Fromage.*
Chicken. *Poulet.*
Coffee. *Café.*
Cold cuts. *Charcuteries.*
Dinner; to dine. *Dîner.*
Dish. *Plat.*
Drinks. *Boissons.*
Duck. *Canard.*
Egg. *Oeuf.*
First course. *Entrée.*
Fish. *Poisson.*
Fixed price menu. *Prix fixe menu* or *formule.*
French bread. *Baguette.*
Grape. *Raisin.*
Grapefruit. *Pamplemousse.*
Green bean. *Haricot vert.*
Ham. *Jambon.*
Ice cream. *Glace.*

Juice. *Jus.*
Lamb chop. *Côte d'agneau.*
Lemon. *Citron.*
Lunch. *Déjeuner.*
Meat. *Viande.*
Menu. *Carte.*
Milk. *Lait.*
Mushroom. *Champignon.*
Napkin. *Serviette.*
Of the house. *De la maison.*
Peach. *Pêche.*
Pepper. *Poivre.*
Pineapple. *Ananas.*
Plat. *Assiette.*
Potato. *Pomme de terre.*
Receipt. *Reçu.*
Salmon. *Saumon.*
Salt. *Sel.*
Shellfish. *Fruits de mer.*
Soup. *Potage.*
Steak. *Bifteck.*
   Medium. *A point.*
   Rare. *Saignant.*
   Well done. *Bien cuit.*
Tasting menu. *Dégustation menu.*
Tea. *Thé.*
Tuna fish. *Thon.*
Veal. *Veau.*
Vegetable. *Légume.*

French/English

A la carte. Literally, "Off the menu," with each dish ordered and priced separately.

Addition. Bill.

Ananas. Pineapple.

Artichaut. Artichoke.

Asperge. Asparagus.

Assiette. Plate.

Avocat. Avocado.

Baguette. Long, thin French bread.

Beurre. Butter.

Bifteck. Steak.

  A point. Medium.

  Bien cuit. Well done.

  Saignant. Rare.

Boissons. Drinks.

Brioche. Buttery roll.

Café. Coffee.

Canard. Duck.

Carte. Menu.

Champignon. Mushroom.

Charcuteries. Cold cuts.

Citron. Lemon.

Côte d'agneau. Lamb chop.

Crème fraîche. Thick, sour, heavy cream.

Crudités. Raw vegetables.

De la maison. Of the house.

Dégustation menu. Tasting menu.

Déjeuner. Lunch.

Dîner. Dinner; to dine.

Entrecôte. Beef rib steak.

Entrée. First course.

Formule. Fixed price menu.

Fromage. Cheese.

Fruits de mer. Shellfish.

Gâteau. Cake.

Glace. Ice cream.

Haricot vert. Green bean.

Jambon. Ham.

Jus. Juice.

Lait. Milk.

Légume. Vegetable.

Oeuf. Egg.

Pain. Bread.

Pamplemousse. Grapefruit.

Pêche. *Peach.*

Plat. *A dish.*

Poisson. *Fish.*

Poivre. *Pepper.*

Pomme. *Apple.*

Pomme de terre. *Potato.*

Potage. *Soup.*

Poulet. *Chicken.*

Prix fixe menu. *Fixed price for a set number of courses.*

Raisin. *Grape.*

Reçu. *Receipt.*

Saumon. *Salmon.*

Sel. *Salt.*

Serviette. *Napkin.*

Thé. *Tea.*

Thon. *Tuna fish.*

Veau. *Veal.*

Viande. *Meat.*

Post Office Terms and Phrases

English/French

A letter (which requires more postage than a postcard). *Une lettre.*

Air mail. *Par avion.*

Post office. *Bureau de poste.*

Postcards. *Cartes postales.*

Stamp markets. *Marché aux timbres.*

Stamps. *Timbres.*

To foreign destinations. *A l'étranger.*

To the United States. *Aux Etats Unis.*

French/English

A l'étranger. To foreign destinations.

Aux Etats Unis. To the United States.

Bureau de poste. Post office.

Cartes postales. Postcards.

Marché aux timbres. Stamp markets.

Par avion. Air mail.

Timbres. Stamps.

Une lettre. A letter (which requires more postage than a postcard).

Recreation Terms

English/French
Beach. *Plage.*
Bicycle. *Vélo.*
Gardens. *Jardins.*
Health club. *Gymnasium.*
Horse racing. *Course de cheveaux.*
Ice skating. *Patinage.*
Jogging. *Jogging.*
Stadium. *Stade.*
Swimming pool. *Piscine.*
Team. *Equipe.*
Tennis. *Tennis.*
Woods. *Bois.*

French/English
Bois. Woods.
Course de cheveaux. Horse racing.
Equipe. Team.
Gymnasium. Health club.
Jardins. Gardens.
Jogging. Jogging.
Patinage. Ice skating.
Piscine. Swimming pool.
Plage. Beach.
Stade. Stadium.
Tennis. Tennis.
Vélo. Bicycle.

SALON TERMS
General Salon Terms

English/French
Beauty salon. *Salon de beauté.*
Beauty salon professional. *Esthéticienne.*
Couture designer/owner. *Couturière.*
Hairdresser. *Coiffeur.*
Signature (a woman's perfume scent). *Griffe.*

French/English
Coiffeur. Hairdresser.
Couturière. Couture designer/owner.
Esthéticienne. Beauty salon professional.
Griffe. Signature (a woman's perfume scent).
Salon de beauté. Beauty salon.

Beauty Salon and Spa Terms

English/French
Body massage. *Modelage esthétique relaxant.*
Exfoliating body scrub. *Gommage.*
Eyelash curl. *Permanente de cils.*
Eyelash tint. *Teinture des cils.*
Facial. *Beauté complète du visage.*
Makeup application. *Maquillage.*
Manicure. *Manucure.*
Pedicure. *La beauté des pieds.*
Resting room. *Salle de repos.*

French/English
Beauté complète du visage. Facial.
Gommage. Exfoliating body scrub.
La beauté des pieds. Pedicure.
Manucure. Manicure.
Maquillage. Makeup application.
Modelage esthétique relaxant. Body massage.
Permanente de cils. Eyelash curl.
Salle de repos. Resting room.
Teinture des cils. Eyelash tint.

Hair Salon Terms

English/French
Blow Dry. *Brushing.*
Color. *Couleur.*
Cut. *Coupe.*
Hair. *Cheveux.*
Hair conditioning. *L'essentiel cheveux.*
Wash. *Shampooing.*

French/English
Brushing. Blow Dry.
Cheveaux. Hair.
Couleur. Color.
Coupe. Cut.
L'essentiel cheveux. Hair conditioning.
Shampooing. Wash.

SHOPPING PHRASES AND TERMS

Shopping Phrases

English/French
Do you accept credit cards? *Acceptez-vous les cartes de crédit?*
How much does this cost? *Ca coûte combien?*
I would like the Export Sales Invoice for sales tax reimbursement. *Je voudrais l'imprimé pour la détaxe.*
I would like the package gift-wrapped. *Je voudrais un paquet cadeau.*

General Shopping Terms

English/French
Accessories. *Accessoires.*
Bookshop. *Librairie.*
Cashier. *Caisse.*
Credit card. *Carte de crédit.*
Department store. *Grand magasin.*
Discount store. *Boutique à reduction.*
Fake jewels; costume jewelry. *Faux bijoux.*
Flea markets. *Marchés aux puces.*
Gifts. *Cadeaux.*
High fashion. *Haute couture.*
On sale. *Soldes.*
Perfume shop. *Parfumerie.*
Price. *Prix.*
Ready to wear. *Prêt à porter.*
Real jewels. *Vrai bijoux.*
Sales tax. *Détaxe.*
Toys. *Jouets.*

French/English
Accessoires. Accessories.
Boutique à reduction. Discount store.
Cadeaux. Gifts.
Caisse. Cashier.
Carte de crédit. Credit card.
Détaxe. Sales tax.
Faux bijoux. Fake jewels; costume jewelry.
Grand magasin. Department store.
Haute couture. High fashion.
Jouets. Toys.
Librairie. Bookshop.
Marchés aux puces. Flea markets.
Parfumerie. Perfume shop.
Prêt à porter. Ready to wear.
Prix. Price.
Soldes. On sale.
Vrai bijoux. Real jewels.

Clothing Terms

English/French
Bathing suit. *Maillot de bain.*
Belt. *Ceinture.*
Blouse. *Blouse.*
Blue jeans. *Jean.*
Boots. *Bottes.*
Coat. *Manteau.*
Dress. *Robe.*
Glove. *Gant.*
Nightgown. *Peignoir.*
Pajamas. *Pyjama.*
Pants. *Pantalon.*
Rain coat. *Imperméable.*
Sandals. *Sandales.*
Scarf. *Echarpe.*
Shoes. *Chaussures.*
Size. *Taille.*
Skirt. *Jupe.*
Sneakers. *Tennis.*
Socks. *Chaussettes.*
Stockings. *Bas.*
Sweater. *Pullover.*
Tie. *Cravate.*

French/English
Bas. Stockings.
Blouse. Blouse.
Bottes. Boots.
Ceinture. Belt.
Chausettes. Socks.
Chaussures. Shoes.
Cravate. Tie.
Echarpe. Scarf.
Gant. Glove.
Imperméable. Rain coat.
Jean. Blue jeans.
Jupe. Skirt.
Maillot de bain. Bathing suit.
Manteau. Coat.
Pantalon. Pants.
Peignoir. Nightgown.
Pullover. Sweater.
Pyjama. Pajamas.
Robe. Dress.
Sandales. Sandals.
Taille. Size.
Tennis. Sneakers.

TRANSPORTATION TERMS
Métro Terms

English/French
Connecting métro lines.
  Correspondances.
Exit. *Sortie.*
Line. *Ligne.*
One ticket. *Billet.*
Pull (on door). *Tirez.*
Punch (bus ticket). *Oblitérer.*
Push (on door). *Poussez.*
Special express métro lines that go into the suburbs and make only a few stops in Paris. *RER.*
Taxi stand. *Tête de station.*
Ten tickets. *Carnet.*

French/English
Billet. One ticket.
Carnet. Ten tickets.
Correspondances. Connecting métro lines.
Ligne. Line.
Oblitérer. Punch (bus ticket).
Poussez. Push (on door).
RER. Special express métro lines that go into the suburbs and make only a few stops in Paris.
Sortie. Exit.
Tête de station. Taxi stand.
Tirez. Pull (on door).

Train Terms

English/French

Big lines (long-distance routes). *Grandes lignes.*
Car. *Voiture.*
Drinkable water. *Potable.*
First Class. *Première Classe.*
Line. *Ligne.*
Nondrinkable. *Non-potable.*
Nonsmoking. *Non-fumeur.*
Platform. *Quai.*
Second Class. *Deuxième Classe.*
Smoking. *Fumeur.*
Suburbs (trains going nearby). *Banlieue.*
Track. *Voie.*

French/English

Banlieue. Suburbs (trains going nearby).
Deuxième Classe. Second Class.
Fumeur. Smoking.
Grandes lignes. Big lines (long-distance routes).
Ligne. Line.
Non-fumeur. Nonsmoking.
Non-potable. Nondrinkable.
Potable. Drinkable water.
Première Classe. First Class.
Quai. Platform.
Voie. Track.
Voiture. Car.

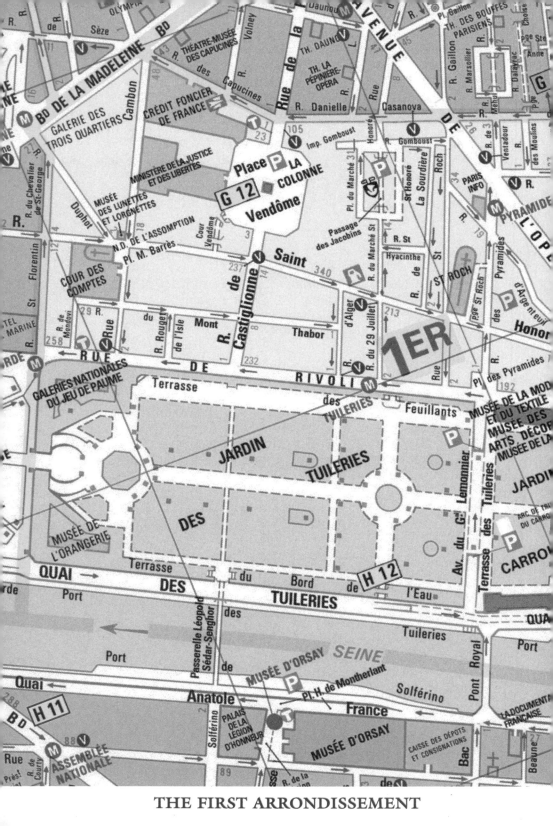

THE FIRST ARRONDISSEMENT

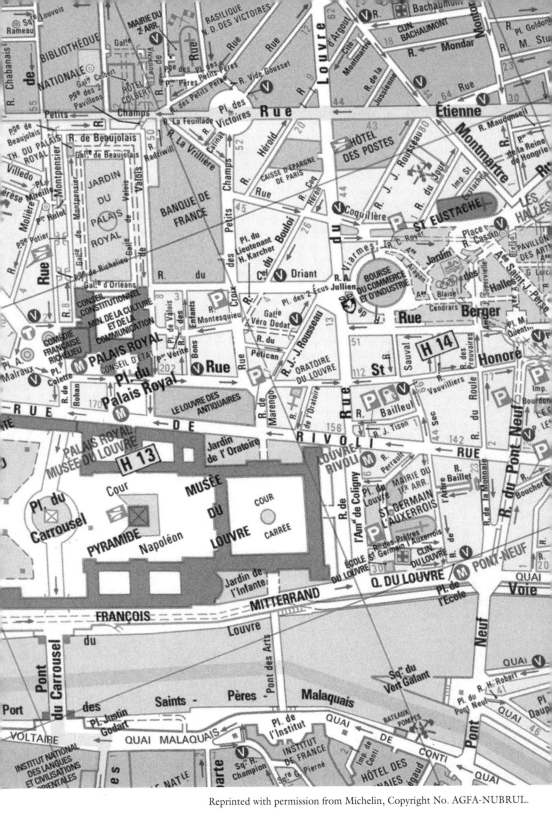

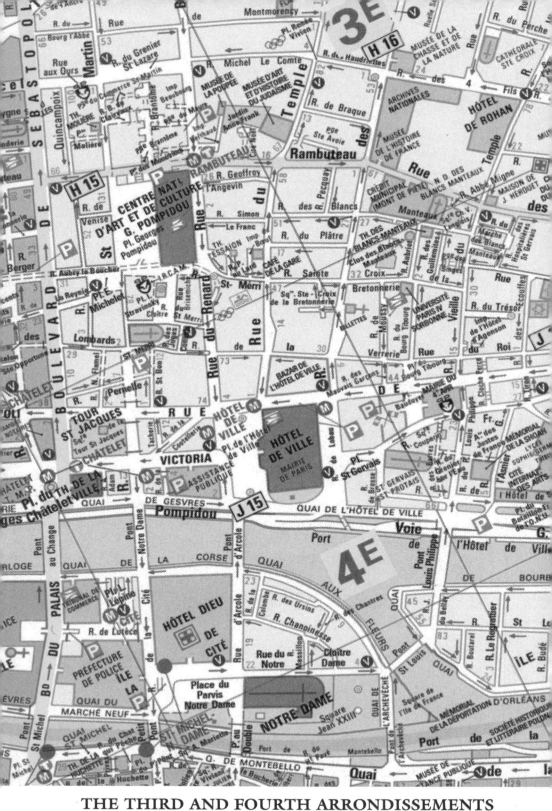

THE THIRD AND FOURTH ARRONDISSEMENTS

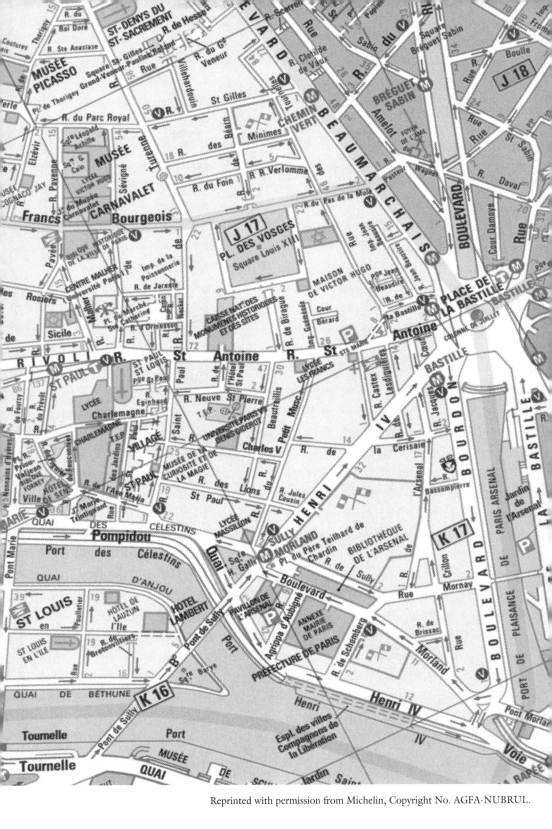

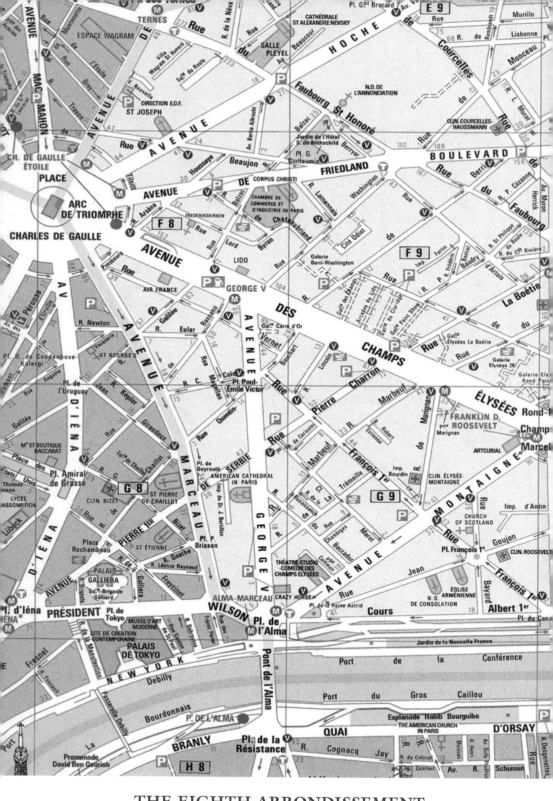

THE EIGHTH ARRONDISSEMENT

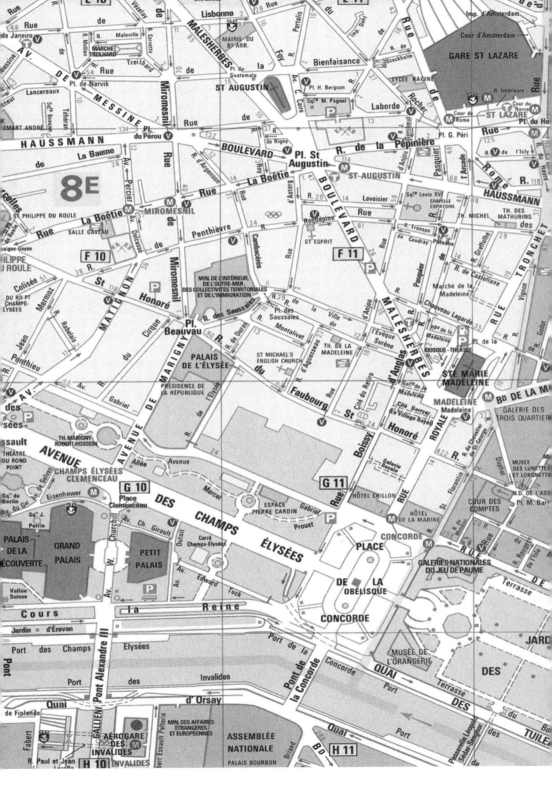

THE SIXTH ARRONDISSEMENT
Reprinted with permission from Michelin, Copyright No. AGFA-NUBRUL.

Suggested Readings

When you're planning your dream trip to Paris, here are five books that will immerse you in Parisian history and current French culture. These books truly make the city come alive. And for those of you who are "slaves to fashion," the stories about the history of the fashion houses and the perfume industry are eye-opening.

Deluxe: How Luxury Lost Its Luster. Dana Thomas. New York: Penguin Books, 2007.

Thomas shares the history of the top designer labels that have become household names, and the conglomerates that now run them. My favorite sections chronicle how these brands started with a single creative person. We learn about Gabrielle "Coco" Chanel, who grew up in an orphanage yet managed to open her own milliner shop in Paris in 1910. Then there's Louis Vuitton, who became an apprentice to a Paris trunk maker when he was still a teenager in the 1830s. Twenty years later, he opened his own business, redesigned the trunk, and an international status symbol was born.

A Moveable Feast: Sketches of the Author's Life in Paris in the Twenties.
Ernest Hemingway. New York: Charles Scribner's Sons, 1964.

Hemingway vividly describes Paris of the 1920s, when writers congregated to work on their craft, share one another's company, and partake in the excitement of the city. In twenty short chapters, the author depicts his struggles as a young writer; offers wonderful descriptions of Paris, from the cafés and parks to the bookstore Shakespeare and Company; and portrays the people he befriended, including Gertrude Stein, Ezra Pound, and Scott Fitzgerald.

Paris to the Moon. Adam Gopnik. New York: Random House, 2000.

Some refer to Adam Gopnik as a modern-day Hemingway. He, too, lived in Paris for a number of years, where he wrote "Paris Journals" for *The New Yorker.* Gopnik's essays on life in Paris use wit and insight to illuminate French culture and explain how it differs from life in the United States. Some of my favorite sections include a description of attending a haute couture fashion show; a behind-the-scenes look at the kitchen of Arpege, a three-star Michelin restaurant; and an exploration of why Café Flore is regarded by Parisians as "fashionable."

Parisians: An Adventure History of Paris. Graham Robb. New York: W.W. Norton & Company, 2010.

A series of "tales" that depict the story of Paris through figures who played an important part in its growth, *Parisians* starts with Napoleon Bonaparte's trip to Paris in 1787, when he was an eighteen-year-old artillery lieutenant, and paints a vivid picture of his evening at the then-infamous Palais-Royal area. Other chapters describe the creation of the underground métro system; Hitler's half-day tour of Paris during World War II; and Marie Antoinette's attempt to escape from Paris' revolutionary crowds, only to become lost in a maze of streets.

The Perfect Scent: A Year Inside the Perfume Industry in Paris and New York. Chandler Burr. New York: Henry Holt and Company, 2007.

If you're a scent addict, as I am, you'll enjoy Burr's thorough description of how modern-day perfumes are created and sold. Burr was allowed to observe and report on the evolution of two new fragrances. His story covers *Un Jardin sur le Nil*, which was designed for the Paris company Hermès, and *Lovely*, Sarah Jessica Parker's celebrity perfume designed for Coty in New York. Burr explains how a scent is created, from the plant to the laboratory; details the debate over the design of the bottle and stopper; and describes the multi-million-dollar launch and marketing campaigns.

Index

Hotel du Lion d'Or Louvre

Hotel du Lion d'Or Louvre is a few blocks from the Louvre Museum and one block from the Tuileries Garden in a shopper's paradise off Rue St.-Honoré. This location can't be beat, and the prices are very reasonable for the neighborhood. The hotel also offers a few studio apartments across the street.

ROOM AMENITIES

- Air-conditioning
- Sound-proofing
- Complementary Wi-Fi
- TV – satellite
- Telephone
- Hairdryer
- Additional bed upon request

SPECIAL OFFERS

- Classic | from 105€
- Standard | from 133€
- Executive | from 153€
- Junior Suite | from 204€

HOTEL LION D'OR LOUVRE

5, rue de la Sourdière 75001 PARIS

Tel : 00 33(1) 42 60 79 04

www.hotel-louvre-paris.com • hotelduliondor@wanadoo.fr

Fat Tire Bike Tours
24, rue Edgar Faure
75015 Paris

Email: Paris@FatTireBikeTours.com
Phone: 1-866-614-6218 (toll-free from North America)
01-56-58-10-54 (calling from within France)